May you be inspired
by life
God Bless
E King
July 2008

Ekua:

Wednesday's Child

VALERIE JOY BROWN

Published by

MELROSE BOOKS

An Imprint of Melrose Press Limited
St Thomas Place, Ely
Cambridgeshire
CB7 4GG, UK
www.melrosebooks.com

FIRST EDITION

Copyright © Valerie Joy Brown 2008

The Author asserts her moral right to
be identified as the author of this work

Cover designed by Jeremy Kay

ISBN 978-1-906050-83-2

All rights reserved. No part of this publication may be reproduced,
stored in a retrieval system, or transmitted, in any form or by any means
electronic, mechanical, photocopying, recording or otherwise,
without the prior permission of the publishers.

This book is sold subject to the condition that it shall not,
by way of trade or otherwise, be lent, re-sold, hired out or
otherwise circulated without the publisher's prior consent
in any form of binding or cover other than that in which
it is published and without a similar condition including this
condition being imposed on the subsequent purchaser.

Printed and bound in Great Britain by:
Biddles, Kings Lynn, Norfolk

CONTENTS

Introduction			v
Foreword by Elsie Dontoh Kessie			vii
1. Childhood			1
2. Ghana	1964–1966		37
3. Britain	1966		51
4. Ghana	1966–1969		60
5. India	February to November 1969		68
6. Ghana	November 1969–1972		88
7. Ethiopia	1972–1974		107
8. Ghana	1974–1979		128
9. Britain	1979–1981		174
10. Ghana	1981–1984		202
11. Britain	1984–1985		228
Epilogue			250
Afterthought			254

INTRODUCTION

Ekua is the Fanti day name for a girl born on Wednesday, a name I acquired, not at birth, but when I was reborn as an African, aged 21 years. I kept it, alongside my birth name of Valerie Joy ever since. I have been privileged to lead a much more interesting and diverse life than my birth might imply!

This is a true account of my life, spent married to a black, Fanti, man, from Ghana, West Africa.

It tells of my life and loves and sorrows of forty years; spent in Britain, Ghana, India, Ethiopia and finally Britain again.

If I have omitted anything, it is to protect innocent people, but I give no such protection to myself!

I have to thank my dear mother, Agnes Anderson Brown, now deceased, for being so generous to me all my life and for all the advice she has given me. I have not always taken it immediately, but after many years and mistakes, I realised that she was very wise and right. I hope you enjoy reading this book. It has been great, 'therapeutically' for me to write it.

CRAVEN PARK, LONDON, 1985.

This manuscript was hand written over a period of six months in 1985; and typed in Kilburn, London in, July 2002: continuing in August 2004. As you can imagine, a lot more has happened since then but that will have to wait for another book.

FOREWORD

When Auntie Ekua (Valerie) asked me to write the foreword for her forthcoming book, I was both honoured and touched. This was not the first time she had asked me to write about a special event in her life. Sadly, the first time was to write and read out a tribute at the funeral of her beloved last child Julien, who she tragically lost nine years ago. I am glad that I now do this in much happier circumstances.

The first time I met her was in 1979 in Ghana, at her home in Ablempke (a suburb of Accra, capital of Ghana). My younger brothers were in the same secondary school with her son, Hamish, and were so close that they were literally part of each other's family. My father and her ex-husband had both been officers in the Ghana Army and Navy respectively. I had been studying in the university, so had not had much opportunity to meet her before then.

However, during the summer vacation of 1979 shortly after my mother's death, I had returned home and formed a close friendship with her then 14-year-old daughter Rosina, who asked if I would braid her mother's hair. I was intrigued – I had attended a secondary school in which the majority of teachers were white but none ever went around with braids in their hair!

Anyway, I decided to knock on her door a few days later as they lived only about half a mile from our home in Roman Ridge. The door was opened by the friendliest and most beautiful white lady I had ever seen.

I am sure this will be the first time she will become aware of this impact on me. Within ten minutes, I realised that she was not just beautiful on the outside, but from deep within. The braiding experience was a complete disaster initially but she would not give up and with the help of some lacquer we got her hair stiff enough to produce a stunning piece of artwork that she paraded around with for weeks.

It was the beginning of a close and loving relationship which I believe has been a gift from God and as my father declared later, "You may have lost your mother, but God has given you another."

Not long after, political upheavals in Ghana meant that she would flee the country with her family and leave a comfortable lifestyle for a harsh existence in England which would include the loss of her marriage, her homes, her mother and child in the following traumatic years.

However, her inner strength and beauty were never dimmed as she held her head high and rose to each challenge and not only completed her Masters degree but was made a Fellow of the Royal Society of Medicine in the last year.

I have not read the book yet, because I want to save the tears and laughter, which I know will come in abundance, for when it is officially public.

I know it will speak volumes to readers about the lives of people who have been affected by events over two continents. It will also follow the journey of a woman who has a deep love for people of African origin and went on to 'mother' so many of us who had lost our mothers one way or the other.

In fact, she is the first to tell you she was born in the wrong country, and I shrugged and smiled so many years ago when she told me she preferred to be called Ekua Brown – it was only a natural progression for her.

Over the years I have observed an incredibly honest and courageous person who has grown from strength to strength, accepting the errors of her ways, loving passionately the people who crossed her path.

A woman, who took the knocks of life with dignity and composure, and then did something truly inspiring and wonderful with it. The most remarkable thing about her was her lack of bitterness and her decision during the lowest points of her life to do something positive with it.

I watched with admiration her persistence and excellence as she undertook adult education and progressed to postgraduate level something, marrying young and having her family young, she had not been allowed the opportunity to do earlier.

Her varied and interesting life is an account that would have been a crime not to document.

Well done, Auntie Ekua; I am sure this book will bring assurance to the Many who are limping through life with the hurts and pain that are being thrown from many angles. All your 'children' are proud of you.

Reader, I am sure this book will show that you can learn to live at peace with yourself again and learn to laugh again.

Elsie Dontoh Kessie 6th January 2008

Chapter One

CHILDHOOD

I was born on 10th May 1944, at the Southern General Hospital, Govan, Glasgow, Scotland; the only girl amongst 38 boys, (so my mother informed me!). I have since read an article that more boys are born during wartime than girls. My case seems to prove that fact. My mother had been expecting a boy, who she had intended to name Ian Douglas, but, much to my mother's surprise, I turned out to be a girl. So they had to find a new name and I was named Valerie; after Valerie Hobson, a forties film star, and later the wife of Profumo, the politician involved in the scandal of the 1960s. Also, Joy, as my mother said that I was a bundle of Joy! So, Valerie Joy Brown, as I was christened at Christ Church, Shooters Hill, Blackheath, London.

My mother promptly called me 'Precious', and I was told that even up to the age of three, I would tell people that my name was Precious. I was born with black curly hair and blue eyes, which changed in my first year, to blonde curly hair and green eyes. (One advantage was that my eyebrows always remained dark so I never had to wear eye make-up later in life.)

We went to London when I was six months. Because of the war, my mother had stayed in Glasgow with her family. In London, mother said, "That I was sitting in my pram and watching the doodle-bugs go over." Mummy said, "That they were terrifying, as long as you heard the buzz, you were all right; but as soon, as the buzz stopped, they would just drop!

Another time, I was in my carrycot in front of the fire, when Mummy, had a premonition and quickly picked me up out of the cot. The next minute there was a bomb and all the fire was blown out of the fireplace. It would have landed on me, if Mummy had not picked me up in time!

My parents: Joseph, Thomas, Brown, my father was born in Greenwich, south-east London, not far from the Naval College and Greenwich Park.

His father was from Kirkintiloch, Scotland but he died when my father was 13 years old. Thus, my father became the head of his family; consisting of Auntie Doris, his eldest sister; and then Auntie Iris; and finally Uncle Fred, the baby of the family. His mother, Elisabeth, first Blazey and then Brown and finally Miller! My grandmother, was from Suffolk, where her father had a farm, at Frikenham, not far from Newmarket.

After a few years as a widow, my grandmother married again to a man called Robert Miller (who we children called Granddad and the grown ups called Pop!) whose wife had died leaving him with four children. So the family became eight children along with my father and his siblings: they were, Auntie Bessie, the eldest; Uncle Bill, the only boy; Auntie Doris (called Doris Miller or Auntie Doll) so, as to distinguish her from my father's own sister Doris Brown; and last but not least, Auntie Edie, who was the youngest and the nicest of them all. Everybody should have an Auntie Edie in their families and the world would be a better place. They all called my grandmother Aunt Sis, and we children called her Nanny.

My earliest recollection is of travelling to Glasgow, for my grandfather's funeral. I was three at the time. We took a black taxi, driven by a neighbour, Mr. Bateman. When we got to Euston Station, as we rushed along the platform to get our reserved seat, on 'The Royal Scot', a steam train, The strap of the carrycot carrying my baby sister, Laraine Carol, born on 12th February 1947, broke; and I was horrified in case something would happen to my baby sister of whom I was very proud. She had the most beautiful blue eyes and dark hair. Well actually at that time she had no hair but as it grew it became dark. Going to Scotland was something that we did two or three times a year.

My constant companion at that time was my cousin Keith Miller, who I called Keithy. He was my father's stepbrother's son, and he was the same age as me, born in July 1944. He was also fair with green eyes, and everybody thought we were twins. We lived in a flat upstairs in a row of Victorian terraced houses, and they lived on the ground floor next door. Uncle Bill had actually got the flat for my parents when it became vacant.

I was a very happy child and it didn't take much to please me. I was so close to Keith that one time, on being taken on holiday to Scotland, I became ill because I missed him. I remember coming home and him bringing me some flowers to cheer me up.

My Mother, Agnes Anderson, was born at Old Kilpatrick, Dumbartonshire, Scotland. My mother disliked the name Agnes; as her mother, Mary Roche, my grandmother, who was a Catholic, had called another baby before her, Agnes, as it was her favourite saint's name, but that baby had died aged six months. So Mummy was known as Nancy for most of her life or Aunt Nan by most of my cousins. Her brother Andrew called her Annie. My mother's father's name was Andrew Anderson, as was my Uncle Andy's and one of my cousin's. So that name was well kept in the family. My grandfather was an inventor, who invented, amongst other things, the bobbin for Singer sewing machines. Though he sold the rights to Singer and got no acknowledgement for it.

Grandma Anderson, my mother's grandmother, was a Hepburn. They were manufacturers of pianos and Grandpa Anderson was the headmaster of a boy's private school. My grandmother, who we called Grandma, had thirteen children, of which ten survived to adulthood: George, who died from TB when my mother was 21; Aunt Mary, who died when Mummy was 13; Andrew, Harriet, Robert, my mother, Tommy, Charlie, Ivy and Violet.

At the age of three I was very ill and was just saved from meningitis, as my mother put it. Anyway, from that time I started with my ear troubles and every so often I had to go to hospital and have an operation on my ears, and then for what seemed ages afterwards, had to go to the Miller Hospital, at Deptford (it has now been knocked down) to have a penicillin injection everyday. At that time the injections had just come in so I owe my life to Sir Alexander Fleming, who discovered penicillin.

I was so brave and never cried when I had the injections so the nurses used to show the grown-ups, who were afraid of injections, how brave I was. The hospital staff, were, really lovely to me: the sisters, porters, ambulance drivers and the tea lady. I used to go so often that they all knew me. I was a pretty little girl with beautiful naturally curly blonde hair, so people used to feel sorry to see me all bandaged up. I used to see an Ear, Nose and Throat specialist called Gwen Evans, and he was always very sad to see me again. The nurses used to bandage my dolly's head for me.

When I was four years old at Easter time, Keith, Gina my other cousin, and I all started school together. We went to Sherington Road School at Charlton, in the infants' class. We used to wear navy blue gymslips and a tie that was yellow and navy, striped diagonally. Everyday we used to skip along the road to school. We were only at Sherington a little while when we were transferred to a brand new school at the Standard, Blackheath. It was called 'Invicta' Road Infants' School.

I presented the bouquet on opening day to Harriet Cohune, a famous pianist, who opened the school. Auntie Freda, Keith's mother, made me a beautiful peach-pink satin dress, which had a tremendous gathered skirt, which I could spin round very nicely, and I spent a lot of time, twisting and twisting and spinning the skirt round. It's just amazing, the simple pleasures that children enjoy!

Now before I go further, I should introduce my family: My mother, who was called Nan, by all who I knew as a child, and Auntie Nan by all the children. Was a very elegant, beautiful lady, with green eyes (like mine) and beautiful auburn hair. She was very strict with us, especially the way we spoke, and as she was Scottish, she spoke with a very cultured Scottish burr. My father was also a very handsome man, six foot two tall with black hair and beautiful blue eyes, (just like his mother's).

But handsome is as handsome does, so they say! My father's life was his sports; and he started my dislike of sports, which has lasted all my life. He used to take us to his sports club, and some of my first memories are of the starter gun going bang and people, including my father, running round a track. I found the whole thing positively boring. Anyway, he used to win medals for every sport, and silver cups, and he won them three years in a row and collected the big cups. Mummy insisted that they kept the big cups in the sports club; it was bad enough cleaning the little silver cups that we had in the house.

My sister Laraine Carol Brown was three years younger than me. She always had dark, straight, fine hair, (in contrast to my blond, naturally wavy hair) and the most beautiful large blue eyes, which always got her away with a lot of things as a child. She just had to beam her eyes on you and you would forgive her everything. Laraine was always very pretty and the two of us – one fair and the other dark – complemented one another. Laraine grew taller than me. We were always very close and had fits of giggles whenever we were together. That completes the family of four, though mostly we were only three as Daddy was never there-always training for his sports, or working. He worked at the South-Eastern Gas Board, at Phoenix Wharf, Greenwich (now the site of the Millennium Dome) and was there for the whole of his working life until he retired at 65. When he was 21 the gasholder blew up and killed hundreds of people, and he was really badly burned. He was in hospital in St Alfredge's at Greenwich (where he met my mother, who had come down from Scotland as a nurse) for many years, which meant that he was unfit for military service during the war; and as he worked in an essential service – gas – he had to continue working whilst all my uncles and aunties were in the services during the war. He joined the St John's Ambulance Brigade and the National Hospital Reserve.

He was very mean and my mother had to go out to work two and half days a week, at the local Co-op shop from the time I was seven years old. She worked half-day Thursday and full day Friday and Saturday, and from that job she bought new furniture for the house and dressed Laraine and me always in the best quality clothes.

When we were on holidays from school in the summer, sometimes, she wanted to take us to the cinema, so we had a great time. She would say, "If I don't pay the insurance man this week, or the Co-op man, we can go to the cinema." So when the insurance man, who was very nice, or the Co-op man knocked, we all had to be quiet and pretend; we were not in, until he had gone away. Of course, as children, we thought it was a great game. It was not until I was much older I realised the significance of that. (There were no credit cards in those days, only HP (hire-purchase) and if you did not pay, the goods were taken back.) Mummy always paid the rent. When we were older, she was able to take a better job, in the City, working as an accountant. Then she was much happier.

My father had a thing about holidays and I suppose I must be grateful for that, as I had more holidays than anybody else in my class at school. First of all, we would go to Scotland to stay with my Auntie Harriet and Uncle Hugh, and my cousins Jean and wee Hughie. In actual fact that was the first home I went to from the hospital when I was born. My cousin Jean, who is nine years older than me, told me she remembers collecting me from the hospital and buying a brown fur rug for my pram.

I used to love to go there as they lived in a huge granite apartment, and the thing that most fascinated me was a big double bed in an alcove in the kitchen. Auntie Harriet would cook lovely fresh fish, and make big round sugary doughnuts. We would have club biscuits, which you could not get in London then, and Irn-Bru lemonade. Uncle Hugh had been a hairdresser and he loved my hair. Mummy said even in the winter he would not let me wear a hat so everybody could see my beautiful wavy hair. We would always take a trip on Loch Lomond, and though I have never really lived there, the beauty of my country of birth and the lovely burr of their accents has always made me nostalgic throughout my life.

Then we would visit all the other aunties and uncles: Uncle Andrew and Auntie Jessie with my cousins Irene and Morris. Everybody would make high tea and bring out the best china; Auntie Vi and Uncle Don and my cousins Norman and Linda; and Uncle Tommy and Auntie Isa, who did not have a child until I was 13 years, when they had my cousin Glen. Uncle Tommy always wore an Anderson tartan kilt, which we children loved. They travelled around the world a lot, and often visited us in London. He said that everywhere he went, people stopped and talked to him because of the kilt. My Auntie Isa was one of the sweetest souls that I ever knew.

Uncle Bobby and Auntie Peggy with my cousins Andrew and Edward. Andrew emigrated to Australia when I was 14 years old and Uncle Bobby and Auntie Peggy joined cousin Andrew and his wife later. My grandmother lived with Uncle Charlie, the youngest, until she died and then Uncle Charlie also went to Australia.

My Auntie Ivy, who I have never seen since I was three years old, lived in Belfast and because of the troubles we never went there. She had my cousins Heather, Pamela, and Peter and Uncle Bob, her husband, who died quite early. I did meet Heather years later at Jean's wedding. Sometimes my father would come to Scotland but mostly we went with Mummy.

The next holiday would be at Hastings where my father's Aunt, Mrs. Wellard, had a boarding house, 'Victoria House' and we would go and stay in the off-season. I remember the pebbles on the beach, all nasty and strong, and a lot of time we would get tar on our clothes, which came from passing ships. The boarding house was fascinating as it had no running water in the rooms and we had to use large jugs of water and a china bowl to wash; and large china potties under the bed and stone hot water bottles. There were lots of aspidistra plants and ferns all over the house. I remember that mummy had us dressed in Anderson tartan kilts and lace blouses, which fascinated everybody as you did not see much tartan in England at that time.

My father is a very strong swimmer and would swim out to sea for miles (he is a Scorpio). Sometimes even when the red danger flag was flying he would be out and, with the sea as black as night, he would still swim!

From that time I got my fear of water and swimming. My father, six feet two tall, would put me on his shoulders and walk into the sea with me, until the water came up to his shoulders. I used to be so terrified and he used to laugh at my fears. To this day I am afraid of water and don't like people with loud laughs.

All the usual seaside things were there like Punch and Judy, donkeys, candyfloss, sandcastles, amusement arcades, but we were too small for most of those. We always met lovely people on holiday.

The most exciting part of the holidays was going home on the steam trains. We always had lunch or breakfast on the train. I especially loved the steam train going to Scotland, and Mummy would say that the train was saying, "Going home! Going home!" as we chugged along. Then in the summer we would go to Leysdown on the Isle of Sheppey, where Nanny, my father's mother, had two caravans that she used to let out. (This was in the days before people went on holidays abroad.) Sometimes all my father's family would come: Auntie Iris, who was my godmother; and Uncle Derek, who had no children; Auntie Joan and Uncle Fred and my cousin June; and Auntie Doris and Uncle Dick and my cousins Sheila and Jean, and later they had my cousin Philip.

We used to go out in the mud-flats with a bucket and collect cockles, and then take a drag net along the shore and get shrimps and eels and Dover sole. (Years later I learned from a man that we got those fish because the shores had been mined because of the war, and nobody could fish.) My Nanny would clean the fish and Mummy would clean the cockles and put them in vinegar, and we would sit shelling fresh peas and eating more than we put in the pot.

One year a terrible thing happened, a family had camped in a tent in front of our caravan. There was a little girl and boy that we used to play with. One evening we went to bed happily in our caravan, called 'June' after my cousin. When we woke up in the morning: a terrible sight, the tent had burnt down in the night with the children and their baby sister in it. I have never forgotten the charred remains and the terrible smell.

After that, we used to go for what my father called a proper holiday, to a private holiday camp in St Austell Bay, Cornwall, Duporth House. We returned there, year after year, and my father was always elected King for the week or two that we stayed. He used to love to get up to all sorts of pranks, and arranging concerts, etc. When I see the TV programme '*Game for a Laugh*', I always think how my father would love that.

I was always very quiet and didn't like loud noises, or loud people, but, as a child I was always full of fun and laughing.

In Cornwall I loved the scenery, and the lovely warm weather. We, Laraine and I used to go riding, on the lovely Exmoor and Dartmoor ponies; and spend a lot of time on the beach basking in the sun, though I never managed to swim. Duporth House was where Lord Nelson and Lady Hamilton used to live when he wasn't at sea. I was always fascinated with Nelson as we lived so near to Greenwich, and I used to spend most weekends in Greenwich Park and The Maritime Museum, where they had the Nelson section. I had seen his clothes with the hole made by the bullet which, killed him at the battle of Trafalgar.

So to be at Duporth and imagine him there was very romantic. I have always had a fascination for history. St Austell is where the new Eden project is and I have a strong desire to visit it again and see the old house again with its private beach and beautiful sand, not like Hastings pebbles!

Living as we did at Charlton, south-east, London, we were surrounded by history. Charlton Manor House still stands: it is mentioned in the Domesday Book, as is our church of St Luke's, which has a Norman tower. When I was very young, there was actually a farm still in Charlton, where they had horses and cows and used to sell milk. It was later sold, and then they built a new council estate, though fifty years on I don't think it is so new.

In fact, Charlton was as near to the country, as you could get whilst living in the town. We were in walking distance of Blackheath, where they still had fairs and circuses every year; and Greenwich Park with Greenwich Palace, where Elizabeth, the First, used to ride and have a tree house, which was still standing until the hurricane a few years ago. I loved the Queen's House, and its golden spiral staircase; not forgetting the Naval College with its beautiful 'Painted Hall', and the artist, standing with his hand out, requesting more money!

Then there was Charlton Park, the grounds that had belonged to the Manor House. We used to go there for school sports whilst at Sherington Junior Girls' School. Also Maryon Wilson Park, which was quite wild and had streams where we would go to catch newts and tiddlers, and have great fun hiding in the bushes. At this point in time there was no fear of children being attacked, and we: my cousins Keith and Gina and I, would spend hours out playing with Keith's dog Smudge. Some sandwiches and a bottle of lemonade, and we would be out all summer holidays. Then we had the open-air lido park where we could swim. It was very cold and as I could never swim it was not my favourite place.

So my early childhood was very happy, with no cares or worries apart from when I had to go into hospital to have my ears done, which from age three to seven was quite a lot; and then the doctor, decided to remove my tonsils and adenoids, and the ear problems stopped. I forgot to mention all the big, bombed houses, where we also used to go, though it wasn't allowed! They had big signs saying, 'Danger, Keep Out' but that didn't stop us, and we would collect bits of broken china or glass or find some beads and imagine what they had been part of?

After 'Invicta' we went back to Sherington, which had been changed into a junior school. The boys were separated from the girls, having the two top floors, and the girls the ground and first floors. The boys had the back playground and the girls the front, and we were not allowed to cross the line. Up till now I had been with Keith, most of my life but now we only walked to school and home together. His brother Rod was five years older than him and as Laraine was three years younger than me, she was until she reached a certain age, too young to play with. So Keith and I and my cousin Gina, Auntie Edie's daughter: we were always together, all being born in 1944. Gina was one week younger than me, and Keith over a month younger. In Scotland, Norman was also the same age as me, born on 4th July, American Independence Day, so very easy to remember.

I enjoyed school and never missed a day apart from illness. At the age of ten I had an accident, in which our neighbour's son Derek Acourt accidentally shot an arrow in my eye. This was a bow made with a twig and string; and another twig as an arrow, which luckily was blunt. This gave me double vision, which I wasn't aware of at first. Suddenly I started fainting and ended up back at the hospital. There I had to do exercises, looking through a machine to gauge the amount of distance between the two eyes. Today I still have double vision but I am able to manage it and not let it worry me too much.

We took the eleven-plus to go to secondary school whilst most of my school-friends went to grammar school. The L.C.C., the London County Council, had built a new experimental school based on the Comprehensive system. Mummy decided that this seemed more like the Scottish system of education and that I should go there. It was a girls-only school combining lots of other schools in the area. We were two thousand girls. So in 1955, the first year it was open, Gina and I went to Kidbrooke Comprehensive Girl's Secondary School, Corelli Road, Kidbrooke (where Jamie Oliver did his school meals programme). Gina still lives around the corner from the school today. Gina and I were not in the same class, as there were about six classes in each year.

The first day, of the first term, of the first year, I was voted Form Prefect, even though I didn't know a soul in the class. It was just my pretty face again. It didn't last very long as after one lesson I tried slipping out the back of the class the quickest way to the locker room and lost my flash! My first teacher was Miss Thomsett and the class was 1T, which didn't mean anything in those days. Gina and I continued to go to school together. We had a really long walk – just less than three miles – which meant that we weren't entitled to a bus pass! Still, I'm sure all that walking did us good; in those days all children walked to school and I'm sure if they did today there would be a lot less obesity in school-children.

Kidbrooke was a fantastic school, brand new building and a hall the same design as the Festival Hall, where we used to have live performances from the RSC company and stage plays. It had all the lighting and stage equipment that you could think of. The school had its own orchestra. Five fully equipped gyms, massive playing fields, tennis courts, and netball courts. We played hockey, which I hated, running around in the freezing cold in just your shirt and a short gym skirt. It also had an artist's studio, kiln facilities for pottery. Fully equipped science laboratories, lecture rooms, and house-craft suites, with fully equipped flats to practise house-craft. Each unit had six kitchen units to practise baking, cooking and general household cleaning including making raw starch – which was later to come in handy when I was in Africa. There was also a millinery department where we learned to make hats, which also came in useful later. You could take City-Guilds Certificates and you could do a secretarial course as well. Along with the academic side of taking O levels and A levels, all in the same school. The school was divided into houses named after the Queen's Beasts. I was in Unicorn house. Every house had a different colour and we wore house colour ties and berets (ours was yellow) as part of our uniform, which consisted of grey skirts and Air Force blue shirts in winter, and checked dresses in summer.

As it was a new experimental school we had visitors from all over the world frequently. Each classroom had a tannoy system. The Headmistress, Dame Mary Green, had come from one of the private schools and she used to wear a cap and gown to assembly. Everyday we had assembly and I loved to sing all the hymns. On the tannoy on the way to assembly they used to play classical music, which I think was a great way to learn without realising that you were learning it. That first year I was in the nativity play, playing a Swedish girl bringing gifts to baby Jesus. The Head Girl, Eileen Butler, played Mary, and she was so beautiful, that I was in awe of her and forgot to put my hands up in prayer. Mummy, of course, had something to say when I came off, but the headmistress was fine.

Whilst I was there Gladys Aylward, the missionary in China, came and gave us a lecture about her life. They made a film about her life, called '*The Inn of Sixth Happiness*' with Ingrid Bergman. That inspired me and I wanted to be a missionary for a while; at least that was after wanting to be a ballerina like Margot Fonteyn, I had ballet lessons from age three; and then a show-jumper like Pat Smythe, that was from my riding in Cornwall.

Since my travels in other countries and seeing how few facilities children had like books etc, I regret that we as the body of the school did not fully appreciate the facilities available to us or utilise them fully. That school was a wonderful idea, but was before its time. In the first year Lady Edwina Mountbatten came and opened our school. I had met her previously with my father, as she was the head of the St John's Ambulance Brigade for many years. I always admired her, and Lord Mountbatten was one of my heroes.

My mother had taught me to read at the age of four, before I went to school, and I have been reading ever since. I must have read thousands of books. I went through the local library, then at Charlton House, and Ruby Kaye the librarian used to take me to the Methodist church with her on Sundays when I was small. It was called Sunfields at Blackheath, and the service was held in the church hall as the church had been bombed. (The church was later rebuilt, but, by that time, I had started going to St Luke's, which was High Anglican.) After church I would go and have tea with her parents and her sister, who had a crippled foot, and play with their dog in the garden, which was at the top of our road. Ruby encouraged me to read, too. I love historical novels as you can learn a lot of history from them. In addition I liked autobiographies and biographies. I read most of the books in that library and also the school library, which I omitted to mention. It was a lovely library to sit and read in. I didn't like detective novels so much as I always guessed who did it and therefore found them boring. I did a lot of painting and pottery at school and was quite good at both.

In the second year, my form teacher Miss Hawkins (later Mrs. Willis) taught French and German. Though I didn't actually learn German, she taught us some in class when we had form time. She organised for us to have penfriends with a class in France that was being taught by a friend of hers. So I started writing to Guy Mailleau in Paris at age 11. I would write in French and he would reply in English. I learned of his family; they were from Bordeaux, in the South of France, but lived in Paris. He had a grandmother; mother, Odette; father, Robert; and one brother, Jean-Claude and two sisters, Françoise and Yolande. We exchanged little gifts and photographs, writing at least once every two weeks. At the age of 14 years an exchange visit was arranged with another class at Pont Audemer in Normandy. Unfortunately the girl I was paired with got sick and had to drop out. When I wrote to Guy and told him, he had been looking forward to meeting me when the school party made a trip to Paris. His family invited me to come and stay with them in Paris instead.

So at the age of 14 years and looking too much like 19 for my mother's peace of mind (I was fully developed very early) Mummy took me to Victoria to get the boat-train. On the train a man, who said that he was going to Casablanca, offered to look after me on the trip. That gave poor Mummy a terrible fright (with pictures of me ending up a white slave in a harem). Luckily we met a lovely girl called Helen, whose mother was also seeing her off, and we arranged to travel together, though she was only going as far as Dieppe. She was studying Pharmacy. We spent a pleasant trip together. The sea was calm and we arrived at Dieppe safely. At Dieppe, very nervous to be on my own again, I encountered a terrible problem. I was travelling in a very smart, fitted light green tweed suit, with a hat of mauve flowers. The suit unfortunately included a tight pencil skirt with a slit at the back.

When I got to the French train and found how high it was, I couldn't get up the stairs in my tight skirt. So, blushing like mad, I had to lift my skirt above my knee and climb up on board, having thrown my suitcase up first. I sat in a compartment with a French family and some French students, boys who were returning from England. They were very nice and kept chatting to me, but I was so nervous, I was always nervous!

After some time and a pleasant journey we reached Paris and Le Gare St Lazare. The boys helped me off with my case. Mummy had bought me some wheels, which were strapped onto the case, so I could wheel the case myself. Unfortunately the straps slipped off and I ended up carrying the case and the straps as well.

So, nervous as a kitten and in a strange country, where people spoke French and mine seemed to have disappeared, I got off the train and walked to the end of the platform. From the crowd, somebody started waving at me. We had previously written to say what I would be wearing. Then Guy came over to me, and said, "Are you the English girl called Valerie?" and I said, "Yes!" one of the only times in my life I ever said I was English (being Scottish or British, but not English) and he said, "I am Guy. Come and meet my family." And they were all there to meet me: his mother, father, sisters Yolande and Françoise, brother Jean-Claude and his sister's fiancé, also called Guy. None of them could speak English, but they were all so nice to me and gave me a tremendous welcome. We proceeded to another train to Rueil-Malmaison, where they lived, in a beautiful modern flat designed by Le Courbusier, a famous French architect. It was 13th July and the next day was Bastille Day. But, unfortunately, after all the nerves on the trip and the relief of arriving safely; as soon as they brought food to eat in the evening, I started vomiting, so the next day I had to stay in bed.

Guy was most annoyed as he had wanted to go out with everybody (I later found out that Jean-Claude, who was doing his National Service, was actually in the parade) and instead had to stay home with me and his grandmother as chaperon. His grandmother was a lovely old lady: a typical French widow dressed entirely in black. Her bedroom contained some beautiful old furniture, a crocheted white lace bedspread and a big crucifix on the wall. I wrote to Mummy to say that I was ill, and terribly homesick, and I wanted to come home immediately. Poor Mummy was frantic. Anyway, by the next day I felt better, and Guy, who was one year older than me, and his best friend Michel took me to see the sights of Paris. I went to the Eiffel Tower, and sent postcards to Keith and Anne Robbins, my best friend, saying that I was having a lovely time.

I stayed for six weeks and the weather was so hot. I saw the famous 'Tour de France' cycle race, as it passed us by. I fell ell in love with the 'Sacre Coeur' in Montmartre, and all the artists, still my favourite place in Paris. We went to Versailles at weekends and to the Bois de Boulogne for picnics with the whole family, who I grew to love so much. Of course at that age and in such a romantic setting, I received my first kiss from Guy and fell in love! There was a song sung by Paul Anka: 'Puppy Love' which, told exactly our story.

Anyway, after six weeks, I returned to London with so many happy and lovely memories (the first of several trips to Paris over the years) and also much plumper, as Guy's mother was such a wonderful cook and I loved all the food and wine that I sampled. We continued to write and I used to wait for the letter from the postman.

The following year, Guy came over to London, and as his English improved he took his Interpreter's exam. He was also learning Spanish and German. He did so well that his father wrote to my mother, to thank me, because I had helped him so much. One thing with him: whilst, if he made a mistake in English, I would quietly correct him; If I made a mistake in French, he would go into peals of laughter, and he made me afraid to speak French for fear of making mistakes. When I was alone with his mother and sisters I would have to speak French to communicate, but when Guy came home I would only speak English to him. So for the next three years I went to Paris sometimes just for the weekend, and Guy came to us in London. I would take him to Greenwich Palace, which he loved like me, and around the various sites in London. By this time he was working for the Societe Generale Bank in Paris.

The last time I went to Guy's family in Paris was for Christmas 1962, as Guy was going to start his National Service. We had a lovely Christmas going with the whole family to Midnight Mass, which was all in French, then having a magnificent midnight Christmas meal afterwards. They had oysters, which I am sorry is one thing I don't like, but I was sitting next to Jean-Claude and passing my oysters to him under the table and he was giving me his empty shells. Guy's father got us tickets for the Paris Opera, where we saw Bizet's '*Carmen*'. It was amazing! I wore a red Chiffon dress and Guy looked really dapper too!

He also took me to the 'Casino de Paris' in Montmartre, where they have the Nude Revues, and was dying to see my reaction, but I just took it in my stride. It was a beautiful show with fabulous costumes and I remember that Lina Renaud, one of their top stars, was singing.

We also went to '*Mutiny on the Bounty*', with Marlon Brando, who was then looking gorgeous and slim. It was all in French but I had already seen it in London before coming. But I didn't tell Guy, because it would have spoilt his surprise as he knew I loved Brando, as we had seen a couple of his films before, both in London and in Paris. It was all very romantic; they were my family and I loved all of them. By this time both Yolande and Jean-Claude were married and there were two babies in the family. Corinne was Elyane's and Jean-Claude's daughter; and Elizabeth was, Yolande's and Guy's (her husband was also Guy). They both had beautiful brown eyes; I have a passion for beautiful brown eyes. Guy's were light brown and really beautiful. He always said that my green eyes were so beautiful.

When it was time for me to go, he took me to the airport and he started crying, "I love you," he said, "and I am never going to see you again!" "Don't be silly," I said, " I will come over when you get your leave." He was almost right, as I would not see him again until 23 years later! As I travelled the world, he was also travelling, but to different parts from me. But I have many happy, wonderful memories of Guy and his family. Every time I hear a song about Paris, then I remember my happy time in Paris, and my Guy!

Whilst my cousin Keith was my constant companion from the age of nine months; when we got to secondary school it wasn't the same, as we were at different schools, and even though we still lived next door, we didn't see much of one another. I then became really good friends with the daughter of one of my mother's friends, Vi Robbins: her daughter, Anne Robbins, who was the same age as me; born on 6th January 1944. Together we dreamed our girlish dreams, as we developed into women. We used to buy the latest pop records and we perfected our own jive with many fancy styles. Her uncle George, who was not married and lived with them, used to take us for drives, winter and summer every Sunday, deep into the Kentish countryside.

Sometimes her mother and father would come and we would have lovely picnics, always in Kent, 'the Garden of England!' I think that we explored the whole of Kent in all seasons, from the primrose time, bluebell time, to catkins, pussy willow, and conkers in the autumn.

Anne's dad, also called George, used to drive us to many rock concerts. We used to go and scream our heads off. We saw many famous pop stars of the sixties: Billy Fury, Marty Wilde (who had been at school with my cousin Rod, Keith's elder brother) Eddie Cochran, Jean Vincent, Duffy Power and Joe Brown to name just a few! One time I remember at one concert, one star that I shall not name was wearing skintight black pants, and as he was gyrating on the stage, his zip burst, revealing beautiful white underpants underneath. He quickly covered himself with his guitar, and finished the number.

We went on our first date together. We had been learning judo and dancing at a local night school at Eltham, one of Anne's dad's friends, Mr. Ray, was the Headmaster and he used to pick us and bring us home. Originally, we had wanted to learn motor mechanics, but at that time they would not allow girls in the class! There were a number of boys at the school that we met at the dance classes. There were seven boys, who were all friends, and they all used to wear the same clothes. I remember a beautiful powder blue jacket, which they all wore, and they looked like pop stars of the 1960s or film stars.

So, three of the group asked Anne and me and Anita, who was a friend who lived across the road, on a triple date. They were going to take us dancing at the 'Embassy', Welling, Kent, which was a beautiful ballroom. We were all very nervous and dressed in our best frocks with frilly can-can petticoats, which was all the rage as when you jive you could see all the frills underneath. We met outside the ballroom and the boys took us to an espresso bar across the road. I had never had coffee before that, so what with the excitement, nerves, etc, I didn't feel too good. Anyway, we went into the dance. My date's name was Kay and Anne's was Leslie and Anita's, Terry. The other boys also joined us inside the hall. Now, one thing I liked to do was dance, any dance, waltz, quickstep, cha-cha-cha, jive, and foxtrot. So when I went to a dance I never sat down, apart from drinking an occasional orange juice, which is all I would drink.

We had a lovely evening and I was quite happy with my date, but Anne did not like hers. So on the next date it was only Anita and me. Then Terry didn't like Anita much, so it ended up with Kay and me. They, the boys, used two old banger cars, so it turned out, that I ended up with seven brothers and we went everywhere together. I was only five feet two inches and the boys towered over me. We had many lovely times together, going to dances, skating, and cinema, which we did twice a week.

The boys would ask me to choose a girl for them to dance with. If we went for a drive, they would all put money in the juke-box for me and let me choose all the records I liked. At this time I always had my hair in a French chignon and would put flowers at the back to match my dress colour; so people called me the girl with flowers in her hair! The boys would buy me chocolate, which I love to this day, and as they passed me sitting in the car they would drop it in my lap. This lasted for over a year, from 15 years till 16 years old. When I was 16, in the summer, Guy came over on a holiday and Kay was jealous of him.

One night he decided to take Guy out and get him drunk, not realising that Guy was used to wine everyday. So the inevitable happened and he got drunk himself. When they came back, with him in that disgusting state, I told him to go and that I never want to see him again. As he was going he pulled Guy down the stairs and they fell down the stairs together!

The next morning all the boys turned up. They had come to find out what had happened. They said that Kay had slept outside on the grass verge all night and all they could get from him was 'Valerie! Valerie!' I told them what had happened and they went away. All this time there was no sexual activity, only a few kisses. After Guy left, Kay came back and apologised and said that he wanted to be friends again, so I said okay and we went out together again. But Kay decided that he was going to marry me, and that if he got me pregnant, I would have to marry him. Life at that time was very different from today, we had no sexual education at school and the TV and films were heavily censored and there were no sexual magazines. I was very naïve and innocent, I had no brothers and had never seen a man naked (though I would always ask my mother why ballet dancers had that bump in the front but she never told me?).

Up to that point, we had never had sex, just kissing and some heavy petting. So one day when my mother was out, he forced me and took my virginity. It was very painful, he could not get it in and really forced me. I didn't enjoy it, so that time I finished with him and didn't see him again ever to this day. Whilst I had a permanent boyfriend, and had started working. Anne had also started working, so I saw less and less of her.

Though when I had Hamish she did come with her mother and bring me a lovely dress for the baby, She eventually married her brother's best friend and went to live in New Zealand, so I have lost contact with her. But I have happy memories of her and her family. Uncle George and her dad died so her mother joined them in

New Zealand.

I left school at fifteen and a half years. Though I was supposed to take my O levels, I left the day I should have taken my mock exams. Something, I have always regretted! It was because my friends were earning money and buying dresses etc, so I also wanted some. In those days it was not difficult to get jobs without qualifications; you could leave a job on Friday and start a new one on Monday!

I was lucky to get a job with 'Continental Telephone Exchange', now part of 'International' at Faraday House, Queen Victoria Street. It was a job that I really loved and I was very happy there, talking to France, Germany, Sweden, Russia and all the other European countries every day. It also meant that I could telephone Guy in Paris, more frequently. Though we had to work Christmas Day and most of the holidays and it was shift work, though only days, as the night staff were all men at that time.

Unfortunately, at the age of 16, I fell in love with a man who was working there and for a few months was ecstatically happy even though he was 42 years old! Then one day he rang me and said, "I don't want to see you again as my wife has come back!"

As you can imagine, my world collapsed. This had been the first serious sexual relationship of my life. He was French and a very experienced lover, and I had really enjoyed sex with him. He had taken me to expensive nightclubs and for really expensive dinners and to the races, at Newmarket etc, and introduced me to a very sophisticated adult life. I had a nervous breakdown; I couldn't go to work for three months, and then, as he was still working there, my mother decided I should get another job, away from him. So I got a job at a firm of chartered accountants in Albemarle Street, Mayfair. There were lots of famous people who were their clients and it was quite exciting to see them all. But the travelling was a bit difficult; I didn't like the Underground. I also had an unpleasant experience with one of the directors, so I looked for another job.

I found a job as receptionist-telephonist at the production engineering division, of Wiggins Teape, the famous paper company, at Southwark Bridge Road, London. I was quite happy there and spent a lot of time with the porter, Mr. Gold, whose office was on the ground floor next to reception. He was an Orthodox Jew and fairly religious. He was not too well, as he had survived the holocaust in Germany. He also did a lot of printing for the firm in the days before photocopiers.

After that affair, I decided that nobody was going to hurt me like that again, so I put my heart on ice, and guarded it carefully. Though I had several boyfriends who took me out to dinner, cinema etc, there was never any sex between us. One thing that I have omitted to say is that I have always been very religious. As from the age of three, one of the neighbours, who taught Sunday school at the local Methodist church, used to pick me up every Sunday and take me to Sunday school with her.

I therefore always loved Jesus, and God has been a real father to me and I would talk to him at anytime.

When I got to ten years old; as I had been christened an Anglican, I started to go to the Anglican Church, St Luke's, Charlton. The Rector was, The Rev Harold Gatehouse Bear, I really loved him; he was tall and dignified with a Roman look about him, and I always wished that my father could have been like him. I was confirmed and then I used to teach Sunday school, along with Laraine, to four-year-olds at St Mary's, which was a brand new parish church at that time. The parish comprised of St Luke's, Holy Trinity, (now pulled down) and St Richard's, and there was a training house, for young ordinates, run by Father Summers, who eventually went to Cambridge.

I used to go to church at 9.30am for communion, then go to the parish hall for parish breakfast, and then go and teach Sunday school at St Mary's. Sometimes on Sunday afternoon I would go with my mother to help her teach Sunday school at St Richard's at 3pm. Then we would go to evensong at 6.30pm. After that, we would go the church youth club until 9.30, where we would have coffee and talk about different things. Sometimes the boys played squash. I was friends with everybody, though nobody special. I did have a crush on one of my mother's friend's son. He wanted to become a priest. His mother had told everybody that he was going blind, so we all looked after him with extra care. He later went to train at Kelham, but was unable to complete and became a teacher instead. It turned out that he was not going blind at all. His mother had just made it up, for whatever reason, I cannot fathom even to this day. But, thank God, he is well and happily married with two daughters.

Now at the youth club we had several young priests with a lot of ideas: John Sharpe, Duncan Ferguson, and Alan Waite. We planned jumble sales and dances to collect money to buy an espresso coffee maker for the parish breakfasts. That led to us starting a club on Wednesday evenings for non-church members. We played rock n' roll, and it became quite a famous place and many stars of the sixties came. It was called 'The 2 K's'. Now the only way that you could get entry was that you had to attend one service on Sunday, and then you would get a ticket. In this way we got a lot of young people to come to church and we hoped that something would get through to them.

It was not unusual to see boys in black leather trousers and girls in all sorts of dresses there. Cliff Richard came at one time, and Johnny Kidd and the Pirates, and many others. After that, we sent John Sharpe to New Guinea as a missionary and everybody took shares to sponsor him for several years. It was quite exciting going to church at that time.

There was another church attached to St Luke's parish: 'Holy Trinity', on the Lower Charlton – Woolwich road. In the vicarage they had a training house for young ordinates. Young lads aspiring to become priests came there to learn Greek and, Latin, and to complete their O & A levels necessary for going to theological college. My friend Josie, who lived across the road, had a mad passion for one of the boys, whose name was Barry. So we all went along with her on Sunday evenings for evensong. The church didn't have a large congregation – only a few old ladies. The priest in charge was Father Summers, who was a real human priest, and we all loved him. There was a pub across the road from the church and he was often in there with the boys.

One day when I went with the gang – boys and girls including Laraine – there was a new boy and he was absolutely gorgeous like a Greek god; he was very tall and very young. He had been to boarding school and been such a devil, that he was expelled. His name was Rodney Mullinar, and his father was a professor at the Royal College of Music. Rodney had a camel hair coat, which he never put on but threw it around his shoulders like a cloak. He also wore a hat. He had a long lock of hair, which spent most of the time in his eyes. He was only 19 years old, but he had the air and sophistication of a mature man. Rodney became my boyfriend and we had a lot of fun together whilst he was at the vicarage. He said that the local priest at home, who was a friend of his mother's, had arranged for him to come on the course, as nobody knew what to do with him.

Rodney had a beautiful cultured English voice and was a real gentleman with lovely manners. I was lucky in the fact that though I loved him and thought he was lovely, my heart did not get involved with him, so I was able to enjoy him and have lots of fun with him without any heartache. Sex with Rodney was amazing and some of the best that I had in my life. But you could sense that he was only in transit and would move on. We used to walk along the road singing. I had a beautiful royal blue coat with a white velvet snood trimmed with swan's down around the face. Rodney was always wrapping it around my face. They didn't get much time off from the vicarage, so one day I was given some tickets to a show and we gave them to Father Summers and his housekeeper, which meant that all the boys, could have the night off.

One day I accompanied him to Christ's Hospital School, in Horsham. His younger brother John was there. He said that his brother's godfather, Vaughan-Williams, the composer, paid the school fees. Rodney's godfather was Sir Adrian Boult, the famous conductor. We had a lovely day and took his brother out to tea at a famous tearoom in town. The school was a fantastic building, hundreds of years old. I remember especially when it was dusk, walking along a long path in the college, arm in arm with Rodney, and wondering where the road was going to lead us in the future.

In the train back to London we did something so daring that it always makes me sparkle to think of it up to this day. We made love as the train was going through a tunnel; nothing ever seemed wrong with Rodney! Another time, he took me to see a friend of his, whose father, was the chairman of BOAC. He had just come back from Tahiti, and he said that he had taken a photo of a girl who looked just like me. So we spent hours going through his slides and he was able to find it. Another time, he took me to his parent's house at Richmond. His father's study had piles of music, all over the chairs, floor and tables. I can't remember if they were all asleep or away or something but I do remember that I didn't actually meet anybody!

One day Rodney came and I was not in, so he asked my sister Laraine, who was 15 years at that time, to join him for a coffee. I was 18 at this time. The next time I went out with Rodney, we were standing on the porch, kissing goodnight; Rodney was one of the most wonderful kissers that I have known. Then Mummy came and opened the door and said, "Here, you pair! You had better come and speak to Laraine. She has been crying all night and says that you pinched her boyfriend!" So Rodney came in to pacify Laraine. He had such a lovely twinkle in his eye, and he was always so lovely, that you just had to forgive him. He was well covered with flesh, not fat, so his nickname was Podgy Pod.

After a few months of enjoying his company, he seemingly didn't pass his exams and departed from Charlton. I heard that a friend had given him a one-way ticket to South Africa. I know that wherever he goes he will spread a lot of sunshine and break a few hearts; I was lucky that mine wasn't one of them. I have many pleasant memories of a lovely friend. Mummy always loved Rodney. He always used to raise his hat to her and say, "Good Morning, Mrs. Brown." He was so sophisticated, like some great Shakespearian actor, so grand. Remember, he was still only 19 years old, so a long way to go. I wonder where he is now and what he is doing?

Father Summers left Holy Trinity to teach at Cambridge and a few years later, I found out, that they had knocked Holy Trinity down and there is nothing but a large gap, but a lot of happy memories to fill it.

Whilst I was working at Wiggins' Teape, I had a boyfriend called Tony, who worked at the head office at Gateway House, St Paul's. One Christmas, he was escorting me to the firm's Christmas ball, to be held at a fashionable ballroom in London. As he lived at Leigh on Sea, and came to work on the train, he decided to borrow a friend's brand new mini-van to take us to the ball. When I heard, I said, "What! I'm not going to a ball in a mini-van. If you turn up to meet me at Charing Cross Station in a mini-van, I will take a taxi and go on my own!"

I was going home to change, but Tony was going to a friend's flat to freshen up. When I got to Charing Cross, Tony was there and he had hired, a beautiful new car, from Godfrey Davies, and as it was snowing, he had to pay an extra charge for it, so I was pacified! The ball was lovely and we had a good time dancing the twist, which was all the rage then. Then we started the journey back to Charlton. It was a nightmare drive; the snow was so thick and ice underneath. Every time we went round a corner the car slid across the road. After a lot of slipping and sliding we eventually reached Charlton. It was three o'clock in the morning by that time. There were no cars on the road, as most sensible people were home in bed. Tony was a lovely escort and took me to many dinners and cinemas and he was a perfect gentleman. (Years later, sitting in an open sided navy jeep, I used to remember Tony and the mini-van. I wished I could have been in that brand new mini-van, at that time, instead of hanging on for dear life, and pregnant to boot!

Whilst I was going to church and the youth club, I had my first meeting with black people. There were Nigerian and Ghanaian students at the local polytechnic who used to come to our church. My mother had taught me never to be prejudiced against anybody and to wish everybody "good morning!" no matter who he or she was or what they did! It did no harm and could do a lot of good. After the youth club closed several boys and girls came back to my house, where they were always welcomed by my mother, who always said, "she wanted to know who we associated with! We played records, usually my darling 'Elvis', to whom this day I am still a devoted fan! (At this present moment of typing, after being dead for 25 years, he is No. 1 in the charts again!) I was a member of 'The Official Elvis Presley Fan Club of Great Britain and the Commonwealth'. His pictures were all over my bedroom walls.

We usually had coffee and chocolate wheaten biscuits, and most people sat on the floor. There was one Ghanaian, who had a stammer and people found it difficult to understand him, but I found that once he knew you and relaxed in your company, the stammer almost left, so I used to spend a lot of time talking to him. He was never my boyfriend, but a really good friend. His name was Hector Ussher. One Christmas I asked him what he was doing for Christmas and he said, "Nothing", so I asked Mummy and she said that he could come to us on Christmas Day. I was actually working that day as I was at 'Continental telephone exchange' and was rostered for Christmas Day! So I wasn't there. Mummy prepared another Christmas lunch for me on Boxing Day and Hector was invited. We waited and waited but he didn't come, so we put some lunch for him in the oven.

At teatime he appeared and said that his cousin had come from Dartmouth Naval College, and though he had told him that it would be all right for him to come to us. He had, had a nasty experience with an English family; and therefore didn't want to come; and Hector said that he was going to the station to see him off, I asked where was he, and he said, "Outside", so I went outside and told him to come in. He was very, very nervous, but after a while he relaxed and we had a pleasant evening. He said that he would like to write to us as a family and we all agreed and also told him that he was welcome to pop in anytime he was in London. If we were in, We were in! And if we were out, we were out!

That was Boxing Day 1960, and though I didn't know it or suspect it in any way, that was my first meeting with my future husband, James Desmond McCarthy, Boham! Over the next three years he would send us postcards from all over the world when he was at sea, and pop in when he had a weekend off and came up to London. At that time he was a cadet in the Ghana Navy at the Britannia Royal Naval College, at Dartmouth, Devon. When we met that Christmas I was only 16 years old and not very experienced with men or the world. He invited me to attend the end of term ball at Dartmouth at Easter time. I was very nervous and didn't want to go, but Mummy persuaded me that it would be a lovely occasion and I shouldn't miss it. So I found myself on the train going to Dartmouth, a bundle of nerves as they say! I wasn't very happy with my dress, which was my confirmation dress in white brocade. I felt that it wasn't grand enough for the ball at Dartmouth, or so I thought. Unfortunately, the train was delayed and was very late. James met me at the station and took me to the hotel and then had to leave me, and couldn't have dinner with me because as a cadet he had to get back to the college!

He said that he would come for me in the morning and take me to the college, and then he left me. So there I was, a bundle of nerves, alone in a strange hotel for the first time in my life. I quickly ate something and decided that the best thing for me was to go to bed. No sooner had I got into bed, when there was a knock on the door. There was a phone call for me; could I come down and take it? So I had to go downstairs in my dressing-gown, and walk through a bar full of men to take the phone. I was so embarrassed! It was Mummy ringing to see if I was all right and had arrived safely. So I told her that I was all alone and very nervous. She told me not to worry and to go back to sleep. I went back to bed and there was another knock, another call. This time it was James, to say that he could not come and collect me in the morning, as he had to do something in the college. He said that I should get a taxi to the college and he would meet me there. I'm afraid that it was all too much for me and I decided that the first thing in the morning I would get the train back to London!

I went to stay with a friend, because if I went home Mummy would literally kill me for being such a goose. I wrote a note and apologised to James, saying that my nerves would not allow me to stay! I spent the rest of the weekend at my friend's house and when I went home I told Mummy all about the ball (which I hadn't attended). She mostly asked questions, which I answered.

My next problem was: what would James tell Mummy next time we saw him? Anyway, it was some time before we saw him, as he was stationed in Malta for a while. When he did come he didn't give me away, and for that I was most grateful and liked him a lot, and so we continued. He would pop in occasionally. Sometimes I was going out dancing with friends and he would sit and chat with Mummy.

Then in 1963, summer, he invited me to his Passing Out Parade and Ball at Dartmouth. By this time I had travelled to France several times to stay with Guy and his family. I was no longer as nervous as before – quite the young lady at 19 years old. So I went to Peter Robinson's and bought a beautiful strapless chiffon evening gown with ruched body and crinoline skirt in yellow with shoes dyed to match, black velvet and silver lame stole, and an Italian crystal tiara. I felt fit for the ball! I also bought a red silk military style shirt-waister dress to attend the parade. My hair, which by now was dark blonde, I used to put in a French roll; and I used flowers to match what I was wearing to cover the pins at the back. For travelling, I bought a shades of purple tweed suit, so felt quite chic, and with a pair of chic sunglasses, was all set to go.

Now, James was a senior sub-lieutenant, so no problem of rushing back to college! The train was on time and James was there to meet me and took me to a very nice boarding house with a lovely landlady to cater for all my needs. We walked around Dartmouth, which is a beautiful place along by the river, and it was lovely in the summer evening. The next morning I took a taxi and went to the college, and James met me and took me to where the spectators stood to watch the parade. I was wearing my red silk dress. James said that after the parade I should meet him at the gymnasium entrance. So, after the parade I went to the gymnasium entrance, but, though there were many people there in groups with their girlfriends and families, no sign of James! So what to do? I asked somebody, and they told me to go and ask the porter, at the Exmouth division. So I did, and after a while James came down, and said, "Oh, it's you!" He had seen somebody in a red dress leaving in a taxi and thought that I had gone.

He took me round the college, which was very interesting, and then we had lunch and went back to rest before the ball in the evening. I put on my beautiful yellow dress and my tiara, and looked really lovely though I say it myself. James came in his mess jacket naval evening uniform, looking very nice indeed. So we went to the ball!

There were two other Ghanaian officers passing out with James: Fred Anatsui and George Bedu-Addo. There were also some new cadets who had just arrived. James invited some friends, a couple that owned a hotel at Torbay, a doctor, Mike, and Belinda his wife. It was very pleasant company. There were several different bands playing in different rooms in the college. Then we all went into supper. Dartmouth is famous for its strawberries served at balls, so we had some of the famous strawberries and, whoops, the whole lot was knocked down my dress by somebody passing. James went up to his cabin and brought some Omo (washing powder) and washed it all off my dress for me. I had loads of champagne and was very happy!

The next thing, as we were dancing, I felt something around my ankles. My dress with the crinoline had three petticoats, and when they did the alterations at Peter Robinson's they had missed one layer, and it had worked down and I had put my foot through the frill! We, James and I, went out into the garden and ripped the rest of the frill off, all round, and left it in the bushes. So if anyone found a frill the next morning at Dartmouth, it was mine!

We had a lovely evening and for the first time in our relationship, James kissed me goodnight. It was very nice and romantic; a beautiful summer night, with all the stars out. I, of course, had my champagne. I am not a drinker but I do love my champagne, Not to get drunk but to get pleasantly mellow. Whatever anyone says, there is nothing like champagne, especially Moet et Chandon, my favourite!

The next morning we went to the Methodist chapel, in the college. James read the lesson, and then he came with me to London, on the train, along with two Nigerian friends of his. One, Abdulai, later became Commander of the Nigerian Navy. James had three weeks' leave, before he had to leave to return to Ghana, so he asked me to take leave and spend it with him. I realised that I was going to miss him when he left. He said that he loved me and asked me to marry him. I said yes and we bought an engagement ring from a jeweller's behind St Paul's Cathedral. Two diamonds and a sapphire. It was all so romantic. I went to see him, Fred and George off, at the West London Air Terminal at Cromwell Road. We had planned that I would join him in November, and we would have a naval wedding in Ghana.

When James and I got engaged in July 1963, he was staying with his sister Anna at Balham, London. I used to visit him there. One day he went out and he said that he was expecting his niece Julie, his sister Elizabeth's daughter, who was only one year younger than him. So, would I let her in? I said, "yes of course!" The bell rang and I opened the door and there was this lovely friendly girl. I introduced myself as "Valerie, your uncle's fiancée". She was very pleased and excited. When his sister came home later, Julie went upstairs to her room with her and the next thing I knew, there was this wild African woman, James's Anna, coming bursting into the room, wrapped only in a cloth and shouting at the top of her voice in Fanti. She was shouting at James, and then she took his cabin trunk and threw it down the stairs. I had no idea what it was all about, till later. James said, "Darling, let's go!" The explanation was this: as James didn't know what to expect from his sister he had not told her that we were engaged. (In Ghana an engagement was as binding as a wedding.) I didn't know this until many years later. Anyway, I was quite horrified at her behaviour, though I thought it was really bad of him not to have had the courage to tell her.

He moved to a friend Daniel Blay-Afful's house, and we had a small engagement party there. Mummy came and the rest were mostly Ghanaians. His niece Julie came and when she met Dan she immediately liked him and later they got married. Then it was time for James to return to Ghana. He didn't see his sister, again before he left!

Six weeks after he left, I went to visit his niece Julie and she had invited an English girlfriend who had never tried African food before, so I told her how nice it was and how much I liked it. The girl reluctantly tried it, imagine my surprise when immediately I ate, I started feeling sick and just got to the sink in time before I vomited all over the kitchen floor. I said, "Oh! it must be the Underground." To this day I don't like travelling on the Underground, but needs must.

When I got home, I said to Mummy, "Funny thing, I was sick today." Mummy took me to the doctor, who confirmed her worst fears, that I was pregnant. I was totally unaware as we had had sex only once and had used contraceptives! Mummy and the doctor, who was an old family friend, wanted me to have an abortion; but I would not hear of it, being very religious and feeling that life was sacred and being very excited to be pregnant. So they gave me some tablets, which should have caused abortion. But when I took them they made me vomit and I never stopped vomiting during the whole pregnancy.

I got a book from Gina (who was also pregnant the same time as me) on relaxation exercises and started doing them. As soon as James returned to Ghana, I received a letter to say that the Admiral in Charge of the Navy had refused us permission to marry. (Many years later when the Admiral became one of my best friends, mentor, father, brother, uncle all rolled into one! I found out that it was not true, but rather James had said that we were already married.) When I wrote to James to say that I was pregnant I did not hear from him for several months. He sent a friend to my mother to offer money for an abortion, (I didn't find that out until several years later). In the meantime I was very ill with the pregnancy; I even had to attend clinic in an ambulance as I kept fainting all the time. I couldn't work so I spent almost seven months at home, hardly going out. I couldn't go to church but Father Bear used to visit me at home.

When my sister found out that I was pregnant with an African she was so disgusted that she left home and went to stay with a boyfriend's mother because she was afraid of what the neighbours would say. The neighbours were more disgusted with her leaving me than with me, and I must say they were all lovely to me. When the baby was born I had dresses and presents from the neighbours. When my father was told I was pregnant he told me, to "Get out of the house!" But Mummy said, She's not going anywhere; this flat is in my name!" That I never knew until that day. I was so upset and went round with Mummy to see Miss Jean Robinson, who was the parish worker. She had always been a good friend to me and I was going to miss her as she left the parish soon after.

From that day until my baby was born I never saw my father again, When he came in I went to my room and stayed there. My mother and my father were not together at this time, they lived separate lives although they lived in the same house. They had nothing in common and were like chalk and cheese. Daddy's life was still his sports and would be until he died.

After some time, James wrote and said that he had married me by African Customary Rights, and he sent me a bible and a wedding ring made from Ghana gold. So from November 1963, according to him, I could call myself Mrs. Boham. He said that he was trying to come back to England to do a course.

In March 1964, I had a letter from him saying that The Ghana Navy – the whole fleet – was visiting Liberia, one vessel – GNV Achimota – would be coming to England for a refit, and he was trying to be transferred onto it. A few weeks later I heard on the news that Sierra Leone, had that day issued a self-stick stamp in the shape of the map of Sierra Leone. A few days later the postman brought a letter and from the top of the stairs; I saw the postcard with that self same stamp, which meant that James was on the way. On 1st May 1964, the day Princess Margaret's son (Viscount Linley was born (there were four Royal births when Hamish was born in 1964), the bell rang and Mummy went down to open the door. It was James. It was a great relief after so many months. He asked me, "Where is the baby?" I was so small, I only looked about five months pregnant and I said, " It's there."

He said, "Well, he can come anytime now!" He had to go back to his ship, which was in Southampton in the drydock, but he said he would come as soon as we needed him. He wanted to get married there and then, but I said, "No! I have waited so long, a few more weeks won't make any difference."

On 6th May, I had a show and the doctor sent me to hospital. On 7th May 1964, at 2.30 in the morning, Hamish was born. I had no pain and in fact didn't know that the baby was actually coming. He weighed 7lbs 5oz and all the nurses and even the doctor were asking where had I put him? As I had been so small at fullterm. I was so thrilled with my son and lay awake looking at him, and I couldn't believe that I had produced anything so beautiful. He had long black straight hair and everybody said that he looked like a Beatle. Nobody suspected that his father was an African, as there was no sign on him and he was very white.

Mummy sent a telegram to James and she came at visiting time. At that time, visiting hours were very rigid – only half an hour and only two visitors at a time. Suddenly, towards the end of the visiting time there was a commotion at the door and a voice said, "I must see my wife!" And James strode in. It was a long ward with glass partitions, and everybody visiting his wife turned and all eyes were on us, and James came and kissed me and said, "You're wonderful, darling." Mummy said that the man whose wife was in the next bed said, "Gor blimey! That was better than the pictures!" I must say that I had long hair and a band in it to match my nightie and everybody thought I was a film star! I received two enormous bouquets of flowers the day Hamish was born, and three days later it was my twentieth birthday so I received some more. All the ward had some of my flowers so as she was leaving I asked Mummy: "Could I give her bouquet to the midwife who had delivered me?" So I gave her the whole bouquet still with its ribbons and wrapping and she was very happy.

After about a week I was allowed home with the baby, because in those days they didn't chuck you out of hospital as soon as you had a baby. We had physiotherapy and post-natal exercises to help you get your figure back quickly. (Today I am amazed by all these young girls who have Caesareans and come out with enormous stomachs which take months to get rid of.) In no time at all, I was wearing my normal clothes. Hamish was very good right from the start; he used to eat and sleep and had the loveliest nature.

On 1st June 1964, we were married by special licence, by Father Bear, at St Luke's Church, Charlton; very quietly. There was Mummy and Sam Adzigbli, our best man; and Deaconess Stonestreet, who had replaced Miss Robinson; and Dan Adjekumsa, who came with Sam. Father Bear asked James if he was a practising Methodist and he said, "Not today!" So we didn't have communion! Auntie Freda, Keith's mother, looked after Hamish for me. It rained heavily all day and it was at eleven o'clock on a Monday morning. I wore a short, Grecian style, white chiffon cocktail dress, with a train over one shoulder, and with a garland, of wax orange blossom flowers around my head. My hair was in a bun on top with the flowers around. I didn't wear a veil. We had a small wedding lunch at home and I made a small wedding cake and we had champagne!

On 7th June we christened Hamish and had a big party in

St Richard's Hall. That was really our wedding reception as well (killing two birds with one stone). All the Ghanaian officers who were in Dartmouth at that time came, including: Joey Amedume, (who became Commander Navy and was later shot, during the 1979 coup). He had a beautiful West Indian girlfriend at the time. Auntie Doll and Maureen and Pauline helped with the party and James had brought gallons of duty free drinks from the ship so the party was well celebrated!

We then rented a house at Wilson Grove, Southsea. The house belonged to an old lady who had gone into a home. The house was full of beautiful antiques and the son didn't seem to realise. There were beautiful carved chairs from India and screens inlaid with ivory and precious stones, silver hairbrushes and combs. All our friends who came nicknamed it 'the Museum'. I met Sally and Jim Addo, who had just had a baby: Donna-Marie; She was the prettiest baby that you ever did see, with lots of hair. Glendora, who was Matthew Lartey's girlfriend, brought lots of stuffed toys made by her patients in the hospital. They were really beautiful: a puppy dog who looked so real if you sat him in the grass, a beautiful white velvet elephant with seat in mauve and jewels, and a lion. Hamish was really happy with those. Mummy came down at weekends so that we could go out and she could be with her grandson.

We were invited to the end of term ball at Dartmouth, by the four who were passing out: Joe Kyeremeh, Joy Amedume, Ben Nubour and Kevin Dzang. We had a lovely time at the ball. I wore a harebell blue chiffon strapless dress with silver embroidery on the bodice. It was a lovely time and I was very happy with my new husband and baby son. We arranged to go and see them: Kyeremeh, Amedume, Nubour, and Dzang off at London Airport; Mummy came down to Southsea to look after Hamish. We got the train up to my mother's and would then go and see them off the next day. We arrived late in the evening to find that my sister Laraine, had her boyfriend Terry staying the night and he was sleeping in Mummy's bed, where we were supposed to sleep, though he lived in Ilford and had a car. My Father came and I told him that we had come to stay. He said, "That we should sleep on the sofa!" James got angry and said, "Come on,

Darling, lets go" We tried to find a hotel, but because it was August Bank Holiday they were all full. So we ended up getting the mail train back to Portsmouth, getting there really early in the morning; and Mummy had Glendora sleeping over with her so we had to wait for them to get up before we could sleep! That was an experience I never wish to repeat.

After doing a short navigation course at HMS *Dryad*, James was now returning to Ghana. He was posted to a brand new corvette, *G.N.V. Kromantse, which,* had been built for the Ghana Navy by Vickers Thornycroft at Southampton, and then had trials at Portland Bill. For the commissioning of the *Kromantse,* James decided that I should wear Ghanaian dress and we bought some material and James sewed it for me. It had a beautiful pattern of white background with big red tropical flowers and I wore an ivory necklace, earrings and bracelet, which had been brought from Ghana for me. James was in charge of the parade, so I was to come with Joe Kyeremeh and his girlfriend Ethel. But Ethel was taking so long to get ready and I knew that James would be furious if I was late, so I got a taxi to the Portsmouth Dockyard, where the ship was alongside. When I got there I was already late and all the admirals had arrived! To my horror I discovered that the slit skirt of my dress was so tight that I could hardly move. So with the guard of honour drawn up and all the admirals waiting I had to make a slow and stately progress to my seat, which was right in the front. I could see James looking daggers at me but it was his fault as he had made the dress!

The ceremony went off well and there were so many admirals and their wives. Anyway, the ratings on the ship were all proud of me, as I was the only one representing Ghanaian wives. The British officers asked me how long had I been in Ghana and I said, "I've never been there!"

That day was the first day that I met Commodore Hansen (the head of the Ghana Navy, who had been transferred from the Ghana Army where he was a colonel) though at that time I was annoyed with him, because, as I had been told, he had refused us permission to marry, which caused so much anguish on my part! But he is such a charming man, a real gentleman and a man amongst men and an

African. Today Uncle David and Auntie Lily are my most treasured friends, supporting me against all odds, but that was almost forty years ago!

So the ship sailed for Ghana, and on 22nd November 1964 Hamish, now six months, and I said farewell to Mummy at Heathrow and flew out to Ghana for the first time.

Chapter Two

GHANA
1964–1966

On 22nd November 1964, Hamish and I took a Ghana Airways flight to Accra, the capital of Ghana. We flew on a Coronado chartered by Ghana Airways from Swiss Air, one of the best aircrafts that I have flown on. The cabin crew was really helpful with the baby. As you can imagine I was so excited. Hamish, who was a wonderful baby, cut his first tooth on the plane going to Accra. The flight took five hours – the shortest flight that I have ever had to Ghana. It was not my first flight, having flown to Glasgow and Paris, but it was definitely the longest at that time. It was a pleasant flight and a really good landing. Arrival at Accra so excited. When we got out of the plane at 6pm it was already getting dark (in the tropics it gets dark just like somebody has switched off the light). When we came out from the plane it was so humid and Hamish started sweating and I had to take off his dress. James was at the foot of the plane, with several of his friends, all military officers. Two of James's friends had started writing to me before I came and one of them was at the airport to meet me: Kwame Asante, who was then Adjutant of the President's Own Guard Regiment. The President was Dr Kwame Nkrumah, who had done so much for the African cause.

Also to meet me were Emile Allottey-Annan, who was in the Air Force at that time; Kwame Baah, who later became Foreign Minister; and Benny, another friend of my husband's. They greeted me nicely and made me feel so welcome and I was so happy to see James again. Emile took us to his house in Dodowa Villas, very near to Flagstaff House where President Nkrumah lived. He gave us his own bedroom to sleep in that night. His brother in law offered to look after Hamish, and so my first evening in Accra I went dancing at the Metropole Hotel where the famous Ramblers International Band played every Sunday at that time. Kwame Asante's girlfriend was a beautiful girl called Cecelia, and we became good friends. Emile's wife was also called Cecelia and we remain sisters to this day (nearly forty years later as of writing). She is one of those special people that you meet in life.

After a pleasant evening dancing 'highlife' we went home to sleep. I slept very well indeed. In the morning we got up at 5am, and ate fresh grapefruit from the tree, absolutely delicious! We went to the airport to take an Air Force flight to Takoradi, where James was stationed. If you have never been in the tropics, I think that 6am is the loveliest time: the sun coming up but nice and cool; all the tropical flowers along the roadside – hibiscus, frangipani, bougainvillea, all colours; flame trees, mango trees, poinsettia; and the birds singing, people walking along, watchmen coming home from work, and others hurrying to work; the tro-tro local buses (which used to mean 'thruppance-thruppance' but now costs a lot more in fares); vans with wooden bodies with all manner of sayings on them written in the local languages, like '(they look like lovers' and) ('God be with You') and 'God is here'. Anyway, I was thrilled and still so excited.

At the airport we said goodbye to Emile and thanked him for his hospitality. In Takoradi we were going to stay with the other friend of James's who had been writing to me – Tom Kutin. He had written to say that his home was mine for as long as I needed, and that James had talked about me so much and he had seen so many photographs of me that he felt that he knew me already. The flight was a good flight and we flew on an 'Otter', which was twin engined, and we flew low over the coast and you could see all the villages along the route, and in that beautiful sunshine it was perfect. The pilot was Kwesi Forsen, who became another good friend. Hamish cut his second tooth on the plane from Accra to Takoradi but made no fuss.

As I said, he was really a good baby, and once he had his dummy, "no problem".

Tom met us, in dashing Air Force blue uniform. (He has been one of my dearest friends throughout my stay in Ghana.) James was in his white naval uniform – the first time I had seen him in white. (In England they wear the navy blue uniform but with Ghana Navy, buttons and emblems.)

Tom took us home, which was a one and a half bedroomed flat at Airport Ridge, the military quarters in Takoradi. I met Tom's wife Regina, who was pregnant with their first child. Everybody made a grab for Hamish and he was really spoiled. Winifred, Regina's younger sister, age 12 at that time, was living with them and going to school. They couldn't have been kinder or nicer. We had lunch, which was yam and turkey tail stew. That was the first time I discovered that people ate turkey tails, and in fact they were imported frozen from Europe. It was Tom's favourite. The yam was really nice, quite like potato. Then I wanted some bread and discovered that most people in Ghana ate sugar bread. You can imagine eating egg sandwich with sugar bread so we had to hunt for what they called tea bread, which was like our normal bread. But it is amazing how quickly you get used to things and I was eating sugar bread like everybody else in a very short time.

Regina, who was a nurse, was one of the most beautiful black women I have ever seen (and when I say black, I mean pure black). She is among the gentlest and loveliest people that I have met. They gave us the small bedroom with a single bed and Hamish's cot and no fan, but we were on the first floor and not far from the sea and I never felt hot – I just loved the sunshine. After a few days Regina's mother, Mrs. Kwasie, and her elder sister came to visit! So you can imagine the situation, but we all fitted in. Regina was on night duty and slept during the day, TT slept on the sofa in the sitting room, and Regina's mother and sister were in the bedroom. We were all very happy and Regina's mother gave me a lot of good advice about living in Ghana. One day Regina cooked fried plantain on a coal pot in the kitchen. I thought it was the most delicious food I had ever eaten. Takoradi is really beautiful with the most enormous trees that you can ever see; the harbour and the ships (at that time there was no naval harbour so the navy ships were in a section of the harbour, with a base on top of the hill); with huge log ponds in the harbour awaiting shipment to Europe, and the sheds in the harbour were full of amazing goods from all over the world. Blue skies, sunshine and flowers everywhere. About a week after I arrived in Ghana, *GNV Kromantse* was to pay a visit to the town the ship was named after. One naval officer, Lt. Nathan Mante, took Hamish and me by car. It was about a one hour drive. Joe Kyremeh and Joey Amedume also joined us. When we got to Kromantse the ship was anchored at sea and the crew had come ashore on surfboats, as there was no harbour or jetty.

There was a big Durbar of chiefs from all the surrounding villages, with their colourful Kente cloth (the national dress) and the chief's umbrellas and palanquins. Somebody grabbed Hamish and took him away. I was terrified I was going to lose him but Hamish wasn't bothered, just happy with all the attention; and people speaking in Fanti, of which I couldn't speak or understand a word at that time! Anyway, after some customary rites were performed and libation to the Gods and some African drumming and dancing, we were taken to the regional office for food and drinks, and afterwards a very colourful day was spent on the beach under coconut trees. With the sun shining we returned to Takoradi.

After six weeks we were given a flat downstairs in the same block as TT's. James was not entitled to married quarters until he was 26 years old. He was 22 at that time, but a friend of his, Lt Kwesi Ayensu, who was the Barrack Inventory Officer (B.I.A.) gave it to him anyway as there were so many empty quarters available at that time in 1964. There were not many married Ghanaian officers at that time.

So we moved into our own flat and I was very happy. We had a batman named Godwin. He was a Nigerian and a big thief, so he didn't last very long! He was taken to court, and when charged and fined he said to the judge in Pigeon English, " The money wey no dey God self no fit take um!" The whole court was in fits of laughter. Then we got a really good boy, who was very young and from Northern Ghana, called Awuni Fra-Fra. He was so good and stayed with us on and off for the next five years. I really loved him and he loved Hamish. He kept the house and himself really spotless. He wouldn't let me get a maid to mess his kitchen so he looked after Hamish when we went out. He went to Worker's College and learned to read and write, and would write letters for all the boys in the quarters. He eventually joined the Air Force.

There were many functions in the mess and they were really nice with Air Force, Navy and Army all together. All the different uniforms looked so grand in their mess undress: Army red, Navy white and Air Force blue. There was a distinct difference between the British officers – the BJSTT. (British Joint Services Training Team) and the Ghanaians. Most of the British chaps were only local temporary acting ranks and, apart from the Commanders, were not that intelligent. James wrote a report saying that a frigate that the Ghana Navy had ordered was costing too much, thinking that Britain was cheating Ghana. He was arrested and taken to Accra, and kept under close arrest. Luckily, the officer assigned to look after him was his own friend Lt. Kwame Asante, so he kept James in his own cabin at the officer's mess. He was taken to Flagstaff House daily and questioned: who chopped the money? What he didn't know was that it was the Ghanaians themselves who had inflated the price and they thought that he knew that. He was just being very nationalistic, trying to save his country money.

In the meantime, in Takoradi, I had discovered that I was pregnant again and with the worry of James's arrest I started bleeding. One day, three Military Intelligence (MI) officers brought James from Accra and came to search our house. They thought that he was in contact with Dr Busia, the opposition leader then in exile in Britain. They found nothing; but one of those officers, Major Sam Acquah, was later to be murdered, along with three judges after the 1981 coup-d'etat.

I decided to go to Accra to stay with Emile and Cecelia, his wife, until James was allowed to return. I flew on an Air Force plane, the Float Otter, piloted by Flying Officer Frank Okyne, who later became Managing Director of Ghana Airways. As I was about to join the plane, Major Aquah joined us and said, " Mrs. Boham, are you going to Accra for shopping?"

I said, "No, I'm going to Accra to stay until my husband comes home!" When I got to Accra, after a few days my husband was released. But then, for months, MI officers followed us. It was funny, as he hadn't done anything wrong at all. But it made him bitter about Nkrumah, who he had always idolised up to that time!

On his return I noticed a change in James; it was as though they had taken one man and changed him for another one. He became very African and the things that he used to help me with in England, he wouldn't do any more. He said, "I had the houseboy to do those things". Sometimes he was very cruel and I used to cry, and he would say, "Crocodile tears!" So there I was, pregnant again. Hamish was only eight months when I got pregnant. On my twenty-first birthday in 1965 we had a wonderful weekend – we had a big party in the house, with a band and so many friends. One Margaret Nkrumah, Lt Peter Nkrumah's sister, sang for me: 'Stay as Sweet as You Are. Then there was a naval ball in the wardroom, where I wore my yellow ball-gown again in spite of being pregnant. There was a play performed by students of 'The University of Ghana, Legon'. It was an African version of Shakespeare's *Hamlet*, called '*The Tongo Hamlet*', written by Joe De Graft, a professor at the university. They used Ghanaian names and costumes and it was really good. I do believe that they actually made a film of it. I have always loved Shakespeare and thoroughly enjoyed it. So I had a really lovely twenty-first birthday weekend.

When I was seven months pregnant we went to Kumasi at the invitation of James's sister Joan. She had married a man who had so many children and when we got there they were all home from school. So she sent us to stay with her next-door neighbour, who once was her classmate at Elmina Convent. Now the situation next door was not much better. The lady had five children with her first husband, who was Indian, and the most beautiful children that you could see: Satie, the eldest; then Devie; Chalie; Ashok; and Pushpa, the youngest. Her present husband also had children from a former marriage as well. They gave us a small room with a single bed, and James, Hamish and I, seven months pregnant, all slept there. But

I must say the hospitality was wonderful, the food excellent. Hamish always used to say in later years that Auntie Satie looked like Wonder Woman. Devie, who had beautiful green eyes, was even lovelier if that's possible? Pushpa, at that time was a beautiful baby who grew up to look a lot like her mother, who was the friendliest person that you could meet. Over the years our paths crossed many times, with Auntie, Sattie's mother coming to stay with us in Accra and cooking delicious Indian food. But that comes much later.

Hamish got malaria there because there were so many mosquitos. When we took him to the military hospital in Kumasi they had no Nivaquine syrup or injection to give him so I decided to take him back to Takoradi as I had medicine in the house. So we got the train. Suddenly, in the carriage, Hamish started frothing at the mouth and his eyes were all glazed and rolling about and he went stiff. I was scared to death and didn't know what to do. Just then the train stopped at Bekwei Station, and the guard on the train, who was an old friend of James (as he lived in the railway quarters at one time when he was a child) grabbed Hamish and ran with him along the platform. We followed regardless of bags etc. It was the rainy season and he ran through a bush path and we followed. I had to take off my shoes as they were slipping all over the place. When we reached the main road someone gave us a lift to the hospital. When we got there the sister in charge was a Mrs. Addoo (who it turned out was a relation of the Addoos that we had known in Portsmouth). She managed to get Hamish's temperature down. Almost the entire village came to see the pregnant white woman, sitting crying in the hospital. After a while they said that Hamish was all right and they said that we could go. The only route was to take a tro-tro (one of the buses with a wooden body built on it) so we took one of those, back to Kumasi. The journey was terrible as the roads were all up and down hill and bumpy. It was not the most ideal way to travel when you are pregnant but we all survived. When we got back to Kumasi we took the sleeper back to Takoradi, where we arrived safely. I was able to treat Hamish with the Nivaquine syrup that I had in the house for malaria. Since that time, 1965, up to the time of writing this, 2002, I have never been back to Kumasi.

A few weeks later James was appointed to be the ADC (aide-de-camp) to the King of Libya during the OAU (Organisation of African Unity) conference in Accra, in October 1965. James decided that it would be best if I came to Accra with him and have the baby in the Military Hospital. Hamish was going to stay with James's cousin Ebo Boham and his wife, Christie. Auntie Christie had been especially kind to me, helping me to try new foods and fruits. She was a seamstress, and Hamish and I would spend many days with her watching her sew, and meeting many of her clients. She had six children. The two eldest boys, PaJoe and Francis, were at boarding school, but the four girls were in the house and totally doted on Hamish: Mary, Joan, Lena and Flo, who was only 18 months. They were lovely, well behaved girls and I had no worry leaving Hamish with them. Ebo Boham was the traffic manager for the Ghana Railways and they had a lovely old colonial type bungalow.

In Accra, James and two other officers were given a married quarter to share for the duration of the conference, in Burma Villas, Burma Camp - the Armed Forces headquarters: Peter Nkrumah, another naval officer friend from Southsea (whose sister had sang for me at my twenty-first birthday party in May 1965), and another army officer whose name I can't remember now. One day they came home after practising for a parade that was to be held during the conference, and I was sleeping. As James came into the room, I woke up and felt a pain. Peter was cooking and they were both very hungry, but I told James, "I think that I had better get to the hospital as I think the baby is coming!"

As we had no car, James rang for a military ambulance and came with me to the hospital. When we got there he said he was hungry, so did I mind if he left me there and went back to eat? I said, " no I didn't mind". I went straight into the delivery room and had the baby. The nurse said, It's a little man!" And I was so disappointed as I wanted a girl. But the next minute she said, "No! It's a little woman!" And I was so happy. She rang James immediately and he and Peter raced back to the hospital. James had just got back when they rang and wasn't able to eat after all.

So he and Peter went out to wet the baby's head. She was born on 11th October 1965. I called her Rosina Yasmin McCarthy Boham. Rosina was James's mother's name. In all this time I have not really mentioned my husband's family. I'm afraid that I was not really welcomed with open arms, but rather left alone by them all. Yasmin was the name I had wanted to call a baby girl, after Princess Yasmin, daughter of the film star Rita Hayworth and Prince Ali Khan. McCarthy was James's family name, sometimes hyphenated McCarthy-Boham, which Rosina now uses as she likes that. But James was always just Boham, at that time.

The staff at Military Hospital were marvellous. I had an air-conditioned room to myself and the food was delicious. All the ward maids were lovely to me, and would bring roses for Rosina everyday. Whenever I went to the hospital for many years after they would still greet me. She was a beautiful baby, just like a doll. She weighed six pounds, nine ounces. At birth, she was covered in a kind of cream like Nivea, which the midwife said was quite normal. It must have been all the chocolate and iced coffee that I had whilst pregnant. The funny thing with Rosina: I only vomited once the whole pregnancy and yet she was the smallest baby. Even, two nights before she was born I went dancing at The Star Hotel, which was the most popular spot for officers at that time. I came home to the married quarters and looked after Rosina myself, but I was able to sleep when she slept, and cook for myself, as James stayed most nights, at the State house with the Libyans. Emile and Cecelia, who were just round the corner, now living in Labadi Villas, came to keep me company in the evenings. When the conference was over we all returned to Takoradi together, and back to Hamish, who was delighted with his baby sister. He was now 17 months old, and he could do everything for himself. He would bring me nappies for the baby, and powder. James decided that with the two babies I needed a maid, although I still had Awuni, faithful Awuni, who was very good. One of James,s relations brought us a girl who stayed only a few weeks, as she was pregnant, as we discovered. One day I went out and when I came back it was to find her fast asleep, and Hamish had emptied a large tin of Johnson's baby powder all over himself, the girl, and the entire room. So we sent the girl packing! Awuni was really good with the children. He would do the washing and pressing and finish by one o'clock, and after lunch he would dress himself in his beautifully pressed shorts and shirt and take the children out whilst we had a siesta, before we went out to any parties in the evening. James closed at 1.30pm unless he was on duty, and he would then sleep at the base.

Mummy sent me some gorgeous dresses and all the baby things for Rosina, through Kwesi Armaah, who was the High Commissioner in London at that time. His niece Mrs. Edna Amagatcher was a good friend of Mummy's and arranged to send them for her. I was very grateful as on James's salary we couldn't afford to buy and at that time. November 1965, there was a great shortage of baby goods in the shops. Even baby milk was scarce! So I breast-fed Rosina for three months. Rosina got colic and after every feed used to scream her head off. I remember one night being so tired and her screaming and James pushing me over in the bed and taking over.

I was always taking Rosina to the paediatrician at Secondi Effia-Nkwanta Hospital, which was a terrible old place, before the new building was opened. The Doctor was a Yugoslavian, and one day he said to me, "Madam, there is nothing wrong with this baby, but there are many sick babies here, and if you keep bringing her, she will eventually get sick!" so I stopped taking her there. We would all still go to Auntie Christie, and I have many happy memories of them all and I was so grateful for Auntie Christie's help. She used to introduce me to new Ghanaian dishes and make sure that she didn't put too much pepper in so I could eat it. I had my first mango from Auntie Christie and it was so delicious that up to now I have a passion for mangoes, and every year in the mango season I would get mango fever from eating too many!

Now another dear friend was Aggie Pumpuni, who introduced me to fu-fu, the traditional dish of the Ashantis, made from pounded yam, or green plantain, and cassava. And she is the best fu-fu maker I know up to date (though nowadays, most people use powdered yam and plantain powder – not the same at all!). Throughout the years, wherever we met up again, in Takoradi or Accra, she had to make me her delicious fu-fu again. Aggie also had four daughters who, apart from the eldest, were the same age as my children, so they grew up together over the years. We always seemed to live near them and at one time in Accra were actually next door, so the children used to run in and out of the houses.

James had two half-brothers who have always been very lovely to me. The eldest, Kofi McClean, was James's mother's son with her first husband. Kofi was born in 1918 whilst his father died from a deadly outbreak of influenza which killed millions worldwide that very same year. Kofi worked with NCR – The National Cash Register Company. He used to bring me tea, butter, chocolate and ice cream for Hamish, though most of the time he was working in Accra. He used to repair my sewing machine for me – by now I was designing and sewing my own clothes, and he has always been a very gentle and lovely friend.

James's other half-brother was his father's son with another woman and he was just a year older than James. His name was Joseph McCarthy Boham and he worked in Kingsway Stores for many years. When we used to go shopping he would put Hamish in the trolley and wheel him around. The only one of James's sister's who I saw in Takoradi was Elizabeth – his eldest sister and the mother of his niece Julie – who I met in Anna's flat all those years ago. Elizabeth was a market woman and had a dough-mixing machine and a store at the Market Circle, Takoradi. She was always too busy making money to really see us often and she looked after Julie's baby, Dan junior, whose father was Dan Blay-Afful. Dan junior had been sent to Ghana to Elisabeth so Julie could study Law in London.

In all James has four sisters: Elizabeth, Joan, then Anna and Wilhelmina. None of them made any effort to want to know the real me. In fact Anna was in London for over forty years. When James was staying with her in London after he left Dartmouth, he didn't tell her that we were engaged; and Julie his niece, who became my friend, was so excited when I told her, and neither I nor she knew that he hadn't told Anna. So Julie mentioned it to Anna, and, boy! Did we see a wild African woman! She stormed downstairs, shouting at the top of her voice in Fanti, which I couldn't understand at all then.

She took James's cabin trunk – a big heavy box, and threw it down the stairs, and told him to get out of the house! James said, "She's somebody's daughter," and said to me, "Let's go, Darling." After that, as you can imagine, I was very, very, wary of Anna. Mummy actually got to like Anna but she had not seen that wild African woman! Though afterwards when James said that he had not told her of the engagement, I did think that was very wrong of him and that he should have left her house! If he was afraid of her reaction on finding out.

James's mother, Rosina Quayson, was an old lady who was always dressed in black and was always going to funerals. She was a trader and used to sell the African print in the remote villages around Elmina, where she lived, and Cape Coast. Elmina was first discovered by the Portuguese in 1492; was the most educated part of Ghana and had two castles, one Portuguese and the other Dutch. She used to sell on credit, and go round collecting her money. Some people owed her for years and used to pay her one shilling a week. She had managed to educate her children from that, as did many other mothers in Ghana. James's father, who was also James Desmond McCarthy Boham, had died when James was four years old, so James stayed with Kofi; his brother and with Anna and Joan, his sisters, as he had no real home of his own. I almost forgot to mention Auntie Grace, his mother's sister. James also stayed with her, and his cousin Kofi Mills. When I went to Ghana in 1964 they were using pounds, shillings and pence. In 1965 Nkrumah changed it to a new Ghana currency – Cedis – with Nkrumah's head on it, changing again in 1966 to New Cedis. It has since been known as Cedis. At that time it was two Cedis to the pound, but it has now devalued to about one thousand to the pound or more!

Takoradi, 1965, in September, a new naval wife arrived from England, to live in a flat on the top floor. Her name was Lynn Lartey and she was Guyanese, with very short hair and a fiery temper, though never with me! When she arrived her things had not arrived and I had to lend her some sheets, cups and saucers and plates to tide her over. She always called me Mistress Boham. She had a daughter, Lucy, who was six months younger than Hamish. Her husband Tom was an engineer officer in the Navy and from Accra. She adopted me as her sister and I think spent more time with me than she did in her own flat. She used to tell me a lot about life in Guyana and all about Obeh! the Guyanese juju. She had lived at Plantation Coverden, on the Demerara River. When she was 16 she contracted diabetes on the shock of learning of her father's death. She had left the house to go shopping and met somebody in town who said "Sorry to hear of your father's death" and she went into her first diabetic coma. So she couldn't even attend her father's funeral. I knew nothing about diabetes before meeting Lynn and she never told me she was a diabetic until I had a rude shock!

Her husband had gone to sea and she was pregnant. She kept being sick and was so weak that I brought her and Lucy downstairs to stay with us. She kept asking for water and then going to the loo all the time and vomiting. When she started vomiting blood I took her to the hospital. As we were going in the car on the way she started going into a coma. She begged me to stay with her and I promised that I would! When we got to the MRC (Medical Reception Center) at Apremdu, as soon as the doctor came she said "I'm a diabetic!" and I thought: "My God!" She was transferred in a military ambulance to Takoradi Hospital, where she lost the baby. The doctor had to give her drips and I heard him say, "We have to be quick, nurse, as she's getting very weak!" A few days later, when she was stable, she told me, "I just coughed and the baby came, Val!" Anyway, she was on her feet again and I watched her carefully and made sure she took her insulin if she hadn't taken it, and had eaten if she had taken it! Sometimes we would drive all around town looking for insulin for her at the various pharmacies.

She was a loving person and we had lots of lovely chats about our respective childhoods in Guyana and England. At times she became quite wild and was always arguing with people, though never with me!

On 24th February 1966 there was the first military coup in Ghana to overthrow the government of President Kwame Nkrumah, whilst he was on a peace mission to Vietnam. On the day of the coup James went to work as usual and then all the British officers started coming home early and we heard that there had been a coup. In Takoradi there was no fighting at all, but we heard that there was a lot of fighting in Accra; especially involving the Presidential Special Bodyguard, who lived opposite Flagstaff House, where the President lived with his Egyptian Fathia, who was allowed to leave the country with her children, unharmed. Life returned to normal very quickly.

Chapter Three

BRITAIN 1966

In April 1966 James was sent to Britain to do a navigation course at *HMS Dryad* again – a Master Navigators course. So he went to the college and the children and I went to stay with my mother in London, who was still at Charlton in the same old house. James found a nice house at Waltham Chase, near Winchester, which belonged to a naval officer stationed in the Gare Loch in Scotland. The village was near the college.

Rosina was christened whilst we were in London by Father Bear, who was now a canon and at St Mary's, Lewisham. Anna, James's sister, was godmother; Joseph, James's brother, was godfather and my cousin Linda in Scotland the other godmother. Anna had a little party afterwards at her house at Streatham.

I was very happy in that house at Waltham Chase. Chicken, strawberry and, mushroom farms, where you could get loose broken ones really cheap, surrounded us. On the course with James were some Malaysian, Iraqi, and German officers. We had some pleasant dinners with them all. James was supposed to go on to the Royal Naval College at Greenwich, to do a Junior Defense Course, but at the last minute was recalled to Ghana.

Top Left: My beautiful Mama (Agnes Anderson, (Nancy)), 1935, taken in Glasgow, before she married my father.
Top Right: Mummy and me on the beach at Hastings, 1945.
Bottom: Raymond (my father's cousin) and me in the field of my great-grandfather's farm at Frickenham, Suffolk, 1946, with me carrying my favourite black doll, an omen for the future?

Top Left: On the mudflats at Leysdown, Isle of Sheppey 1947, collecting cockles and seaweed.
Top Right: Mummy, Laraine and me in Greenwich Park, 1949.
Bottom: Nanny and Granddad, Mummy, Laraine and me outside Mrs. Wellard's boarding house at Hastings, 1949.

Top Left: Uncle Mac, Laraine and me in Greenwich Park, 1949.
Top Right: The Grecian Flyer, the only bike that I have ever ridden. Laraine sitting on it in Greenwich Park, 1950.
Bottom Left: Laraine and me wearing our Anderson Tartan kilts outside Mrs Wellard's, Hastings in 1952.
Middle Right: Mummy, Laraine and me in the sea at Hastings, 1952.
Bottom Right: Me riding Twinkle, an Exmoor pony at Duporths, St Austell, 1953.

Top Left: Me in fancy dress competition as Miss Duporth, they lent me the cup and sash, Cornwall, 1954.
Middle Left: Nanny's caravan June at Leysdown with Laraine, Mummy and Janet Acourt, 1954.
Bottom Left: Mevagissey, Cornwall, with Mummy and Uncle Mac, 1954.
Top Right: Auntie Iris's garden at Letchworth, with my cousin June, Nanny, Laraine and some neighbour's babies, 1958.
Bottom Right: Paris, le Sacre Coeur, taken by Guy, my French penfriend, 1961.

Top: Warner's holiday camp, Ryde, Isle of White, with almost all Daddy's family except Uncle Fred, Auntie Joan and June. I am in the middle now aged 14, 1958.
Bottom Left: Playing tennis with Laraine at the sports ground, Greenwich, now the site of the Millennium Dome, 1958.
Bottom Right: Nanny's garden at Shooters Hill, taken by my father's cousin Adrian, 1961.

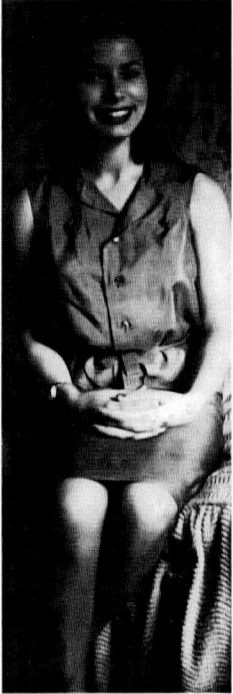

Top Left: With Auntie Vi in her garden at Linevale, Clydebank, Glasgow, with wee puppy Rajah, 1961.
Top Right: Paris on the left bank of the Seine, 1961.
Bottom Left: Sitting on my bed at home in Charlton, 1963.
Bottom Right: Folkestone, August 1963.

Top Left: James and me on our engagement, July 1963.
Top Right: 1st June 1964, my wedding day, James and me with Mummy.
Bottom Left: 1st June 1964, my wedding day with Dan Adjekumsa, at home in Charlton.
Middle Right: Southsea, with James, Mummy and Bemi and Aki Tedjuso, now a famous Nigerian Architect, 1964.
Bottom Right: Takoradi, Ghana, early 1965, Hamish and I.

Top Left: James, Rosina, aged 1 month, Hamish and me, Takoradi, November 1965.
Top Right: Rosina and me at Rosina's christening at St Mary's, Lewisham, where Father Bear was then a Canon, 1966.
Bottom Left: Laraine with Terry her first husband, 1966
Bottom Right: Mummy and me with Hamish, Rosina with Auntie Anna (her godmother) and Uncle Steve, 1966.

Chapter Four

GHANA
1966–1969

So on 22nd November 1966 we returned to Ghana. We stayed with Emile and Cecelia in Accra and then went to Takoradi again, where we were given a house at West Tanakrom. In December 1966, whilst we were staying at West Tanakrom on our return from Britain, a new friend entered my life. Her name was Volda Morgan and she was from Trinidad & Tobago. She had come to Ghana, for her wedding, to an army officer called Major John Owusu. He was an Ashanti. She arrived just two weeks before the wedding and had been so keen to bring her wedding cake that she left her wedding dress in London. After a lot of frustration it arrived on time. We had a lovely military wedding with swords at Apremdu, the army camp where John was stationed, and then a reception in the mess. She was given away by Osei-Boateng, and the chairman of the wedding was Colonel Acheampong, who later became Head of State.

She was a beautiful bride; she was really lovely with lovely long hair and a beautiful slim figure. I bought her a China tea set as a wedding present, with butterflies all over it. I liked it so much that later I went to buy one for myself. All these years later Volda still has the set in her glass cabinet in her house in Tema. After staying for three months Volda returned to England to continue her nursing and to do a midwifery course.

February 1967. James had one older sister, who was his father's daughter with his first wife, who had died. She used to sell plantain in the market at Secondi and lived in the family house at 1st Street, Secondi. She had dropped out of school, so was an illiterate, but she was very nice and was the only one in the family, who made me feel welcome and part of the family. She loved Hamish and called him her Papa! She had visited us three weeks earlier, wearing a beautiful green brocade Ghanaian dress and the Tooku – something like a hat wig which had gold ornaments stuck in it – and wearing lots of gold necklaces and bracelets. She was going to Elmina to be made an Asafohene, which is a kind of military leader in the traditional sense in Ghana, as women used to lead in war as well as men. She had been so proud of herself as seemingly her father had done it before so she was carrying on in his footsteps.

Then one day Elizabeth, James's sister, came as we were eating. She said, "That we should finish eating" and then she told us that this sister had died! Now in Ghana a funeral is a big celebration and has to be really grand. This sister, whose name I have forgotten (how terrible of me!) had gone to a wake (keeping an all-night vigil) for a friend who had died, and sat up with the body all night. In the morning she complained that she wasn't feeling well, went to hospital and died of high blood pressure, which had not been diagnosed up till then! So this was my first experience of a death in the family. Normally they wear black for funerals, but as this was sudden and unexpected, they wore white. I was not informed of this and ended up wearing purple, though as I was a foreigner I was excused!

The body was laid in state in an elaborate four-poster, brass bed covered with beautiful white satin and white net curtain hangings. I had never seen a dead person before that and it was quite an experience, especially as they had laid her out in the same beautiful green brocade dress that I had seen her wearing the last time I saw her alive. All the family members sat down in a room, and the mourners had to go round and shake hands with them all, and sit down with the family for a while to show their sympathy. The immediate family had strips of the deceased person's cloth tied around their wrists to show who were the actual mourners. We didn't stay for the entire night of wake keeping and I suspect, me being a foreigner, they spared me that too!

The next day we went to church for the funeral service and then on to the cemetery for the burial service. I was amazed to see how popular she had been, as there were so many cars and tro-tro that we blocked all the traffic. Her son Kwesi, who was 16, was among the people who carried the coffin. He was weeping frequently and was a very tall handsome lad, who later came to stay with us for a while in 1970, until he got a job with Black Star Line (the national shipping line) as a seaman.

A month after the funeral they have a Memorial Service, and everybody dresses up and then goes to church. Afterwards they have beer and food, and people then donate money to pay for the funeral. One year later they go and put a headstone on the grave. One thing that I noted is that while they spend so much money on the funeral, once they are in the ground they don't bother much with the cemetery. Each new funeral party has to go and weed the cemetery before the burial. The wild African bush grows fast, and wreaths beaten by the rain and wind and faded by the sun would be thrown over the whole cemetery. At least in England cemeteries are pleasant places – almost like parks, with the grass cut neatly: at least the few that I have seen.

On 17th April 1967, we were all packed to go to Akosombo, where James would be on attachment to the VRA, (Volta River Authority), the hydro- electric project. Because of the coup we couldn't leave on that day as there was a curfew. Thieves came in the night and stole my sewing machine and James's tape-recorder, but we were very lucky as because of special security stops, the thieves were stopped and we got the things back.

So now we are at Akosombo. For the first time, we are out of military quarters. The quarters at Akosombo were very nice and well furnished with air conditioners and open plan kitchen. They had been built for the American engineers who had built the dam. The lake formed by the dam was said to be the largest man-made lake in Africa. Anyway, with the hills behind it reminded me of Loch Lomond in Scotland, though of course the climate was totally different. It was very hot, and very humid because of the water in the lake. We were also plagued by black flies, which used to come through the netting. They used to bite the children on the legs a lot, so the children were always covered in bites.

James was sent to Akosombo to plot the navigable path for the new proposed water transport. This was difficult to do, as there were still trees under the water where they had been flooded. Fishing was also difficult – though there were a lot of fish in the lake, especially tilapia – as the nets would get caught on the underwater obstacles. James and his colleagues plotted the course to Kete-Krachie and then James was recalled to the Navy. This time we were sent to Accra.

Accra 1967. When we returned from Akosombo, I had just had a minor operation and was not so well. Laraine came on holiday to Ghana at that time. Mummy had sent me some new dresses through Laraine and there was one yellow silk dress, which I liked very much. Laraine went to Aburi, the botanical gardens, for the day, taken by Edwin Sam – an army officer and James's relative. We were supposed to meet them later at the Star Hotel for a dance, but when we got to the Star Hotel they were not there. Anyway, I had my coke and James ordered a beer. After a while he suddenly said to me, " I am going to get you a taxi so you go home on your own."

I said, "What are you talking about?" and he said, "My girlfriend is here and I am going with her, so I want you to go home." He started pushing me towards the entrance of the hotel and I had tears streaming down my face. When we got to the entrance, Benny, who had been one of the officers who came to the airport the day I arrived in Ghana in 1964, was just coming in. When he saw me crying he said, "What's wrong, ,Valerie?" and I told him, and he told James off and told him to take me home, and put us both in a taxi. When we were both in the taxi, James said, "That he was not coming back to live with me in the house. I could stay there with the children." I was crying all the time! I never knew the truth or the purpose of that. He didn't leave or go back to the hotel that night, but I never wore that yellow dress again as it had such unhappy memories.

We had been very lucky, or so we had thought, to get a brand new married quarter, which had all new furniture, fridge, cooker etc.

We couldn't believe our luck! One of the British officers had been there and moved back into an older quarter. As I have previously said, "Whilst in Akosombo I had a minor operation for some women's complaint." I should have been all right after that but as soon as we moved into the house I started bleeding very heavily and had to go to hospital for three weeks and I was bleeding all the time. In the meantime, Hamish used to say to me, "Mummy, there was a man in my room last night," and I used to say, "Don't be silly." My sister, Laraine came on holiday in August 1967 with a friend and she slept in the children's room whilst her friend slept in the spare room. She said that, "She saw a funeral procession going through the wall in her room." Then another friend, Lynn Lartey, who I have mentioned earlier, who was Guyanese and, married to Tom Lartey, another naval officer, and who was my friend from Takoradi, came to stay. She was a diabetic and had recently lost another baby. She had been flown from Takoradi in a coma. When she was released from military hospital she came to stay with me for a few days before going back to Takoradi.

We hadn't seen one another for such a long time, so we had to get up to date with all the gossip. We were talking till one o'clock in the morning, when suddenly, I saw a man's face in the window. First of all, I thought that it must be a thief. The face kept smiling. After a while Lynn saw it too, and then we realised that it must be a ghost. We were very scared, and Lynn got up to put a cloth across the window and broke the bottom louvre window glass, and then the shadow started coming through the window. We got up and fled downstairs to the sitting room. After a while I saw another face in another window downstairs. I decided that I must be imagining it and ignored it. The next thing, Lynn said, "Do you see it?" and I said "Where?" and she pointed to the same window! So we fled into the outside toilet, which had wooden louver windows and therefore nothing could reflect. We stayed there till 6am when the sun came up!

Up until that point in my life I did not believe in ghosts or spirits; but having seen it with my own eyes, though I was scared, I was still interested. I therefore started reading all the books that I could find on the subject. The next thing was that the houseboy, still Awuni, started complaining that all sorts of funny things kept happening in his room.

The iron went hot when it was not on and so many other things; the lights went on and off and James, who was very sceptical, admitted hearing footsteps in the night. The Catholic Chaplain, Father Owusu (who later became Archbishop of Sunyani in Brong-Ahafo, Ghana) was living in the house opposite, so we got him to come and try and exorcise the ghosts, and we put in for a transfer to another house. We were very lucky in the fact that James got promoted to Lt-Commander at that time, and we were therefore eligible for another type of house. In the meantime we discovered that the house had been built on an old military cemetery and that explained a lot.

In February 1968 we were lucky to move to the new house in Burma Villas, also in Burma Camp – the M.O.D. HQ (Ministry of Defense, Headquarters). James was made Adjutant of the 24th February, Revolutionary Parade. He had to ride a horse, something that he had not done before; but he learned very quickly at the Cavalry Regiment. He did very well and it was a grand parade at the Black Star Square. I went with Col. & Mrs. Techie-Menson – Charles and Nancy, who were good friends and neighbours that I had made since arriving in Accra.

In fact it was Auntie Nancy who looked up which day that I was born and gave me my Ghanaian day name of Ekua, or Auntie Ekua – (Wednesday born) and from then on I was known as Ekua, hence the title of the book! The Techie-Menson's house was opposite ours. They had four children: one girl and three boys, and Hamish and Rosina played with them. I was now pregnant again. This was a baby who was planned and in fact it took me five months to get pregnant from the time I decided that I wanted another baby. Hamish was now four and Rosina almost three. They went to nursery with Charles and Nancy's younger children.

James was now the Director of Personnel at the Naval Headquarters. At this time they decided to sack the British officers from the Navy, as they always complained that the Ghanaian officers had no experience and also never gave them the chance to acquire any! Most of the British officers were the dregs of the Royal Navy, who were given local ranks for Ghana alone. Anyway, an Indian admiral, Krishnan, was called in to review the situation as it was felt that the climate and conditions in India were more similar to Ghana than Britain's. So Admiral Krishnan and Commander Vasant came to Ghana. Admiral Krishnan, who became a really good friend, was really roly-poly like Humpty Dumpty. We held many pleasant dinners for them, and were invited to the Indian Embassy and the Indian community in Ghana (which was quite large) any time they had a dinner for them. At that time I had a lovely Indian friend in the Embassy, Mrs. Kukraja, and her husband. I had always enjoyed Indian food in restaurants in London, but what Indians prepare for special occasions in their own homes is really lovely. I was fascinated to eat a sweet covered in real silver tissue, and many others.

James and another officer, Cdr. Nathan Mante, went to India to tour the Indian Navy training establishments, to see which ones would be good for Ghanaian needs. James had a very nice tour of India and even went to see the Taj Mahal! In May 1968, when I was five months pregnant with Julien and James was away, I flew to Takoradi on an Air Force flight and stayed with Ebo and Christie Boham for a few days. After a very pleasant stay in which they gave me their own bedroom to sleep in I returned to Accra. When the plane landed I said to the pilot, "Thank you for a nice flight and perfect landing." A few days later the pilot, who shall remain unnamed, arrived at my house in a taxi. He said, "That the taxi was for him" (which meant that he had money), that he liked me and would I go to the May Ball at Legon, the University of Ghana? I of course said "No!" but was really flattered that being five months pregnant, somebody could still fancy me. I never told James about that incident!

When James arrived back from India he had met Imoru Iyana (a big Ghanaian politician at that time) who had invited us to his house at Cantonments, a suburb of Accra, just opposite Burma Camp. I had not really met any northerners up to that time, apart from Awuni our houseboy. We became frequent visitors to Iyana's house, and his current girlfriend, Lillian, who was half Lebanese and worked for Ghana Airways, became good friends with us, as did. Iyana's daughter Sandra, a lovely girl. We were privileged to be invited when he had almost the whole house of northern chiefs visiting.

I loved the northern dances with their xylophones and the beautiful smocks and embroidered leather boots (they rode a lot of horses in the north) and the long pointed beards of the chiefs. At that time, the Inspector-General of the Ghana police was a northerner, and he was there. Whilst, the northerners were dancing, it was the custom for people to pin money on their clothes. There was plenty of food, and I had a lovely day in spite of being pregnant. Later on Imoru Iyana was accused of planning a coup and sent to jail! So that stopped our visits, though I used to meet Sandra in town.

Almost as soon as James returned from India I had my new baby Julien Douglas (it was supposed to be Duncan, which means a brown chief, but James got it muddled when he went to register him) McCarthy Boham, born on 6th August 1968. I had no pains again and nearly had him in the toilet. I just got to the hospital and twenty minutes later he was born in the ante-natal room. He was eight pounds and his tummy was so fat. He was beautiful, and his hair was a little lighter and slightly straighter than Hamish's and Rosina's. I came home when he was four days old and James's nephew, Lt Henry Smith, was getting married that day; and I was so disappointed that I couldn't go, as Henry was a special favourite of mine. But after the wedding the bride and groom came to see me in the house. The day after the wedding in Ghana it is the custom for the bride and groom to go to church in the wedding dress but with a hat instead of a veil. They also came to see me in the house after church. One month after Julien was born we had a grand christening and Henry and his bride were there. In fact, Henry took all the photos for me with my camera. It's a funny thing with babies: the first one you take pictures all the time and the second one you take less, and when you come to the third you hardly take any at all.

Then James was nominated for the Staff College in India along with another naval officer: Lt-Commander Alfie Obeng. My sister Laraine came from London again when Julien was born and stayed with me until we left for India. Before going to India, we left for London to stay with Mummy. Arriving just in time for Christmas. James went straight to India and we stayed six weeks in London.

Chapter Five

INDIA
FEBRUARY TO NOVEMBER 1969

If any of you have any idea how it is to travel alone on a long haul flight, with a baby of five months in a carrycot and two toddlers, of almost five years and three years, then you can imagine what I went through on that trip! But I must give all praise to Air India and their staff; they were really wonderful. We flew London, Moscow, Delhi, Bombay, and Madras. We stayed overnight in Madras and then flew Indian Airlines, their internal airline, to, Bangalore and then, Coimbatorre. On the aircraft the stewardesses came and took the baby and the children from me, and let me sleep. That was greatly appreciated. They provided milk, disposable nappies and plastic pants as well as toys and games for the children.

When we arrived in Madras, that was my first view of India and the passport official read my name and said, "Welcome to India, Valerie" and that really gave me a good feeling when we went through customs. Airline staff met us and a car was provided to take us to the hotel that was provided by the airline. I loved Madras, which is a really old Indian city, though we didn't see much as we were all so tired. When we got to the hotel we bathed and then went to sleep. Julien's baby milk went off in the heat so the only thing that he could have was glucose water. So overnight; until we reached Staff College at Wellington in the Nilgirie Hills, Madras State, South India; Julien had nothing but glucose water.

When we arrived at Coimbatore, nobody to meet us! Then an

Indian driver approached with a letter from James to say he wasn't sure if we were arriving or not? so as he had an important lecture, he was sending the driver to pick us up. We thought that we had arrived. When we left the airport we found an ancient box wagon, which was a wooden chassis on an old army jeep. The seats were stuffed with sawdust and straw and was most uncomfortable! So we got in and started the drive. It was so hot in Coimbatore, which has temperatures of 125 degrees (F), at times; and even the rivers dry up. We saw a cracked riverbed, and we were all sweating profusely to say the least – perspiring was just not adequate a word. We drove through the town with its buffalo carts and old 1950 model cars, or so I thought; lovely palm trees and flowers everywhere; the beautiful colours of the saris; and the bustle of coolies crossing the roads carrying loads. What I didn't know at that time was that Wellington was about 10,000 feet above sea level and we had a three hour drive from the airport, gradually getting colder and colder.

We came to the hills and started driving up. The road was really narrow and in some places no other car could pass as sometimes a buffalo had given up and sat down and blocked the road, and he couldn't be moved until he was ready, or until they could force him to continue! The vegetation was beautiful, but so many hairpin bends. It was tropical jungle and in the distance you could hear tigers roar; in the hills the sounds carry for miles. The sunshine through the trees was beautiful. Julien slept through it all. He kept waking up and seeing that we were still in the car and went straight back to sleep after a little glucose water. After three hours we arrived at Wellington, aching all over from that terrible vehicle! From the outside the house didn't look too bad; but inside the floors were cement, and in the kitchen was a fire wood range; and no bath or even a shower, just a sunken square with a hole in the wall! The beds were ancient wooden beds and the mattresses were made of cotton.

The bearer, or head servant, was Chinapa, who was a nice man with a pleasant smiling face. We all sat down on the sofa, in the sitting room and he made us some tea, the panacea for all ills. As the tea was grown and dried locally on the next hill, it was especially delicious! Nilgiri tea is exported all over the world. It is Orange Pekoe, and we drank a lot of it over the next few months and even took some home to Ghana. It was so cheap it was unbelievable! Then James arrived with his cousin Major Edwin Sam, Major Ted Utuka, and Lt Commander Alfie Obeng, who were the other Ghanaian officers on the course with him. One thing: it was not Ghana because even the other ranks' quarters were better than that! In India too you have to have so many servants because of the caste system! It was supposed to be done away with but it wasn't in 1969. So we had Chinapa, the bearer, who was in charge of everybody else and did the cooking and marketing; then Rajama, the ayeh; and a small girl to help her called Elizabeth, who was about twelve years old. Then a dhobi – a washerman who collected the washing and took it away and washed it in the local stream and brought it back the next day; then a sweeper, who swept and washed the floors and did nothing else and was supposed to keep out of everybody's way, as, coming from the lowest caste, her shadow should not fall on anybody, especially those of the highest Brahmin caste. Then there was a gardener who did the garden. The houses were on top of a hill and you could see people working on the tea plantations on another hill. There was also a little hill railway on another hill, with two engines – one at the back and another at the front. It was really fascinating to see it chugging up the hill.

Milk was brought to the door in churns, and Chinapa made curd (yogurt) everyday and woe betide the milkman if he put water in the milk. (When you make curd, if there is water in the milk, it sits on the top.) We got real cream off the top of the milk. It was not pasteurized or sterilized or anything but we used to boil it. It was a lot more fatty than the milk that we get in the UK. A fish man used to come round selling fish off a wooden platter, which he carried on the top of his head. He used to bring shrimps and a delicious pinky fish, of which I could never get the real name but it was very nice. There was rationing there so we had a ration card and had to line up at the depot to collect once a month. White flour was really scarce – we only got two kilograms a month – so the bread they made was mixed and it was better to eat chapattis. Julien's first words were 'cow' and 'papatis', as the cows roamed all over the place. Sometimes you would open the front door, and there was a big cow going moo! By tradition the Hindus, who worship the cow believing it to be a reincarnation of one of the gods, were not even allowed to push them away.

We ate Indian food all the time. As there was so much variety that you never get bored with all the dhaals and lentils, I could quite easily be a vegetarian. The market was fascinating and had everything – all tropical fruits and vegetables and all temperate as well; so we had mangoes and, grapes and we could even get wild strawberries, which were small but very delicious. With one rupee, which was (one shilling and two-pence at that time,) you could get a very good meal for the whole family for the day!

The Moslems kept one corner of the market. There you could buy beef, which was very cheap and mostly tough, from old cows, as they weren't allowed to kill below a certain age. In the other corner the Hindus sold pork, which the Moslems of course do not eat. The market was well laid out and really clean. Though the beggars and coolies constantly pestered you. I made a lovely friend who was from Zambia. Her father was the Bishop of Lusaka, and her name was Felli Kasote. Her husband Dunstan, an army officer, was also on the course. We were very grateful to them for more reasons than one. As the college was so far from Delhi, the Ghana High Commission, who were supposed to pay us, were so many months behind with James's salary, and Felli and Dunstan used to give us money to feed the children. Years later I heard that there was a big scandal about embassy staff who put the salaries in an account, didn't pay them for a long time, and collected the interest on the money. This became a rather large amount in the end, and in the meantime the students were suffering!

After two months, two more Ghanaian wives joined us: Justina Utuka and Adelaide Sam, Edwin's wife as they had just got married. They had travelled from Ghana together and shared a house together with their husbands. Justina was a lovely, quiet and gentle lady, and Adelaide was a really new bride. I also made many lovely Indian friends, two of whom were very close to me. One was Prema Raina, whose husband was an Indian Army, officer, and who had three children at that time. She was from Kashmir, and used to wear long dangling earrings on a chain, which always fascinated me. The most striking thing about them as a couple was that they were so happy, yet theirs was an arranged marriage and they had never seen one another until the wedding. Prema means love, I was told, and she was really lovely.

Her next door neighbour, Amita, was also a good friend and she dressed me in her own sari and taught me how to wear it. She also put my hair up for me. Her husband was much older than her and she had one small daughter at that time. I used to go to them for coffee and lunches when the men were away. It was Prema who decided that she wanted to go for painting lessons at the local Catholic convent, so we all decided to go. (There was no television where we were in India at that time and if there was, most of the time there was no electricity – only a small hydro-electric system on a local dam.) So women used to paint and embroider, and would gather together to sing, play instruments and recite poetry, Indian of course, which was nice, like Victorian England. Others would gamble and play mahjong all day and night.

So we all started the painting lessons, two mornings a week. We were taught by an old Portuguese nun from Goa, called Sister Dolcette; she was a very good artist. We worked in oil and I discovered a talent, which I didn't know I had! At school I had done well at art but only with poster paint. We started painting flowers on satin and I painted a beautiful orchid. The teacher would call everybody's work rubbish. But when I called her to see my rubbish, she would say, "It's not rubbish, it's good!" The Indian ladies started painting pictures of the Virgin Mary and baby Jesus. So I thought, as the only Christian there, I had better do something special. So, from a picture of an Old Master, which Sister had, I painted Christ with a crown of thorns. It was very good and Sister was very pleased with it. Years later when I looked at it, I couldn't believe that I painted it; there was such a look of agony in the eyes – definitely my masterpiece, which, unfortunately, I lost in a bizarre way many years later!

Then I started doing machine-embroidery with another sister. This involved using a treadle machine and embroidery hoops, also doing a lot of pulled thread work; and I made some lovely things this way. Justina and I also went for tailoring lessons with one of the colonel's wives, Mrs. Morley. Col. Morley later became a General. We learned how to take the measurement and how to work out the size of the neck and armholes. I later made some beautiful tailored suits, and sewed many dresses and Ghanaian outfits for myself.

We used to have a lot of functions in the mess, and it was a breathtaking occasion. The Indian ladies were so beautiful in their evening saris, with all the jewellery – it was all real – passed down from generation to generation, as part of their dowry: diamonds, rubies, sapphires, emeralds and more. Earrings, necklaces, bracelets, head ornaments, nose ornaments, and a chain worn across the front of the saris, all matching sets! The food was amazing too, with so many dishes from all parts of India. When people say curry, it basically means stew. As all areas of India use different spices and different ways of cooking, there is not just one curry! I gave a demonstration of a Ghanaian dish at the ladies' club, which took place at the Gymkhana club. It was for groundnut soup, or peanut soup, as most people in the West call groundnuts. It can be made very hot if you like! Or with no pepper at all according to taste.

GROUNDNUT SOUP

Ingredients
1 jar of peanut butter (smooth)
(Or you can roast and grind the peanuts yourself in a coffee grinder)
1 large onion
3 large fresh tomatoes
Pepper to own taste!
Salt
Tomato purée
1 whole uncooked chicken

Method
Mix the peanut butter with some water, gradually adding 3 pints, until it is like milk (it mixes better with boiling water).

Put in a large saucepan.

Cut the chicken into pieces (size depends on personal taste).

Add to the milky mixture, put on the stove (or whatever you use for cooking and turn it on! It can be made in a pressure cooker though I haven't tried a microwave – they didn't exist in 1969!

Chop the onions or grind in a liquidizer.

Chop the tomatoes.

Grind the pepper.

Add the salt and tomato purée.

Put all in the pan and bring to the boil, watching all the time as it is inclined to boil over!

Let it slow boil until you see drops of oil on the surface of the soup. You can also boil it down thick and eat as a stew.

(Note of caution: if you eat it before it is properly cooked, i.e. if you eat it before the oil appears on the surface, it can give you a running stomach. But if it is properly cooked you will have no problems!)

You can eat it with rice, yam or potatoes; Ghanaians usually eat it with fu-fu, which is pounded yam or pounded plantain and cassava, and is really delicious.

I also gave a demonstration of gift-wrapping. I used to cut petals and make a paper rose for decoration; I also made them in material to put on my dresses, like a brooch.

Admiral Krishnan came to the Staff College to give a lecture. He had about an hour to spare, so he asked to come and visit me. He caused quite a fluster as the Commandant and the Commander of the Naval Section of the Staff College, didn't know exactly where our house was! Anyway, he arrived and I made tea for him. He said to me, "I'm sorry, Valerie, that the house is not quite what you are used to!" Whilst he was in Ghana he had visited our home many times and was aware that it was superior to the Indian married quarters. The Indian officers were very surprised; as I was later told that, the Staff College houses, were among the best, in the Indian Armed Forces! All the Indian wives had been so happy with the houses, but I had said nothing to them about the houses in Ghana. I was greatly honoured by the Admiral's visit and appreciated his kindness in remembering us. It made the Naval Captain treat James with a little more respect! In India there is a lot of colour prejudice and the fairer skinned you are the better!

Around this time, Julien had pneumonia and I used to give him a teaspoon of whiskey with some honey and hot water and gradually give it to him on a teaspoon. One day, we were going to Dunstan and Felli's for lunch so I gave him some before we went out, and when we came back later in the evening I wanted to give him some more. When I looked at the bottle the level seemed higher than when we went out in the morning, so I said to James, "Funny thing, I could swear that there is more in this bottle, than before we went out!" James said, "Wait a minute," and he drank some. We then discovered that Chinapa, the bearer had taken some, and had added water to make up the level and some saffron powder to make the colour look right! James was so furious, he said, "If you want to drink my drink, at least leave it in a fit state for me to drink it!" So he sacked Chinapa. In India, in Madras State, at that time they had prohibition, so no alcohol at all, but there was a concession for the Staff College and most officers had an allocation. People kept dying from making all kinds of illicit alcohol from all sorts of things, including banana skins, etc.

We had a new bearer called Cruz, who was very moody and not as pleasant as Chinapa, but they were all stealing food from us, to feed their large families. They went home with large baskets everyday, but as the food was so cheap it didn't really affect us. When you have servants, there are a lot of things that you have to turn a blind eye too! Or your life would be constant nagging or getting upset. I always tried to look after my servants well by treating them with respect and giving them clothes and always feeding them when they were at work. At least I knew that they had one meal a day.

The Ghanaian Ambassador, in India, Major-General Steve Otu, invited all the Ghanaian officers and their wives to be his guests in a beautiful hotel in Cochin, so we flew down to Cochin together. We met him at the airport. He arrived after us. He was very pleased to see me wearing Ghanaian dress. He took us to dinner in the hotel and there was a striptease artist who turned out to be a man! He looked so beautiful and it was a total surprise at the end. We had a lovely weekend in Cochin, the height of which, for me, was to have a real bath! At Wellington we only had our bucket and cup. General Otu was great fun and became a good friend. I was able to tell him that in 1964, when President Nkrumah had sacked him, we were celebrating as he had said that we should move out from our married quarter because James was not 22 years and therefore not eligible, and he said, "Well! I didn't know you then, Valerie, did I?" Cochin was very similar to Kete in Ghana, with palm trees and plantain and lots of mosquitoes. In the harbour they had boats like Chinese junks, carrying cement I do believe. They were building a harbour or something then. But the hotel was great and equal to any anywhere else in the world for high standards. We all had a really good time. On the plane going back to Coimbatore, there was the most terrible turbulence I have ever experienced on an aircraft – up and down, dropping several feet at a time. It was the most frightening, trip that I have ever experienced; even flying over the Himalayas, on the way to India was not as bad as that! It was the Monsoon season.

James travelled with the Staff College; all the combined service officers Army, Navy and Air force; on a three-week tour of India, which included a trip to Sikhan in the Himalayas. While he was away I went to the library, and collected so many books, as James didn't like me to read when he was home! I had just discovered the '*Angelique*' series by Sergeanne Golan. I found it really enthralling. I had collected three books in the series and read one after another; I am a very fast reader. About 1am, as I was reading, I suddenly felt a pulsating in my head, and when I looked up from my book; I saw a cloud of smoke in the corner of the room by the doorway. I could not believe my eyes. As I looked, the smoke started forming into a figure. I could see hands crossed, I was really scared. I closed my eyes and put my head down and then I kept repeating, "Whoever you are, I don't want to see anything! Go away!" I kept repeating this over and over again and suddenly I felt relief on my head and when I opened my eyes and looked up, there was nothing there! This is no made up story; I really and truly experienced this! I told Commander Frank Green, who was a retired Indian naval officer who lived in Coonoor Village just down the hill from the Staff College. He and his wife, Doreen, had become our friends during our stay in Wellington. Frank was a psychic. He told me that what I saw was the astral body of my husband and that he would be in trouble in September sometime! He couldn't tell me anymore, as I hadn't watched or listened to anymore.

When James returned he had a cut finger. He said, "That his fingers had been so cold, that he cut his finger while riding in the Himalayas and didn't even feel it!" It was a really deep cut and took a long time to heal.

Then the climax of the whole thing for me as a wife: the Ladies' Club in the Staff College, decided to give a fashion show of all the different costumes of India, and all the foreigners were to take part! We had British, Australians, Canadians, Americans, Malaysians, Zambians, Iraqis and many others from smaller countries, along with us four Ghanaians. My fellow Ghanaian wives were very shy and reluctant to take part, but I persuaded them, and I taught them and also Felli my Zambian friend, to walk. So Mrs. Sam, Adelaide, wore a beautiful everyday Ghanaian cloth dress, Mrs. Utuka, Justina, wore Kente, (the traditional hand woven cloth of Ghana), and I made a beautiful gold lame Ghanaian evening dress made in the Jerome style, which was popular then, with wide sleeves; with a turban style, headdress and a small matching cape. I made it myself and Felli wore Zambian dress and we all looked fine. I walked to the head of the catwalk and then removed the cape and trailed it on the floor behind me on the way back! It was a really glittering evening with the British, Canadian, American and Australian wives all wearing beautiful evening dresses.

The Indian dresses were fantastic, with wedding dresses from all over India with all the beautiful jewellery, and so many different ways of wearing the saris, and chemise with trousers. All the participating wives were awarded, the College Emblem, a small silver brooch in the form of an owl. We were so proud and felt like we had graduated from the college, too!

Then it was time to leave India and all my good friends; I have omitted to mention a few friends. I cannot close my chapter on India without mentioning Cdr. Frank Green and his wife Doreen and their three children. He was a retired Indian officer, an Anglo-Indian, and he used to tell people's fortunes. He was very accurate and predicted that Ted Utuka would be shot, and he was later when he became a general in 1979! Frank never charged any money but did enjoy being invited to dinners and lunches because when we were in Madras State, as it was then (it became Tamil Nadu whilst we were there), we had prohibition! So the only time that he could get a drink was in the College as the officers had a special concession. He also said that James would become the head of a large organisation with lots of ships and James said, "Commander, Navy?" and Frank said, "No, but that James would be Military Attaché somewhere in Africa though he couldn't say where.

James said, "When will I divorce my wife?" and Frank said, "You will not divorce her, but if you are not careful, you will lose her to a prince or plenipotentiary!" Needless to say, I am still waiting for my prince! When we left Wellington we flew to Bombay and spent a week in the naval mess, in accommodation for married officers. We did some shopping and sightseeing and then started our flight back to Ghana.

We flew from Bombay to Dubai and I carried some Kashmiri lampshades on my back all the way to Ghana. We stopped in Dubai for one hour to refuel, then went on to Bahrain and finally landed in Beirut, where we were to connect with Ghana Airways. Beirut in 1969 was a pure paradise. The sky was blue, the sun shone, and there were beautiful new hotels all round the beach. It was a typical French town like Paris, with amazing shops, restaurants, roads and beautiful cars; but with an Arab influence.

The first thing that the children and I did, as soon as we got to the hotel was to spend, at least half an hour, having a soak in the bath! The whole time in India, the only time that we had, had a real bath was when I was in the hotel in Cochin. Otherwise we had to use a bucket and cup. We had a heating element (like a kettle element), which hooked on the bucket, to heat the water. This only worked when the electricity was on. Most of the time we used candles and James had to study by candlelight, and the cook used the fire wood range or kerosene stoves. So it was heaven to have a real bath! A friend in the Ghana Embassy in Beirut, Mr. Vidal Buckle, came and took us round the shops and then home to his house for dinner. The next day we took Ghana Airways and flew straight to Accra.

Top Left: James and me, London, 1966.
Top Right: James in his Lieutenant's uniform, with Hamish, Rosina and me, London, 1966.
Middle Right: Christmas 1968 with Daddy at SEGAS Christmas dinner at the Coop at Woolwich.
Bottom Left: Laraine, 1967.
Bottom Right: Laraine with Aviv, my nephew, born prematurely 1970 at Lewisham Hospital Prem. Unit.

Top: Ghana 1971, with Kutin–Mensah, editor of the Graphic newspaper, showing two Americans around the press.
Middle Left: The Ghana Navy hockey team with Lt. Steve Boateng, 1971.
Middle Right: With James, now Commander Boham (NOIC), Takoradi, and Lt. Boating before presenting the hockey trophy to the winners, 1971.
Bottom Left: Admiral Nanda, the head of the Indian navy inspecting a Guard of Honour at the Naval base ,Takoradi, with Lt. Peter Nkrumah with the sword drawn and Lt. Col. Fred Akuffo, then commanding the Sixth Battalion, Ghana Army, and Commander Boham (James behind) 1971.
Bottom Right: A tea party in honour of Mrs. Nanda, the admiral's wife, Takoradi, 1971.

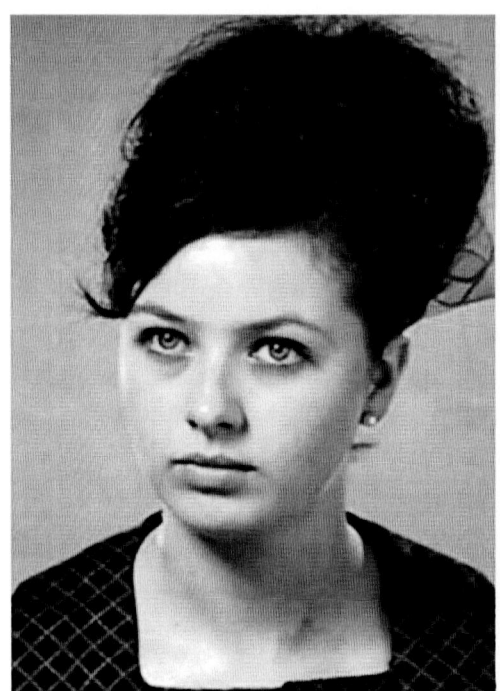

Top Left: Laraine Carol Collins, my beautiful sister, 1972.
Top Right: Reception at the Korean Embassy with Mrs. Lee, the Military Attaché's wife (my friend), Addis Ababa, Ethiopia, 1973.
Middle Right: Col. and Mrs. Need, the British Military Attaché, Addis Ababa, and me, 1973.
Bottom: Reception at the French Embassy with the Togo Ambassador to my right and my good friends Raymond Petit and his wife Kathrine to his right, Accra, 1972.

Top: Takoradi, 1974, James and me.
Middle Right: Christmas party for State Fishing Corporation staff, Christmas 1974, with Mummy in Accra.
Bottom Left: Mummy and me at a Garden Party, Accra, 1975.
Bottom Right: James, Mummy and me with Breid Amamoo, with my painting of Christ in the background (now lost) New Year's Day 1975. Accra house (SFC).

Presenting a Kente stole to one of the Norwegian captains' wife, Accra house SFC (State Fishing Corporation) with James now the Managing Director, 1975.

Top Left: My father looking like the Pope, Greenwich, South-East London, a pageant for the St John Ambulance Society of which he was a member, 1975.
Top Right: Accra, 1975, with my friend Dora, Cdr. Mante's wife. James took a lot of retired Navy personnel to the SFC.
Bottom Left: James, Mummy and me, 1975, Accra.
Middle Right: Mummy and me with Bried holding Julien after the party, 1975.
Bottom Right: Group of SFC staff with Hamish and me in the middle, 1975.

Top: Kutin-Mensah with a German guest and SFC staff at the Tema house (the first house that we owned).
Bottom: James and I and guests at the lunch table in Tema, Ghana.

Top Left: Glasgow, Scotland, summer of 1977, Hamish, Rosina and Julien with Lesley and Lorna, my cousin Norman's children, and Rajah, now a very old dog.
Top Right: James' mother, Rosina Quayson, with her sister Auntie Grace in Elmina, Ghana, and Hamish sitting in the car, 1977.
Bottom: My favourite photo of my son Julien when he was really happy in the garden of the Accra house (the second house that we had built and owned ourselves), 1977.

Chapter Six

GHANA
NOVEMBER 1969–1972

When we landed in Accra, we used for the first time the new airport building, which had just been opened. In the building the air-conditioning was working full blast and it was like the North Pole. Since then it has broken down and has never been repaired. We were better with the old airport, which had loads of fans, which always worked. Now we had a new civilian Government led by Dr Busia, as there had been elections whilst we were away. There had also been, a small earthquake, which didn't do too much damage, but there were a few cracks in some walls. We were met by, Lt Cdr George Bedu-Addo and Monty Provencal. Monty took us to stay with him until we got a married quarter.

After a week we got a house, which was not in Burma camp, but a private hiring near the Saint Hotel by the railway crossing. We moved in with no curtains etc and the BIA (Barrack Inventory officer) had to buy material and get them sewn. James had to do some special assignment at the Navy headquarters and then in February he was promoted to Commander, and given the post of NOIC (Naval officer in Charge), Takoradi, Western Naval Command.

So we moved back to Takoradi. We inherited a huge mansion in Sekondi, overlooking the lagoon and the sea. Down below us was the cemetery and we used to hear all the hymns whenever there was a burial. The house was enormous – an old colonial bungalow, with an immense entrance hall and a complete guest flat downstairs, and a kitchen, sitting room, four bedrooms and two bathrooms upstairs. It was in need of painting but they said there was no paint in the store. James now had a Mercedes-Benz staff car and flew the NOIC.'s flag; he had most of the ships in the Navy under him. But it seems that the power went to his head as from then on we grew more and more apart. He would stay out late saying he was working, and all the usual things. We had all the prestige but no money to go with it. Sometimes we would be in that staff car with the flag flying and not a penny in our pockets.

In the house now we had naval ratings, a cook and two stewards and we had a maid, Ekua, who was the niece of one of the naval ratings, who brought her to me age eleven and told me to train her. As the children were all at school we sent her to school at the local Methodist school. When she came to me she couldn't speak a word of English and had no schooling at all. When she left, you would have thought that she had been in England.

Whilst at Sekondi, we had a visit from an Indian Navy submarine and I had to get the ratings to scrub down the walls as there was still no paint and it was so bad, we had a reception for them in the main hall. The house had so many snakes and scorpions that I told James that we should move back into one of the senior officers' quarters in Takoradi, and as soon as one became available we packed to move. I felt more at home in the modern bungalows. It was only three bedrooms, but it was lovely.

We then had a visit from the Commander of the Indian Navy, Admiral Nanda. It was an official visit so there were parades and a party in the officers' mess, and I gave a very grand dinner party at the house. We had the naval band and dinner was outside on the veranda. I presented him with one of my paintings of Elmina Castle. The Regional Commissioner and the Chief of Police and all the service commanders in Takoradi: they all wore their mess kits and looked so nice with the white Naval uniform and the red Army and the blue Air Force uniforms, along with the black police uniforms.

My father came to visit us in Takoradi for three weeks. Now my father was very mean and all my life I never asked him for anything. James said to me, "I'll ask your father to bring me some cassettes."

And I said, "I won't ask for anything and I won't be disappointed." So my father came and James was waiting for his cassettes, and he said to me, "Did he mention the cassettes?" So I said, "No! You asked him for them, so you can ask him for them." So he said, "Mr. Brown, did you bring the cassettes?" So he replied, "Well, Jimmy, there were so many different numbers on them that I didn't know which one you wanted so I didn't buy any." (If that had been my mother she would have got one of each to make sure that she had the right one!) Then he said to me, "I've got a bottle of scent for you!" So I thought: things are looking up! But he couldn't find it. On the day he was leaving he found the bottle. It was about the size of a walnut. Years later my mother said to me, "Did you like your perfume?" and I said, "Yes!" She said, "Do you know how you got that?" and I said, "No!" and she said, "He went to a dance and won a Boots token and asked me to get some perfume that I knew you liked, and I even had to add money!"

When my father came he thought that he was coming to the jungle, so he came with an old colonial type linen jacket and we couldn't take him out to any of the formal functions as he was so big that he couldn't wear any of James's suits; and though he had loads of suits, he didn't bring one with him.

We were really broke during his stay, and he had wanted to see Accra but we had no money to buy food in Accra. So we had to arrange to take him straight to the airport from Takoradi. Unfortunately, for us his flight was delayed to the following evening, so what to do? We had arranged to stay at Flagstaff House, Nkrumah's former residence, now a senior officers' guesthouse, so I said to James, "Daddy has money, so drop us at Continental Hotel for breakfast", whilst he went to see if he could borrow some money from a friend. We had breakfast on the terrace in the beautiful garden at the back of the hotel.

Then, at a party in the Regional Commissioner's residence in Takoradi, I had met a lovely Irish lady who was the wife of the Junior Minister for Lands, and we had really enjoyed our chat, so she used to ring me sometimes and she said to call her if I came to Accra. So I rang her and said, "That I was with my father," so she said, "That she would send her car for us". So I rang James at Naval Headquarters and told him to pick us up from Breid's. He said, "That he had, had no luck yet, but he would keep trying".

Mrs. Breid Amamoo is lovely. She is full of mischief and you never know what she will come out with next; and if you play along with her stories it becomes quite an adventure. I have had many lovely times with her over the years up to the date of writing, 1985. She has two lovely daughters, Samia and Suzie, and her husband Joseph is also a brick as he plays along with her most of the time. She is someone that I am glad to have had the pleasure to meet and my life in Ghana would have been a wee bit empty without her. Anyway, she entertained us royally! My father was so impressed. James came to pick us in his staff car; scrambled egg, cap and still no money, so I said, "Drop us at Star hotel and I will try to get Daddy to buy lunch." So he dropped us, but Daddy wasn't playing ball this time. I said, "We can have lunch here, Daddy" and he said, "Oh no! We'll wait for Jimmy to come back." Finally James turned up and, success! So I said, "We are not eating here because it's too expensive", so we went to a little milk bar restaurant which had just opened up and was run by one of James's schoolmates: Dan's Bar at Adabraka. Then we went back to Flagstaff House to rest before the flight in the evening. James had been able to borrow 20 cedis (ten pounds at that time) and it wouldn't last long. When we got to the airport my father, who normally drinks only beer, said, "He wanted a double gin! A friend of James's was supposed to meet us at the airport to buy drinks but he hadn't turned up. Then the next minute I saw Mr. Anaman, who came over smiling and I said, "Mr. Anaman, you know my mother in London. Meet my father." And he said, "Oh, let me buy you all a drink." So, saved! As my father was going through the barriers he pressed some cedis into my hand – 19 cedis – so we still owed one cedi. I hoped he enjoyed his stay. I think he did, but it was not really his cup of tea! More prestige than anything!

When we were in India I had learnt tailoring so I now started designing and sewing my own dresses for functions. I made a lot of lovely long dresses with the Ghanaian cloth. And when Julien was born I had cut my hair, which was really long, and made a wiglet with it. So I used to curl the wiglet, plait it and style it myself, so when I went to parties I looked really grand.

In Takoradi I made friends with the Harbour Master and his wife – Fred and Joan Hancock – and they used to come and watch films with me at the naval base, when the ratings watched the films. The naval officers' mess was in Sekondi, which, was a bit of a trek; so James used to go and work in his office and I watched the films with Fred and Joan. On other occasions we got the film and watched it in the house. We sat outside and the screen was a whitewashed wall. Fred's sister was married to a Norwegian and she used to send him raw herrings marinated in sauce and, one I really loved, in a fruit sauce; so anytime they got some they would always invite us. At this time I became friends with the Flemish wife of a Nigerian captain of a Black Star Line ship. Gabriel and Marina Eguwe. She was the illegitimate daughter of an American Indian G.I. and a Flemish woman during the Second World War. Marina had a serious complex but she trusted me and we were really good friends. I used to invite her home for fu-fu and they used to invite us on board the ship for a film show, lunch or dinner. She used to give me so many provisions from the ship. One day Rosina saw some apples in a bowl and she said, "Uncle Gabriel, please could I have an apple?" and when we left the ship a whole carton of apples had been put in the car for her. They had five children at that time but they only had one or two with them on each trip.

I also met Mrs. Glenda Butah, who was a Welsh girl married to one of James's officers, Lt Joe Butah, and we became good friends. She was expecting her first baby and used to come to me everyday. As she lived in the officer's quarters, with most of the other naval wives, I used to visit them all and stay about twenty minutes and then go and have lunch with her.

Her baby boy, Justin, was born four days after my sister had my nephew, Aviv – born on 13th April in England – but I didn't know for some time and had no idea as Aviv was not due until June! Justin was a lovely baby and Glenda used to bring him over to me whenever she was anxious about him. Two weeks later I received a letter from my sister Laraine that said, "Well! I don't know if you are an auntie or not! I had a baby boy, three months premature. He is 3lbs 2oz, and is not expected to live." Well, as I am pleased to write, he did survive; his name, Aviv (which means spring in Hebrew) Shachneay. When I first met Glenda she was really fat, and one day when she came for a visit as she was walking away from us to the car, James said, "My God, she really is fat!" A few days later when she came for afternoon tea, and Joe had gone to play tennis, we were chatting nicely as we did on many occasions, then Hamish started laughing and he said, "Mummy, I'm going to tell on you." (He was about eight or nine at this time.) I had no idea what was coming out next! And he proceeded to say, "Auntie Glenda, Mummy and Daddy said that you are so fat!" I was struck dumb and could not raise my eyes; I wanted to go through the ceiling or through the floor. Then I glanced at Glenda and she said, "Yes, I've always been big!" and I really loved her for that – it relieved all the tension. After she had the babies, contrary to everybody else, she actually lost weight and became very elegant, as she really knew how to dress her figure. She had lovely eyes (like Elizabeth Taylor) and thick black hair that she always kept well trimmed.

The Chief of Defence Staff, Air Vice Marshall, Mike Otu. (the brother of Steve Otu, who was Ambassador when we were in India) was retiring form the Armed Forces so he was visiting all the units on a farewell tour. He was accompanied by his wife, Auntie Bea, or Mama, as everybody called her. She was the loveliest lady, who was able to retain her dignity as the General's wife; but was so nice to everybody, you felt as if she was indeed everybody's mother! When I was in Accra I had attended meetings of the Armed Forces Wives' Association and greatly admired her.

They arrived and there was a grand parade. In Takoradi, there was the Air Force Station, the Naval Base and The 2nd Battalion, one at Apremdu and the other in town: the Parachute Regiment. The Station Commander, Air Force Base, Col. John Barnor, and his beautiful wife Doris; he was the senior officer in Takoradi, so he was Commander in Chief, Takoradi.

At Apremdu were Col. & Mrs. Ted Utuka, (who had been with us at the Staff College in India). At 6th Battalion was Col. Parker

-Yanney – with his wife Hannah, a very elegant lady, who were both good friends of ours. And James, Commander Boham, (my husband) was the Naval Officer in Charge, Takoradi (NOIC). There were many parties in all the officers' messes for the Otus, and then the men were going to have a mess dinner.

So I suggested to the other ladies that as the men were having their dinner without us, we would have a dinner especially for Mrs. Otu and ourselves, so we all agreed to prepare certain dishes and bring drinks. We had our dinner in Mrs. Doris Barnor's house, and we had a lovely time amongst ourselves.

I have mentioned that I had a cook from the Navy. Well, I won't mention names, but this cook every morning would say to me, "Madam, I'm just going to the junction for my breakfast" and I would say, "Okay." What I didn't realise was that his breakfast was Apeteshie (the local gin!). One day the steward came to tell me that the cook was lying in the gutter, so I said, "Is he hurt?" and smiling, he said, "No, Madam!" so I went to see; and discovered that he was so drunk that he was unconscious! So I rang my husband at the base, and he sent the Military Police (as the cook was drunk on duty). They picked him up by his arms and feet and threw him in the jeep and took him to hospital, When he had recovered he was put in the guard room. I then got a new cook, who would remain my friend for years. He was a northerner, called Diera. (I'm not sure that is the correct spelling.)

Takoradi 1970

There was a plane crash in Takoradi, and the pilot was a good friend Flt. Lt. Uri and a lovely chap. They crashed deep in the bush during the rainy season; and by the time the rescuers managed to get to them they did all smell rather bad. So we had a funeral service for them in one of the hangers at the Air Force base, with empty coffins and their photos on top. There were five killed altogether. James was representing Commander Navy, Commodore Quaye, so I went with our driver. The funeral was so grand that there was nowhere to park and there were hundreds of people in the cemetery. I tried to enter and soon realised that there was no way that I could get to the graveside; and returned home. Just as well I did! When James came home he went straight to the bathroom to vomit. He said, "That the stench of the bodies was so terrible that only the overpowering smell of the Chief's perfume saved him."

Sometimes we used to go and visit James's mother Rosina Quayson in Elmina, which is a fishing village with two castles. It is the first place in which the Europeans landed, in 1492. There is a beautiful Portuguese castle, St George Da Mina, and a Dutch castle and there is nothing more beautiful than to see the Portuguese castle from the beach. With the brightly coloured canoes on the beach, and the palm trees; the sunshine and the sea, it is a real tourist attraction, and I don't know why nobody has developed it up to now!

When we went to Elmina we would go round to see all the old ladies. Elmina has a large number of old ladies but not many men. We would give them all something small (money). There was one old lady who was almost a hundred. She was all sinews and bones but she could walk with the aid of a stick and she could see and always recognised me. She would always say, "Jesus, Mary and Joseph bless you!" After all the visits we would go to the Elmina Motel for something to eat and drink. On the way back we would buy kenkey – the local food prepared from corn in plantain leaves; then bunches of plantain, yams, garden eggs, tomatoes, onions and pepper from the villagers, who would normally sell by the roadside. It was a lovely drive with palm trees and thick bush on either side of the road and the lovely warm sunshine with glimpses of the sea and various villages as we drove along the road. It took about fifty minutes to Elmina from Takoradi – James being such a fast driver. Sometimes we would get stuck behind a timber lorry transporting huge tree trunks to the harbour for shipment abroad. The size of those logs has to be seen to be believed, and it would be difficult to pass on the narrow roads (this was long before there were any motorways along this stretch of the road). But James would go full speed and pass them. I was always terrified of his driving as he went so fast but if you made any protest, he would drive even faster. I remember putting my hands up in prayer and he just said, "Don't be ridiculous!"

During this time in Takoradi, relations between James and I were more for official purposes. He took me to all official functions and I gave whatever dinners, teas, lunches and coffee mornings that were required of me, but we never went dancing together as before. He started staying out late. One night he came home and undressed in the children's bathroom and crept into bed without putting the light on. After a while I got up and went out of the bedroom. I looked through his clothes and found that his hankie was full of lipstick and make up used by black women. I started shaking and was so upset. I never drink but I went and got a good shot of brandy to control the shock and the shaking. After, I had calmed down a bit I went back to the bedroom and put the light on. He said to me, "Did you go for a drink of water?" and I said, "No! I went to find this" and showed him the hankie. Then the floodgates opened and I howled and howled! I said, "that I was leaving him!" and he wrote out a cheque for my fare home!

The next day one of my best friends at that time, a West Indian girl married to an army officer: Mrs. Cecily Awudu rang. As soon as she rang I broke down crying on the phone, so she said, "That she was coming immediately." She came to meet me packing and she said, "What are you doing?" and I said, "I'm going! He was out with a woman last night!" She said, "You're not going! You're not leaving these children. Come on!" When James came home at lunchtime he took the cheque and tore it up! Not that it would have made much difference if I was really determined that I wanted to go as we had a joint account; though I never really used it unless James was travelling, but I stayed! Most of this was played out in front of the stewards. My husband at times would not talk to me for days, and glare at me when he came home. So one of the naval stewards decided that he would be funny with me so I said to him, "Eshun, because my husband doesn't talk to me, doesn't mean that you can abuse me, Any more nonsense and you go back to the base!" As working in the house was much easier for him, he stopped his nonsense!

A very good friend of James's who was much older than him even though they were in the same class at school, was Apow. He was a lovely gentle soul who was also a good friend to me. There was a funny incident my first Christmas in Ghana, and because of that, every year Apow used to bring me a turkey for Christmas. Christmas 1964, I had wanted a turkey, and James had a friend who had a farm, who said that he would give us a turkey to buy for Christmas. We went to the farm to collect the turkey and after some time James came back with a goat. So I said, "What's that for?" and he said, "For Christmas" and I said, "I've never in all my life had goat for Christmas!" and was most indignant! What I didn't know, because they had been speaking Fanti all the time, was that the turkey had run off into the bush as it was a free-range farm and they hadn't been able to catch it, but they had agreed to catch it and bring it to the house later! When Apow heard the story he made sure that I had my turkey for Christmas every year. Whenever he came he would bring yams and plantain, as he knew that I liked them, and he would always give me ten cedis, which at that time was a great help. When he came next time I told him about the girlfriend and he said, "That he would talk to James". James was going out with Apow and I wanted to go with them, but he said, "No!" When I persisted he punched me in the face and cracked my front tooth! He then went out. Apow was in the car and didn't see him punch me! The next day I had a bruise on my face and told everybody that I walked into a door!

One of James's school-friends, Dr. Fifi Dadzie, had just returned from studying Aquatic Biology in Russia, and was getting married. He asked James to be his best man so we all went to Accra for the wedding. He was marrying a very beautiful young lady called Phillipa Morker. She was working for the Ghana Broadcasting Corporation at that time. It was a lovely wedding and she made a beautiful bride. We invited them to come and stay with us in Takoradi in our guest house for their honeymoon, so they did and we had lunches and dinners in their honour. One day they came home laughing! They used to take Julien, who was three years old and really sweet, out with them. They said, "That as they were going out they saw James coming home in the staff car and Julien said, "There goes Daddy. He's going home to shout on Mummy!" and that was the life! I could never do anything right and he shouted on me or didn't talk to me for days. I used to get him to talk by saying, "Come on, what have I done now?" and if I said it long enough he would finally blurt out what he was annoyed about! In public it was all smiles and he would call me Darling and put his arms around me and kiss me, but when people left it was a different story!

About once every three months his mother would pop in for a very short visit and occasionally we would all drive her back to Elmina and visit her sister Auntie Grace. Kofi, his brother, would come whenever he was in Takoradi and we always saw Joseph in Kingsway Stores and occasionally he would come over for lunch.

Glenda Butah, who had just got married to Joe, had been living in a married quarter belonging to a friend who was overseas. When he came back they had to find another quarter. James had to go to Accra to take over from Commander Navy for a couple of months, so I said that Glenda should stay with me. We were talking late into the night so I said that she should sleep with me. We both went off to sleep. Then I was woken by the most peculiar noise and I realised that Glenda was snoring, not just snoring but it was so funny that I couldn't help but laugh. I put my head under my pillow and was laughing for most of the night. The snoring went from high to low and was very constant. The next morning she said to me, "Did I snore?" and I said, "Yes!" She said that she had forgot to tell me and that she had been snoring since she was a baby. One time a neighbour was visiting her mother and hearing the snores said, "My god! Your husband snores" and her mother said, "That's not my husband, that's our Glenda!" But it didn't deter our friendship.

One morning my next-door neighbour Mrs. Tina Laing came over. She said that she was going to visit a friend, another Air Force officer's wife, Mrs. Arkhurst, who had just had a baby; so she asked if I would like to come. I agreed and so we set off. It was only three houses' walk away. When we got there I met a very interesting young lady who had just returned from nursing in Libya. We had a very interesting and absorbing conversation about her life there. She then said, "I like you so much!" and I said, "I like you too!" Her name was Miss Pat Attafuah and she was staying with her fiancée in Sekondi so we agreed that we had to meet again!

When I got home that very lunchtime James said, "By the way, I bumped into one of my old school-friends who has just returned from doing medicine in Russia, so I invited him and his fiancée to lunch tomorrow." Imagine my delight when his fiancée turned out to be the very same Pat that I had met the day before. I won't mention the doctor's name as he is past history. So therein began a wonderful friendship and Pat is my dearest sister up to this day! We had many pleasant times with Pat and the doctor but trouble brewed and they separated. But nothing could separate me from Pat. She got a job working at The Parkinson Howard Hospital in Tema and she also acquired a pretty one-bedroomed house at Tema with the money from her bonus from Libya, and I really admired her pluck.

In December 1971, just before Christmas, we heard that James would be transferred to Accra, to the Naval Headquarters, in Burma Camp as the Chief Staff Officer (CSO). So on 7th January 1972 the children and I packed all our belongings and went to Accra. Luckily we had a bungalow at Juba Villas, where our old friend Joe Kyeremeh was living and he was posted to Takoradi to take over from James as NOIC. We just settled down a little and all the children slept in my room, with me and Ekua the maid, too! The children thought that it was great fun to sleep on the floor so they collected all the cushions from the sitting room and they all slept on the floor. James rang me at about 10.30pm and asked if we were all alright, and I said, "Yes, we are all fine!" At about 3am – I'm not quite sure of the time – I thought I heard a couple of shots and I thought: you must have been imagining it! At about 5am, my next-door neighbour, who was my good friend Aggie Pumpuni (who used to make my fu-fu), came over with the houseboy. She said, "There's been a coup. What do we do?" I said, "Nothing! We have to keep the children in the house and not let them go to school!" This was a difficult task as Aggie's children, apart from the eldest, were all the same age as mine. In fact we had even been admitted in the hospital at the same time before so they really loved each other. Whether in Takoradi or Accra, we always seemed to be in the same place at the same time and only a few houses away. This time it was right opposite across the road. They even went to America on the Staff course the same time that we went to India on the Staff course. So we had to lock the children in either one house or the other! As we were standing outside the house an officer, Yaw Boatche, passed. We asked, "What is happening and who is doing it?"

He said, "It's Acheampong!" and I was really surprised because he had always seemed so quiet and nice – not at all the type to make a coup! Definitely, not a rebel; In fact, very nice indeed – a teacher by profession.

The whole day we listened to military music and the occasional announcement that said that they would broadcast at 6pm. So six o'clock we were all glued to the television; all the telephones had been disconnected as soon as the coup took place as we were living in the Burma Camp military quarters, Accra Ministry of Defence.

They played the national anthem and then we saw some officers seated at a table. I immediately recognised Acheampong and Kwame Baah, who was Julien's godfather; Tony Selormey, and Barney Agbo.

Acheampong started announcing the names of members of the National Redemption Council. (NRC), and then we heard him announce: "Commander James Boham, Naval Commander." We were so shocked in the house as we had no idea! Aggie came over and said, "You've got a post!" I said, "I know, but I don't know whether I like it or not!" James at this point was still in Takoradi and we could not communicate. Anyway, by next day the phones were reconnected. By the time that James got to Accra, a few days later, he no longer had the post as people had been lobbying and succeeded in getting him out!

Acheampong, who was a good friend, said, "That he would send him to London as Ambassador, but James said, That he preferred a service appointment. Then he offered to send us to Korforidua as Regional Commissioner but I said, "I won't go there!" Then the final solution, to which we all agreed, was to go as Military Attaché to Ethiopia in the Ghana Embassy and to be a member of the Liberation Committee for Africa. The reason most people were against James was that he was married to a foreigner and I think that he really hated me from that time on. But he didn't want to disgrace himself by just ditching me.

One thing I omitted to mention: whilst we were in Takoradi James had met a French Diplomat and he and his wife became very good friends of ours. They were a great comfort to me at this time. Their names were Raymond and Catherine Petit. He was First Secretary at the French Embassy in Accra, and he was half-French and half-Vietnamese, his mother being Vietnamese. His wife was from Iceland. She was a tall, beautiful blonde, like a model! She was also a Taurean like me and we got on really well.

With all the problems of the moment I started bleeding again and had to be admitted to the hospital for a D & C. I was not pregnant as I had, had the loop fitted after Julien was born. The day James was to take me to the hospital he was nowhere to be found. Then I heard that he had driven Col. Techie-Menson and his wife Nancy to visit Charles's mother in Apam, in a white Mercedes-Benz that they had got from the castle car pool, about three hours drive there and back. I was so upset that I rang Catherine, and she and Raymond came and took me to the hospital. When James came back in the evening he was mad! Why should I get Catherine and Raymond to take me to the hospital? He hadn't wanted them to know. As I mentioned before, in public he was all 'Darling, Darling' and was the perfect, attentive husband; but in private he could be really wicked mentally. In April I left to go to London before going on to Ethiopia; James was going to a conference in Kampala, Uganda before going on to Ethiopia. Catherine and Raymond came to see me off. As they had diplomatic passes, they were able to see me right onto the plane. Nancy and Charles Techie-Menson also came to the airport.

London 1972 – Anna's place

When I was leaving for London James said, "That his sister Anna had been complaining that since we got married we had never stayed with her; so he would like me to stay with her when we went to London! Whether this was true or not I don't know, because James was such an accomplished liar and he would make you believe him no matter how far fetched the story! (The first lie he told me was on our marriage certificate; he said, "That his father was a doctor") when his father was never a doctor. He even said that he was a heart specialist! To make it very grand. I didn't discover that this was a lie till many years later in Elmina. We were attending a funeral and his nephew Mike Issilfie, laughed when I said that James's father had been a doctor. He said, "That James's father had run transport".

When we arrived in London Anna and her husband Stephen met us and took us to their home. She went to buy Kentucky Fried Chicken for us, and she gave us a comfortable double room. Now, one thing at that time: you could only bring fifty pounds sterling out of Ghana, so that was the only money that I had. Anna was working as a nursing sister. She said, "that we should use whatever food was in the kitchen and feel free". Now the children had been used to a car all the time, and anytime Anna and Stephen were going out, they wanted to go, too. But they never offered to take us out anywhere and I didn't ask because, as I mentioned before, she was the wild African woman who threw James's trunk down the stairs way back in 1963 when we first got engaged. She would lock the telephone in her room when she went out. I used to hear the phone ring and knew that it was Mummy, and would have to put on all the children's coats and walk with them round the corner to the phone box to ring her. I was not very happy but because she was James's sister and he had asked us to stay with her I had to put up with it. He was coming to London for a few days before going to the conference in Kampala.

When James arrived the telephone was plugged in our room and she started cooking for him everyday. So when I told him what had been happening before, he didn't believe me! Now James didn't have much money on him either and as he needed some underwear, shoes, shirts etc. he said that, "When he got to Kampala he would send me some travellers cheques as they would give him some imprest.

On the night James arrived Anna and Stephen went to collect James's other two sisters, who were in London at that time – Joan and Wilhelmina. The next thing, I heard them say in Fanti, (their language) (thinking that I didn't understand, though I had picked some up by this time), "Brother Ebow," (James's Fanti day name – Tuesday born) "since Valerie came she has never once asked to come and visit us," and they were complaining! So I surprised them all and said to Joan, "When I was in Ghana, when did you, Joan, ever come to visit me? You only came to see your brother and when your brother left for work you joined him in the car, and never spent five minutes with me on my own! If I come to my own country and have no car and three small children to look after, should I ask to see you?"

That left them all speechless. The next day James left for Kampala. I rang my father and I was crying and he said to me (and he never normally swears), "I don't know what the bloody hell you are doing there in the first place. Come home and I will leave the money for a mini-cab!"

So I told Anna that I had no money and was going to my mother so she would look after the children whilst I went to work! A few days later I had a call to say that a letter had arrived for me so would I come and collect it? When I got to her house one of her tenants came and gave me an empty envelope with no traveller's cheques or letter in it! To this day I don't know the truth of it, but normally if a letter was opened here, the Post Office would stamp it: 'Letter open, contents missing' and the postman would ring and tell you that the mail was received damaged.

James did an investigation and he said, "That the American Express travellers cheques were traced to Anna's account." I am not saying this – only repeating what James told me. Anyway, after a lot of hassle my father gave me fifty pounds and I was able to buy a few things for the children before we left for Ethiopia.

In London there was the excitement of seeing my nephew Aviv for the first time. We arrived on 7th April and so were there in time for Mummy's birthday on the 12th and Aviv's first birthday on the 13th. He was a beautiful baby with big blue eyes like his mummy and my father and grandmother (Nanny, Daddy's mother) and I spent a lot of time nursing him. Laraine was living with Roni, Aviv's father, who was an Israeli. My father said, "That, If he had any more daughters, he would have 'the League of Nations'. And, of course, we had to choose those with the most prejudices against them – the Jews and the blacks. Anyway, my nephew was lovely. They had a flat at Falconwood and Laraine was working whilst Mummy looked after Aviv. I had a lovely time with Roni and Laraine – the first bit of freedom for a long time and I felt quite young again!

One day Roni took us to Golder's Green to one of his Israeli friends, who was a very good hairdresser, and we all had our hair done. I had mine straightened for the first time in my life, always having very tight wavy hair. Then we went to an Israeli restaurant and had Israeli food. In the evening we decided to go to the launderette to wash the children's clothes. Now I was quite the 'bush girl' about washing machines as in Ghana we always had the houseboys who did the washing, so I had never used one before as when I was a child Mummy always sent everything to the laundry. So I put too much powder in the machine and the next minute bubbles were coming out all over the floor. Laugh? We all laughed until our sides were splitting. We had to wash the clothes again without soap. After such a lovely day and such a good laugh, when we arrived home Mummy said, "That James had rung from Kampala and was most annoyed that I wasn't in. He would ring back at eight in the evening. Eight o'clock came and he rang. He immediately started on me. "Where had I been? Why should I leave the children with my mother and father? If all I wanted was to go gallivanting, I should send his children to Addis Ababa on their own and not bother coming at all!" I immediately started crying, and was crying for ages after I put the phone down. Roni, Laraine, Mummy and Daddy were all mad! Roni said, "I shouldn't go at all and he would help me look after the children".

We had to go to the Defense Office, in the Ghana Embassy, Belgrave Square, to arrange our flight to Ethiopia. The Defense Advisor was Arnold Quainoo, who is now General Quainoo, and the Force Commander in Ghana at the time of first writing in 1985. He said that I would have to spend the night in Rome, as Ethiopian Airways didn't fly to London direct at that time! I wasn't very happy, as travelling with three children was no joke!

The day we were leaving I had decided to go to the shops at

Woolwich for some last minute things for the children. Just as I was about to leave there was the Embassy car with Warrant Officer Asante to say that they had just realised that I needed a visa for Ethiopia. I had asked earlier and they had said that as James was now a diplomat I didn't need a visa. So I had to leave the packing to Mummy and Daddy and ask them to get the children ready and dash to the Ethiopian Embassy for the visa. Because the Embassy had rung them, they did everything quickly. At the last minute they asked for photographs and I had none so we had to dash to one of the photo machines and then dash back to the Ethiopian Embassy, before starting back home. I decided to dash to the shops as planned and went to the manager of Marks and Spencer's in Woolwich, explained that I was travelling in two hours, and he was marvellous; he got all his staff to help and I bought everything I needed for the children and myself. I was so grateful, to that manager. So, then speeding home, collecting my emerald ring from the jewellers on the way! I quickly, changed my dress, and grabbed a sandwich. I hadn't eaten all day and neither had Warrant Officer Asante and the driver, who were both so nice to me. Then the children piled into the car, checking passports, tickets, money etc. and we were on our way to the airport. Warrant Officer Asante was from Q-movement so he checked all my baggage, and Colonel Quainoo saw us off.

We had a pleasant flight to Rome and as we arrived at the airport I heard 'Ethiopian Airways, Addis Abebe' (the Italian pronunciation) so I said, "There is a flight" and went straight to the Ethiopian Airlines desk and there was this lovely Ethiopian young man. He went and collected our baggage from the other plane and put it on Ethiopian Airlines and directed us to the departure gate. Now I was wearing very high heels and carrying a large bag and suddenly Julien, who was three years old, said, "Mummy, carry me!" So I had to pick him up. Because I was walking slowly because of carrying him, I didn't notice that Rosina was walking ahead and the next thing she was walking through the wrong gate and the air hostess just let her pass. I put Julien down and said, "Stay there and don't cry" and told Hamish to look after him and then ran like mad to get Rosina just before she boarded the plane to Malta! Anyway, we got our

Ethiopian Airlines flight and less than half an hour after we landed in Rome we were on our way to Addis Ababa. Now earlier on in the book I told you that Air India was the best airline for travelling with children. Well now I'm not so sure; Ethiopian Airlines was so good. The staff were so nice, they played with the children, took Hamish to see the captain in the cockpit, gave them chocolate, and they gave us food so often that you couldn't eat anymore. I would definitely recommend them to any traveller, especially if you have children.

Chapter Seven

ETHIOPIA
1972–1974

After a very pleasant flight we landed in Addis Ababa. I now had what you would call a travel bug for exotic places. I was so excited and so were the children. The airport staff were very nice and welcomed us to Ethiopia. We had landed at about four o'clock in the morning and there was hardly anybody at the airport, which was completely deserted. When we came out there was nobody to meet us but that was my fault, as we were supposed to have spent the night in Rome and arrived later. So, what to do? There was a chap sitting at the Bank of Ethiopia desk so I explained my plight and he was really kind. He got the phone book and started ringing all the Ghana Embassy residences in the book, but unfortunately they had all moved! By now it was 6am. So I said to him, "Could you give me a reliable taxi-driver to take me to the Ghana Embassy?" He agreed so we got into a taxi, which was a bit dilapidated by Ghanaian standards. When we got to the Embassy, the watchman (sabanya), when I told him I was the commander's wife, got really excited and agreed to show us the Warrant Officer's house as he didn't know our house as it was a new one!

When we got to Warrant Officer Twenaboah's house, his wife came out all excited and said that he had gone to the airport with my husband, so she showed us the house! When we reached the house the maid (mamity) also got so excited and took us into the house.

Now this maid, Adimasore, was to turn out to be the nicest servant I ever had and also a good friend. After a while a car came and it was James with Warrant Officer Twenaboah, Warrant Officer Vedomey and Staff Sergeant Adra: James's staff in the Defence Office.

Now in Addis the weather is most peculiar – one minute you are hot and the next cold. It's also about ten thousand feet high. The day I arrived, 1st June, was our eighth wedding anniversary so we opened a bottle of champagne – Moet et Chandon, my favourite, which James had put on ice. We put the children to bed and sat and talked about what had happened since we last met. Then we went to bed. As soon as I lay down, I felt my head spinning and realised that I was going to be sick so I spent the whole night in the bathroom. What I didn't realise, was that because of the high altitude you can't drink as much as you normally do!

The next morning my head was spitting and Adamasa came wailing, "Oh Madam, Master left a bottle of champagne in the freezer and it's frozen and broken."

I said, "Thank God!" as the last thing I needed at that moment was any more champagne! A few days later James sent the car for me to go and see the shops. As we got to a certain square, I saw all the people lying on the floor and said, "My god, they've all been shot!" and the driver, named Taddessi, said, "No, Madam. It's the Emperor, he pass" and when I looked up the hill I saw a cavalcade of maroon Mercedes-Benz's driving into the palace! I later discovered that nobody was allowed to look at the Emperor and they had to prostrate themselves in his presence.

One thing that many people don't know is that it's very difficult to cook at high altitude. When I arrived in Addis, I had no idea. One day I decided to make a chocolate cake for Rosina as she doesn't like fruitcake. I mixed everything as normal and put it in the oven. The oven had a glass door so I was able to watch, and also an oven light. The cake rose nicely and then flopped down. I couldn't believe it. So I mixed another one and it happened again. At one of the cocktail parties I was telling somebody and she said, "Oh yes! It's the altitude. You have to get high-altitude baking powder and put more flour to make it solid." As I don't like cakes much I gave up and discovered mielle feuille at the patisserie, which was Italian: layers of wafer thin pastry with cream, chocolate, coffee or any flavour you liked. So anytime we needed a birthday cake or sweet we ordered one from the patisserie! Another problem was cooking meat, as the boiling point is never quite reached; so I had to cook all meat in a pressure cooker, which halved the cooking time.

You could get corn in Addis so I decided to make kenkey for James, but they didn't have a mill to grind the corn as they did in India. So, I borrowed a large mincer from Mrs. Philapina Ashiabor, who turned out to be a good friend, soaked the corn for three days, and started grinding slowly. It took a long time as the mincer only took a little at a time, and lots of bits got all over the kitchen. When James came home and saw the mess he started shouting, so I said, "Okay! I was trying to make kenkey for you and if that's all you can do, I will never make kenkey for you again!" And I didn't! We couldn't get plantain in Addis; but I used to make tatalai with bananas, and adding salt and tomatoes and onions and pepper; and it came out quite nice. Tatalai is similar to fritters. It is fried in palm oil and eaten with beans.

In Addis it is difficult to get sea fish. It only comes from the Red Sea once a week so everybody used to dash to the fish shop as soon as the fish arrived. The Ethiopians themselves never eat fish – always meat. You could get lake fish and I used to buy it and soak it overnight in saltwater and that made it taste much nicer. The Ethiopian food is dabu (bread made with rye), almost like German or Russian black bread; and ingera and What (a stew). Ingera is like a very large chapatti of an oatmeal colour with the consistency of an English crumpet though very thin. It is sour in taste and is eaten with a hot spicy stew (What) which is very red and is quite delicious once you acquire the taste! They eat it on a basket table with a round top, on which many layers of ingera are laid, and the What (stew) is placed on the top. You tear the ingera from the end and eat with your fingers as you do with Indian chapattis. The waiters get putting more ingeras as they get eaten up. After the meal they have the coffee ceremony. They take green coffee beans and roast them on a small charcoal fire. They then grind the beans and brew the coffee on the fire. They burn incense, frankincense and myrrh crystals to ward off evil spirits. They also make a delicious tea with cinnamon, and the local cheese is quite delicious – similar to Gruyere or Emmenthal, the Swiss and French cheeses. There were plenty of vegetables and a lot of artichokes, and; you could also get fresh strawberries. The meat was very cheap and the butcher always gave you loads of meat for the dogs, free!

We had three dogs in Addis, all of them inherited from diplomats who were leaving. There were a lot of thieves, so we had a sabanya (watchman) as well as the dogs. We had two German shepherd dogs and a cross dachshund who was a female, and she ruled the roost. Her name was Pickle, short for piccalilli; and the dogs were Ras, which means 'Lord' in Amaric; and Bobby, who was pretty hopeless – only howling like a wolf when a train passed. Ras was so big and looked so fierce that even men would ask me to chain him up before they got out of their cars, but he was a big softy. Pickle was the one who might nip you in the ankle! Pickle slept in the kitchen and the others were outside with the watchman, who had a little hut at the gate.

One day I was entertaining several of the Embassy children, to lunch. They were all playing in the garden when the gate opened to let in a car, and a mad dog ran into the compound! Adamasa the mameta was screaming. I just grabbed the children one by one and put them in the house and not one of them even cried or protested. The watchman managed to chase it out with sticks and we quickly closed the gates. There was a lot of rabies in Addis. There were also a lot of lepers, as the biggest leprosarium in the whole of Africa was in Addis. They used to let them out to beg for food. It was quite terrible to see them, all bound in dirty white bindings; you could have taken one and put him back in Bible days and he wouldn't have been out of place! There was a lot of tension in the air as all the time we were there, people were expecting a coup or something any day! As it happened, there was one almost a month after we had left.

When we first arrived, the Ambassador was away, so I couldn't go and call on him officially for a few weeks. In the meantime I met a very interesting lady, Mrs. Lucy Riby-Williams (Auntie Lucy) and she was so kind to come round in her car and take me round to show me where to buy what. She also took me to the famous Makarto

Market. She had an Ethiopian friend called Teresite Solomon, who she introduced me to (she was the secretary to the Ethiopian Airways manager at that time) and Terasite and I also became good friends. The children could not start school until September when the new term started, so every morning I used to teach them reading myself so that they wouldn't fall behind.

James brought them a donkey so they were really happy. We eventually gave it back to the old Ethiopian man who we had bought it from when they lost interest. The house that we had originally, we had to leave as when we lit the fire the whole house became full of smoke, as there was a fault with the chimney! James went round and found a very nice house, which had a twin next door where there was an American family from the Embassy, but they left shortly after we moved in. Then a Burundi couple, Margaret and Salvador Nduruhutse, moved in and the wife became my very good friend. She was beautiful and the Burundi national dress was lovely chiffon in pastel colours. Everyday was a round of glittering parties; this Embassy, then that. There were over fifty Embassies in Addis and what with their National days and Military days, sometimes we had to attend at least three receptions and invites to several dinners; but I loved it all as I love mixing with people of all nationalities.

The British Consul's wife Mrs. Anna Dolman was a lovely lady who really made my stay in Addis enjoyable. She used to have coffee mornings on Tuesday mornings and we used to help some of the diplomats' wives to practise their English. We also did a lot of sewing and eventually had a bazaar in aid of the Cheshire homes in Addis. I met a lovely old lady there whose husband was a Polish count, and who was working for the Emperor. They had been in the Congo during the war and she had been raped by soldiers. It had affected her badly and she was so emotional she used to cry at times. She loved me and said that I was so beautiful. One thing I always remember: her face was so lined and she said, "The lines on my face are the lines of my life." I often wonder what happened to her as she was still there when the coup took place?

Another lady that I met at Anna's was called Anne. She lived just down the road to us and Anna asked her to pick me up and bring me when she was coming. Her husband Tim was working with an insurance company in Addis. The owner of the company's wife, a beautiful Ethiopian lady, used to make pictures by gluing seeds onto a board and they were really good. During the bazaar she asked me to take care of her stall whilst she had a break, and to my horror I discovered that the glue was melting in the sun and the pictures were on the move. We had to frantically move them into the shade and lie them down flat on the ground; they were new pictures and the glue had not fully dried out.

I then met another lovely lady who became so dear to me, in fact my second mother. She has given me help and sound advice over many years since Addis – Mrs. Linda Gardiner (Auntie Linda). Her husband Dr. Robert Gardiner was the Secretary-General of the United Nations, Economic Commission for Africa (UNECA). Linda is a very cultured West Indian lady, and I had just met her eldest daughter Charlotte (a doctor) before I left Ghana as she had married a friend of ours, who we had met when we were at Akosombo. He was a civil engineer with the Volta River Authority (VRA) – Mr. Kwame Kyame-Kumi. Charlotte, was a beautiful girl who was expecting her first baby so Auntie Linda left Addis for a few months to look after Charlotte in Ghana when she had the baby, a little girl called Linda or Yaa Konadu – an Ashanti name as Kwame was an Ashanti.

The children had eventually got into the English School in Addis but James decided that the standard was not good enough, and through a friend of his who came to stay with us in Addis as she was working with Ghana Airways – Miss Margaret Moses (who I discovered later was his girlfriend), he arranged to send the children to St. John's Preparatory school in Ghana. Now I had no idea at all what St. John's was like at that time!

Auntie Lucy Riby-Williams's sister Rose came on leave in Addis with her small son; so we arranged for the children, Hamish and Rosina, to travel with her. Julien, now only four years old, would remain with us in Addis. TT was to meet them at the airport in Accra and he would be responsible for them and they would stay with him and Regina, during the holidays. We paid all their school fees and sent parcels of meat, bacon and sausages from Addis to TT through the Ethiopian Airlines manager in Accra, Mr. Mills, who was most helpful.

So Hamish and Rosina left. I was so upset. Mrs. Elisabeth Bentum, whose husband was Mr. B.A. Bentum (of ILO Addis) (International Labour Organization), was with me at the airport and I wore my dark glasses to hide my tears. The next day Mrs. Anna Dolman came and picked me up and took me out as she said, "She knows how it feels when your children go off to school for the first time!" Julien became the chief in the house and he spent most of his time with adults, so he started talking about very serious subjects; and people started calling him 'Old Man' because he had an old head on young shoulders. Uncle Robert (Dr Gardiner) used to call him 'Haile Selassie'.

Princess Anne came on a visit to Addis Ababa and stayed with Emperor Haile Selassie and there was an official garden party. I wore a beautiful fitted silk dress that I had made in India and a pale lemon organdie picture hat that I had bought in C & A's in London, who I had always found were marvellous for hats. Mrs. Anna Dolman was wearing a lovely black hat and I said, "That's lovely!" and she said that she had bought it in C & As" and I said, "So's mine!" Unfortunately Princess Anne had been bitten by a stomach bug, which is all too common in Addis as there are thousands of flies; so she couldn't stand very long, and shook a few hands and had to leave. She wore a beautiful patterned yellow dress and hat and looked lovely in spite of her problem. In the evening there was a ball but, though she came, she had to stay in a private room, as she was not well enough. Immediately on her return from Addis she announced her engagement to Mr. Mark Phillips.

We were always having delegations to various conferences in Addis in Africa Hall, the UNECA headquarters. One friend came to stay with us, Col. Enoch Donker; and he was a member of The Tema Development Housing Committee, so we gave him a deposit to put on a Tema house for us. We had called Addis 'Operation Last Chance' as we didn't expect any overseas postings after this. So we saved all our monies to buy a Mercedes-Benz to take to Ghana and a cooker and fridge-freezer etc. so we could set up a new home, as up until that point we had stayed in furnished military accommodations.

We had only provided our bed linen, crockery and cooking utensils. I used to sew for a few friends in Addis, and in return, they would buy me material and I would sew dresses for myself. As I bought no new dresses for myself (as we were saving all our money) Addis was fairly cheap to live, though not as cheap as India!

There was a Defence Conference and The Chief of Defence Staff, G.A. General Ashley-Larsen, led the delegation so we had a lunch for them at the house along with the Principal-Secretary, from the Ministry of Defence in Ghana. We finished lunch and were sitting down having coffee when somebody said it was hot and suggested opening the window, so James wanted to open the door to the veranda. I said, "Don't open it!" but he did anyway. The next minute we were swarmed by thousands of flies and everybody had to grab a magazine to swat them away. The flies all sat on the ceiling, which looked like tiny polka dots. After the guests left, Adamasa and I used four tins of fly spray to kill them and we swept up a pile of flies!

So that's Addis and the flies!

Rear-Admiral David Hansen G.N. (retired) and Auntie Lily Whitaker came on a visit to Addis and stayed with Auntie Lucy and Uncle Jimmy Riby-Williams. Uncle Jimmy, the loveliest gentleman that you could meet, was Uncle David's cousin and they had both the same nature and manners – really gentle cultured African gentlemen. Auntie Lily and I became great friends. Today I call her my big sister. She is full of fun. She was very beautiful with a fair complexion. She had been one of the first television announcers on GBC TV, Ghana, had studied television producing, and directing, and had produced several programmes. We had many parties for them: in the Embassy, in our house, at Uncle Jimmy's, and various other homes. Everybody wanted to give a lunch or dinner for them and they stayed for over a month, so that was a lovely interlude.

The Ghana Ambassador in Addis, was Mr. Yaw Turkson, who I think was really a credit to Ghana: a career diplomat who behaved very correctly. His wife Tina was a black American and very elegant. The Ethiopian Ladies' club, had a bazaar and the Ambassador's wife asked me to help with the decoration of the Ghana stand. We were invited to tea with Haile Selassie's daughter, Princess (I can't remember her name), who was very gracious and talked to us all very nicely. There was a raffle at the bazaar and I had bought tickets, a whole book, as it was for charity. The prize was two of Auntie Linda's (Mrs. Gardiner's) paintings. She is quite an accomplished artiste and is well known in Africa as Araba Kromante. Anyway, I left before the raffle was chosen and then later, when Puplampu came, we asked who won the raffle and they said, "You did." So I became the proud owner of Auntie Linda's paintings: two abstracts in acrylic.

Whilst we were in Ghana we were friendly with Dr. Lule, who was the Secretary-General of the African Universities Association. He came to a conference in Addis. He came to the house and brought a letter for James from Miss Margaret Moses. James wasn't in but I invited him to come to lunch. Something told me to open that letter – a thing that I had never done before. It was a love letter from Miss Moses to James. I was furious and burned it! When James came home I told him,"You had a love letter from your girlfriend and I burnt it." I also sent her a letter telling her to refrain from writing to my husband in future, I was so shocked that he could have let her stay in the house with me. Professor Lule had no idea about what was in the letter. He later became President of Uganda for a short while after the overthrow of Idi Amin.

One of my best friends in Addis was Miss Helen Orwang, who was the Cultural Attaché in the Uganda Embassy. She was about six feet tall and so beautiful that she should have been a model for *Vogue* magazine. Margaret from Burundi, Helen and I were together at all functions and receptions. In May 1973, we had the tenth anniversary celebrations of the OAU (the Organisation of African Unity). One of our good friends in Addis was Dr. Peter Onu, a Nigerian who we had met when he was Ambassador to Ghana and who was now the OAU Secretary-General in Addis.

The Heads of State from all over Africa came to Addis and I saw and met most of them: General Gowan from Nigeria; Nyerere of Tanzania, who complimented me on my Kente (Ghana traditional cloth): Oyld Daddah of Mauritania; and all the others too numerous to mention. It was a very *Grande* occasion with a Foreign Ministers'

Conference and then the Heads of State. Col. Kwame Baah was Ghana's Foreign Minister, and he headed the Ghana delegation. He was Julien's godfather and was one of James's friends who met me at the airport when I first arrived in Ghana in 1964.

So we had lunches, and cocktails and receptions at all the Embassies as well as lunches in our house for the Ghana delegation, for about ten days. On the Heads of State speech day the wives were all invited and I went with Margaret, but the Ethiopians had so many security people, that we couldn't get a seat, and went home and watched it on the TV. President Idi Amin was the clown of the whole show – a great giant like a big bear with a huge grin. Unfortunately for Helen, he took a fancy to her so she had to keep out of his way and eventually got a transfer to Paris. We really missed her; especially Julien, who was very close to her. We had many happy lunches together in her house or in ours.

Another lovely friend I had was Auntie Doll (Dolores Acquah) and her husband, Uncle Kwame (Black Label), so called because he never drunk anything else but Black Label whisky! Doll was a French-Canadian by birth but a naturalized American and had met Uncle Kwame whilst he was working for the UN in New York. He now worked for the OAU. She was white and had the loveliest silver white hair. She was about fifty and had never had any children. She read a lot, like me, and I used to get lots of books from her which she got from the Book Shop in Africa Hall, run by a Philippino lady, Mrs. Teddy Omari, whose husband Dr. Peter Omari (a sociologist) was Uncle Robert's Deputy Secretary-General at the UNECA. Doll was Uncle Robert's secretary and she was the fastest and most accurate typist that I had ever seen, and this was before computers. She loved me and called me her baby. Julien loved her and used to play with her hair and she let him tip the contents of her bag on the floor and she didn't mind. They spent most weekends and Christmas with us. Uncle Kwame had been married before and his wife had died and he had three lovely daughters, two of whom were with them in Addis: Essi and Florence. His eldest daughter was called Valli and she was in Ghana.

Uncle Kwame and Auntie Doll decided to take us out to lunch

one Sunday as they were always coming to us. They said that they knew a nice restaurant in the country outside Addis that served Austrian food. As I love Vienna snitzel and apple strudel I was very keen. We arrived at place that looked so old and dusty, as if it hadn't been swept for a hundred years. James refused to drink his beer from the glass and drank from the bottle instead. He also wiped his knife and fork with the napkin. The food was arranged in a buffet, so we helped ourselves. As we were eating, dogs and cats were roaming in and out of the room with the accompanying flies. After a while a chicken jumped on the table and started pecking at the food and I said, "Thank God that didn't happen whilst we were getting our food!" and James said, "How do you know that didn't happen before we arrived?" The next minute the cook came. He was an old man who looked very much like Haile Selassie and his Ethiopian dress was as black as coal with food stains and grease all over it! I am pleased to say that I suffered no ill effects, and the snitzel and apple strudel were really delicious.

Another good friend that I had was the Somali Ambassador and his wife. One day when James was away in Tanzania (he was a member of the African Liberation Committee, based in Dar-Es-Salaam) they invited me out to dinner and they said, "That they would come and pick me up." I dressed up and waited and waited and they didn't turn up! The next day Charles Vandyke, James's cousin (who was First Secretary in the Embassy) rang to tell me that the Ambassador had been arrested (Ethiopia, had not signed the Geneva Convention, and there was no diplomatic immunity), and that was the beginning of the Ethiopia/Somali border problems.

Another story from Addis, and this is just repeated hearsay: is that there is a certain tribe in Ethiopia, and when the men come to manhood, to prove themselves they must cut the private parts off another man. And there was a rumour going round; that at one time that they had brutally done it to an African ambassador! I don't know the truth of that? But that was the story!

Another friend that I had in Addis was Mrs. Elisabeth Bentum, the wife of Mr. B.A. Bentum, formerly of TUC Ghana and now with ILO in Addis. We visited her and her seven children very often.

One day we went to the house, to discover that Mr. Bentum was travelling and Elisabeth had been admitted to hospital. The children were left with an Ethiopian maid and a small maid from Ghana who couldn't speak English let alone Amaric! So I packed them all up and took them home with us. Unknown to me, this upset some of the other Ghanaian wives, who then felt that they should also do something! So when I went to visit Elisabeth in the hospital she asked if I wouldn't mind sending the baby to another friend, so I agreed and sent the Ghanaian maid as well. The Bentum children were the most well-behaved children that I have ever seen as they bathed, dressed themselves and got ready for school without any problem so they were no trouble at all. In fact, the baby had been the most difficult. Julien, who had been alone at that time, was delighted to have so many friends to play with and really missed them when they went back home. When Mr. Bentum returned from a conference in Geneva he came and said, "I don't know how to thank you" and he gave me a gold watch as a present.

Kwame Asante, who had been another one of James's friends who had been at the airport to meet me in 1964; was now the Minister for Labour and was coming to Addis for an ILO conference. James and I didn't know quite what to do, as Kwame was a really good friend who would normally come and stay with us, as James always stayed with him when he was in Accra! We decided to play it by ear: if the Ambassador had him stay with him at the Residency, all well and good; but if he put him in the hotel, we would bring him home. The Ambassador met him and put him in the hotel so when the Ambassador had left James brought him home to stay with us. The Ambassador had not mentioned lunch or anything. At about 12.30pm he rang to say that he had rung the hotel to invite Kwame to lunch and was told that he was with us! We had just been about to sit down to lunch, so Kwame said, "It's up to you, Valerie, do I go or stay?" and I said, "You should go!" There was another round of parties with all the Ghanaians in Addis who wanted to meet Kwame; also many receptions with the ILO. Among the ministers was Princess Elisabeth of Toro, who was the Ugandan Labour Minister.

On another occasion another friend from Ghana came to stay with us. I will not mention his name because of the story that I am going to relate! James took him out and one thing with James: he would not take the key with him so I used to have to get up to open the door for him whenever he came home! Now the house and the garden were in a funny situation. The distance between the back door and front door was an equal distance and James never came in the same door every time, so sometimes the back and other times the front. So I used to stand in the middle of the corridor and whenever I heard footsteps, go and open the appropriate door. This particular night I heard footsteps at the back first and went to open the door and, lo and behold, there was the friend standing there with an Ethiopian girl! He was intending to spend the night with her in our house! James came to the front and I blew my top and told them to take the girl away immediately, which they did. The man, who was a married man and whose wife I knew, didn't know what to say to me the next morning, so I said, "I don't blame you for what you did. I blame James. If he agreed to let you bring the girl home, he is the one to blame!"

In Addis there were many military attachés and we used to meet in each other's houses for dinner. I loved going to the Soviet Embassy. They all lived in a compound. They were really nice people, and there was no cold war with Ghana so we got on very well. The food was delicious. I learned how to make chicken Kiev from one of the wives. One of the military attachés was called Gregory Rublev and he said to me, "If you remember the Russian ruble, you will always remember my name. "Another was called Col. Podkivkov and he was a Hero of the Soviet Union. He had so many medals he made most of the others feel naked in their uniforms. He had fought in World War 11. We always had caviar, black, red and grey; and Russian champagne, which I love! Then we would go to the Israelis and the Americans and the Italians, Germans and French, and of course the British. The only two Africans were James and the Egyptian; and then there were the South Koreans, Col. Lee and Col. Park, whose wives, with their beautiful silk national dresses, were very good friends of mine; and I used to help them pronounce English words. Everybody got on really well and there was a tradition that when someone was leaving they collected and presented them with a silver cigarette box engraved with their names. (Unfortunately ours was stolen when we had thieves at a much later date in Ghana.) It had great sentimental value as it reminded us of happy times with all the other military attachés.

A funny thing about me is that I have an international look and with my permanent tan and my Ghanaian accent, nobody could tell where I came from? I remember going to three parties in one night and being mistaken for first of all an Israeli, then an Egyptian. At the Egyptian Embassy an old lady came running to me as she thought I was someone that she knew, and then realising that she didn't she said, "Excuse me, I thought you were an Egyptian friend." So she asked where I was from? and I said, "Ghana, as I was in the Ghana Embassy in Addis" so she went away and then came back and said, "By marriage?" and I said, "Yes, by marriage." From there we went to a reception given for President Shaka Stevens of Sierra Leone, who was visiting Addis, and somebody thought that I was an Anglo-Indian. I think that as I have green eyes and light brown hair, which I mostly kept blond, and had a permanent tan through living in the tropics; I could be mistaken for several nationalities. People always said that I was beautiful and I managed to keep my figure after all my babies by doing exercises and not eating too much. I always do my own hair, and had a hair-piece made from my own hair when I cut it after Julien was born, and I used to make fancy plaits, ringlets and curls with that. I found that in the heat you must have your hair either very short, or long and pinned up.

When I arrived in Addis I had discovered a present from my Flemish friend Marina, the Nigerian Captain's wife. One time in Takoradi, I had set her hair for her and my dryer was not working so I sat her out in the sun to dry her hair in the garden. She had sent me some Carmen electric rollers and a standing hair dryer. I must say that the electric rollers were a godsend for all the parties – I would put them in for ten minutes and then take them out and allow the hair to cool down and, in twenty minutes, lo and behold, a beautiful hair-do! I have been blessed all my life to have very thick, naturally wavy hair that I have had to tame and smooth; so I never needed a perm, which saved a lot of money. So, as I do my own hair and sew my own dresses and don't drink (apart from the occasional champagne) or smoke, I was very cheap to keep!

Nobody guessed that I was British. I even had one Scottish naval officer, who came to Takoradi on a Royal Navy ship, who I could tell from his accent was from Glasgow. He asked me, "Where are you from?" and I told him to guess! And he said Swiss, Scandinavian and never guessed the truth until I told him; and he was so surprised to discover that I was from Glasgow, too.

James had discovered, in a cupboard in the Embassy, a film projector and some films that had no labels on them. So he brought them home and we watched them and were pleased to discover many films of Kwame Nkrumah at The All Africa Conference and then a film of all the help that Ghana gave to the Congo – teachers, police cars and so many things; and a beautiful colour film on Ghana. So we started to give film evenings to some of our Diplomatic friends. Everybody loved the films and was surprised to see how developed Ghana was.

Margaret came to me one morning and said that her husband had been ordered back to Burundi, and she had received word that if he went back to Burundi he would be killed. So they didn't know what to do. He applied to stay in Addis but he was refused by the Ethiopian Authorities.

The Burundi Embassy staff cut off the electricity and water to the house, and as they had two small children, and though James was away in Tanzania at the time; I told them that under the cover of darkness they were to pack and then come over the garden wall and stay with me, as we had four bedrooms and Hamish and Rosina were in Ghana, so it would not be a problem. I then went to see Dr Robert Gardiner to seek his advice. He was not very happy at me letting them in the house but said that he would speak to the UN High Commissioner for Refugees. In the meantime they were to keep quiet and lay low! The next thing was that her husband went out and got drunk and came home and started shooting at the watchman next door. He then came into the house and handed me the gun and told me to hide it from him otherwise he would shoot his wife! I was petrified, as Julien was passionate about guns at that time so I hid it well, and realised that I had bitten off more than I could chew. The next day, Uncle Robert called and said, "That he had spoken to the UN High Commissioner for Refugees, and he had suggested a way out. Margaret's husband should agree to return to Burundi and on the way get off the flight in Rwanda, where he had arranged asylum for him. He had to change his appearance on the plane so that the Burundi authorities in Rwanda would not recognise him." He agreed to do this but Margaret said, "That she and the children would continue to Burundi, as they would have no problem there." Then the Ethiopian secret police turned up looking for her husband because of the shooting incident. I said, "That he wasn't here" and they produced a paper in Amarhic, which they wanted me to sign. I refused. "They explained what it meant but I said, "That unless it was written in English I would not sign it," so they went away. The next morning we saw them all off on the flight to Burundi. Uncle Robert came to the airport with me. Margaret's husband was going to shave off his facial whiskers, which he had all over his cheeks – not a beard but on the side of the face – and get off in Kigali, the capital of Rwanda. The next day the Ethiopian special police came back and I was able to sign their form for them, as it was in English, that he was not in the house. So, 'All's well that ends well!' When James came back he was not very happy with what I had done. "He said it could have caused problems between Ghana and Ethiopia.

One evening we went to a dinner at the Malaysian Embassy, a lovely dinner, and I got on so well with the Malaysians and Indonesians. When we left the party and were driving home, James said to me, "I don't want you any more. I want you to go!" I was so shocked; I had been so happy and now I was brought right down. I started crying and he said, "I'm fed up with you and your crocodile tears." As we reached the house there were two police cars with their headlights on a dead body lying in the road in a pool of blood. So that was the end of my lovely evening! The next day I rang Mummy, who was in Southend with Laraine and Roni, and I asked them to send a telegram to say that Mummy was not well and I should come immediately: I just had to get away from James. He was not happy but eventually he bought a ticket for Julien and me to go to London for one month, for I was so unhappy and just had to get away from him.

When I arrived in London (Ethiopian Airlines now flew direct to London) the same young man who had helped me transfer flights in Rome was there and he said, "Hallo, Madam", and I said, " Hallo, are you here now?" And he said, "I hope you liked my country?" Arnold Quainoo, who was then the Defence Advisor in London, met us at the airport and took me to Liverpool Street Station to get the train to Southend. When I was leaving Addis a funny thing happened. Bob Kotei, who had been in Addis for a conference, had bought Julien a toy gun that was black plastic and looked so realistic. Julien had wanted to take it with us and I had said no! But he had slipped it in my hand luggage without my knowledge. When they had searched my baggage at the airport they pulled it out from my bag and made such a big fuss, calling first one man and then another so I said, "Look, if it's a problem, just send it to the Ghana Embassy." So they said, "Okay, don't worry, Madam!" When we arrived in London and we were going to the passport section a stewardess came running after me, and there was the gun with a big label on it! I hooked it on one finger and forgot about it. So all the way through customs, passport, baggage and meeting Arnold, this gun was hooked on my finger and I totally forgot about it. When Laraine met me at Liverpool Street Station, she said, "My God! What are you doing with that?" so I explained and she said. "That those guns had been banned in England as somebody had used one at the Indian Embassy and was shot because the police had thought it was real!" So much for that!

I had a lovely time with Mummy and Laraine, Roni and Aviv, and went to spend a few days with Auntie Vi and Uncle Don in Glasgow. The weather was gorgeous as it was July. Uncle Don was a great rose grower and his garden was beautiful. I also spent a night with my cousin Linda and went to visit my cousin Irene, and my cousin Jean came to visit me at Auntie Vi's and we visited all the aunties and uncles. When I was leaving, Uncle Don had disappeared and he came back with the first bud from one of his prize roses. It was yellow. He had wrapped it in foil with cotton wool and it was really special, as it was from a new rose that he had created.

Linda took us to the airport in her little sports car, and we discovered that the plane was delayed so we had to wait at the departure lounge. When I walked in the first thing I saw was a very dear friend, Major Emile Allotey-Annan, (who was the person whose home I had spent my first night in Ghana with his wife Cecelia way back in 1964.) We were both so happy to see one another. Emile was in the Defence Office at the High Commission in London, with Arnold Quainoo, and had come to Glasgow on military business. I kept looking at my rose and Emile got a little jealous, as I was giving it so much attention, and I tried to explain why it was so precious to me. Emile gave us a lift home from the airport in the embassy car that met him.

I decided that I had better change my appearance, cut my hair, and smarten myself up, and some of my aunties gave me some of their evening dresses. So when I returned to Addis I was looking very different, so different that James didn't recognise me when we arrived at the airport. I saw him outside through the window and was waving at him, but because of my hair he didn't recognise me and walked away; it was quite funny! And I later learned that he had gone to check the manifest for my name to see if we were on the flight. He came back when he saw my name and by that time I had got my baggage and come out. There was no mention of him asking me to return again; but there were many phone calls with Ethiopian girlfriends asking to speak to Commander.

Our sex life was pretty boring, and James was no lover – he just had sex. I had sent for some sex manuals before I left and when I came back they were nowhere to be seen. He used to have sex almost every night apart from when I had my period, but would never try anything adventurous and would leave me unsatisfied and totally frustrated. James had requested that Chief Petty Officer Abban should come and be his secretary in Addis in the Defense Office, but about this time he decided that the office in Addis was a waste of money and wrote to the Ministry of Defense to close the office, so Chief Petty Officer Abban was sent to the High Commission in London instead.

Auntie Doll and Uncle Kwame were going on leave in America, so they gave up their house and came to stay with us. When they returned Doll was looking very thin and frail, though she had never been fat. When I told her that we were returning to Ghana, she said, "Oh baby, what am I going to do without you?" Auntie Lucy and Mrs. Coleman (Auntie Baby) and the Ambassador's wife arranged farewell tea parties for Julien and me. Terasite arranged an Ethiopian meal: ingera and What, (stew) and she also presented me with a beautiful evening Ethiopian dress and shama (shawl). She had been a lovely friend to me. Sometimes when she came to lunch James would shout at me and she would cry buckets of tears. She used to come and take me to the Haile Selassie theatre, to see films in her little Fiat car. I always think of her whenever Ethiopia is mentioned in the news. I heard that she is now married and I wish her great happiness across the miles.

We were too stay with Fifi and Philippa in Nairobi in Kenya for one month, before James would join us and we would return to Ghana together.

James had gone to Somalia so Terasite and some of the Ghanaian ladies came to see us off. Terasite was crying and she made me cry, so I couldn't see where I was going when I went through customs. Helen my Ugandan friend had already left, and so had Margaret; and that had been a real adventure! When we took off from Addis we got birds in the engine and had to land again until they sorted it out.

Nairobi – Kenya 1974

We reached Nairobi, which had a nice little airport and was warm, but because of the high altitude could also be cooler at times, like Addis.

Julien and I were met by Philippa and Steve (Fifi) Dadzie, (who, if you remember, was James's best friend from school, and James had been best man at their wedding and they had spent their honeymoon with us in Takoradi.)

Steve was working at the University in Nairobi as an aquatic biologist, and Philippa had just had a baby boy, Ato. They had a nice little house and they welcomed us warmly. They took us to the shops and there were many Indian shops where the material was so cheap, that I bought quite a few lengths for making dresses. I also bought two sheepskins, which were really cheap – about 20 Kenya shillings at that time. They took us to visit a few friends who were teaching with them. We went to visit the Ghana Ambassador in Nairobi, Brigadier Crabbe, who had been Station Commander in Takoradi when I first arrived in 1964. He always wore a kind of cowboy hat, which had always fascinated me, and he entertained us all nicely.

One day Philippa had run out of tea and we went to an Indian supermarket. There was no price on the tea and when she asked the girl on the desk, the girl was so nasty and you could tell that it was racial prejudice. She was most surprised when the next thing I said was, "Who do you think you are? Have you been to India? I have, and there's nothing there to make you feel superior to Africans!" She was really shocked, as you can imagine.

Philippa and Steve took me to a UN dinner with them. I can't remember what it was in aid of, but I was most surprised to find that there were hardly any black people there. Though Kenya was an independent country at that time and had been for a few years. There were lots of Europeans and Indians; but apart from our table on which, there were three Kenyans, one of whom was a Government Minister, there were no blacks anywhere else. I was quite shocked to see that, coming from Ghana where black people are everywhere and even in Ethiopia. Philippa and Steve had wanted to take me to one of the safari parks, but as I have always been terrified of lions, ever (since my father used to take me to watch the lions being fed at the lion house in the zoo at Regent's Park. I never forgot the stench of the lion house and the lions prowling back and forth and roaring when they smelled the meat arriving.) My father found it fascinating and he always had to take us there at one o'clock to see them being fed. So I certainly didn't want to see lions roaming wild around me! So we went for some drives in the countryside around.

I remember that they took me to the shanty-town where the indigenous Africans lived just outside Nairobi. I was shocked as it was so ramshackle. The one thing I loved about Nairobi was the market. Every day they would price the goods and display the price on a board marked with chalk, so no bargaining or cheating; and they had scales to weigh each item, which were checked regularly by the market inspector. Julien and I spent three lovely weeks with Philippa and Steve and baby Ato; then James arrived from Addis. We all went to the airport to meet him and when the plane had landed I saw some of my Israeli friends from the Embassy in Addis. Ethiopia had broken diplomatic relations with Israel, because of the Arab boycott, and so they were all going home. I was glad to see them but sad to think of the boycott. So we brought James home. When we were eating lunch James said, "Did you get my message?" And we all said, "What message?" He said that he had sent a message through the High Commission in Nairobi, to tell me that Auntie Doll had died. She had died the week after I left, of cancer. I was so upset that I couldn't eat again and Julien, who had been sitting there said, "Mummy, is Auntie Doll really dead?" and I said, "Yes, darling, she is now up in heaven with Jesus." Well, Julien, who was still only four years old, but had loved Doll so much, started crying. He sobbed and sobbed and he made us all cry and I had a good cry too and I could hear her saying, "Baby, what am I going to do without you?" when I was leaving. Well now she wouldn't have any problem as she would always be with Julien and me in our hearts!

James had been to Nairobi many times and took us to do some last minute shopping and we encountered a street fight, where people were clubbing each other with wooden batons, and I was shocked at that too!

Finally it was time to return to Ghana and I was really dying to see the children: Hamish and Rosina by this time. We flew Ethiopian Airlines for my last time, landing at Entebbe, Uganda: and Cameroon and Lagos before reaching Accra. The three of us: James, Julien and I, were really happy to be back in Accra.

Chapter Eight

GHANA
1974–1979

Kwame Baah, who was Foreign Minister, then, had done us proud. A staff car met us and a married quarter was available immediately. We just had to collect our things from the quartermaster's store and we were in business. No sooner did we arrive than James was appointed by Col. Frank Bernasko, who was Minister of Agriculture, as the Managing Director of the Ghana State Fishing Corporation, at the HQ in Tema. In the meantime various old friends had been popping in to welcome us back and I was delighted to find that Volda was now back. She came with John to visit us and brought us twelve crates of eggs and two chickens, which was a big treat. She had started a small backyard poultry in her married quarter at Michel Camp, Tema. She now had two boys: Victor and Kwaku, who was only about 16 months at this time. We had sold the Mercedes-Benz that we had bought in Addis and ordered a new one from Germany, as the sea route from Addis would have taken too long to arrive. So we got a brand new green Mercedes-Benz and it cost us two thousand Cedis. At that time, on the road, we didn't have to pay duty as we had been out of the country for over a year and diplomats were given that privilege.

I just settled in the house in Burma Camp, a huge five-bedroomed old-style colonial mansion, and we went to collect the children from St John's Preparatory Boarding School. It was so lovely to see them but they were so thin and they had their heads full of lice so we had a job to get them cleaned but we managed it. So we were one big happy family again. I had got my old cook Diahera back from the Navy and James got his old driver, Chief Petty Officer Osei, who had been with us in Takoradi when James was N.O.I.C. (Naval Officer in Charge).

Julien had the little problem of letting Hamish, now ten years old, be the eldest again as he had been ruling the roost on his own for almost eighteen months, but they all loved each other and were happy together. Rosina was now eight. They invited TT's children to come and spend the weekend with them; up till that time they had been spending the holidays with them. I made them all milo and poured plenty of milk for them all, and Rosina said, "You see, my mummy used three tins of milk for one time, not one tin for three times!"

I was not very pleased when I saw St John's and how the children had been living there! But there was one helper who had been so good to the children, especially Rosina; Sister Mercy. She even had Rosina sleeping with her though Rosina had a bed-wetting problem at that time, and she really mothered Rosina and Hamish. James didn't want to disrupt their education by moving them to another school, but we made sure that they came home every weekend, and they had lots of provisions, and we brought their washing home and did it at home. Julien said, "that he wanted to join them!" So he did. We moved into the Fishing Corporation house at the Kotoko Hill at the Airport Residential Area in January 1975, and we started our extension of our own Tema house at the same time. It was a nice house, very modern and very new. The furniture was black leather and we had orangey lemon cushion covers and some nice brocade curtains, which were cream with bamboo leaves in the pattern. The entire furniture, cutlery etc, was from the Fishing Corporation and we also had a lovely garden, so most of the office parties were held in the garden with lights in the trees.

This was the time when I made another lovely friend, Miss Henrietta Pinto, who was the catering officer with the Fishing Corporation. She was very good at her job and had worked for

President Kwame Nkrumah in the past. Her fish cakes were excellent and if we had a party, she arranged all the food and even trained and provided girls to serve, and she was very strict with them; everything had to be correct. They all wore evening dresses and looked very smart. She would always hide some food for us to eat later as I would be looking after guests and hardly eating anything, and James would be the same. With Miss Pinto's help we gave many lovely lunches, cocktail and dinner parties, and even weddings of friends. For the next five years she became a mother to me and a grandma to the children, always turning up with cakes she had made for them, and she knew that Rosina didn't like dried fruit so she made plain sponge for her.

I also met for the first time my very dear black twin sister Doris Adjei, and it turned out that Miss Pinto was her aunt though I didn't discover that for quite a long time. James's friend Jimmy Edwards, who was an agricultural officer at the Ministry of Agriculture in Accra, had been asked to look after a friend's wife whilst he was away on a course in Paris, France. So one day Jimmy came to the house with this beautiful girl who was pregnant. We liked one another immediately. At that time she was working as a secretary to the Minister for Agriculture, Col. Bernasko, who was the one who had appointed James to the Fishing Corporation.

So Doris used to come and visit me whenever she could and then she had her baby, a beautiful little girl just like her mother, called Nana, and they both used to visit me. I used to put camphor balls all around the room to keep away ants and insects and when Nana started crawling she found them and used to put them in her mouth; so we had to watch her like a hawk as she always remembered and each time she came, would make a beeline for them and dive under the furniture to get them. It was quite funny to see. If you took your eyes off her for a second, she would have got one!

At the Airport house we had lovely neighbours; Baba Alargi and his wife Naa and their children; and next door, Mr. Parker, who was the Managing Director of Shell (Ghana) Ltd), and his wife Ester and their children. So the children had good friends to play with when they were home, and we used to visit them for drinks and they would also visit us, and when we had any parties we also invited them.

Other neighbours just across the road, were the American Military Attaché Col. and Mrs. Dodd. Mrs. Dodd arranged lectures on Ghana history and always invited us, and we had dinner at the same time. They seemed to have a fascination for mixed marriage company, as we always seemed to meet other mixed marriage Ghanaian couples there. They had no children and had a big fat cat, called Asmara as they had also been in Ethiopia. Mrs. Dodd had the lectures compiled into a book before leaving Ghana, and the American Women's Club published it. I was lucky to receive an autographed copy, long since lost. They had a beautiful collection of china and ornaments collected on all their travels and I helped her pack them when she was leaving Ghana.

When we were staying at the airport house, James arranged a ticket for Mummy to come over and she came and spent six weeks with us. She was very happy in her air-conditioned room and as she had brought evening dresses with her we were able to take her to all the parties. The British Military Attaché's mother was also in Ghana on a visit, as were a few other mothers, so the British High Commissioner's wife, Mrs. Margaret Stanley, arranged a luncheon for mothers and their daughters who were visiting Accra at that time. So Mummy and I were invited. We also took Mummy to a military parade and to the wedding of Dr. Wilberforce, an old school-friend of James's. He had just finished at the Ghana Medical School and was married in the chapel at Legon, University of Ghana.

Rosina, who was now a lovely girl of nine, was bridesmaid to Araba, a friend of mine, whose father was Nana Nketsia, Chief of Effia-Nkoma, Secondi. Her husband Ted Bernasko; a pharmacist, was the brother of Col. Bernasko, the Minister for Agriculture. We had met him in Addis when he came on a visit and he worked for an American pharmaceutical company. On our return to Ghana he had became a regular visitor along with Araba his fiancée, who had just returned from studies in America. Dr. Maya Angelou was her godmother in Greensburg, North Carolina, USA. So when Araba was getting married she asked Rosina to be one of her bridesmaids. Rosina had a beautiful yellow dress made by Araba's Auntie

Anna, her father's sister, who lived in London and was a dressmaker. Araba had so many bridesmaids as Auntie Anna had brought so much material from London and kept making dresses as long as it lasted, or so it seemed. I'm sure she had about six if not more?

Araba wore Kente for her wedding with a beautiful lace top and she looked lovely. The wedding was at the University of Ghana, Legon and it was very grand indeed! I wore a turquoise blue chiffon dress with a yellow chiffon hat with yellow daisies round the large brim. We had two weddings to go to on that day, the other was a military wedding held at Arakan Barracks, Burma Camp, officers' mess, Captain Rider, James's niece Alberta, who used to baby-sit and stay with me quite a lot when James was travelling was the chief bridesmaid. She wore a dress with white background and a big pink flower pattern on it, and she looked gorgeous that day.

As the bride and groom were coming up the stairs of the mess, the wedding cake suddenly toppled to the ground. There was a loud gasp from the guests, but somebody was able to hide it from the bride and groom and it was quickly re-arranged! The following day we had a lunch for Ted and Araba in our house as her father's house was in Secondi and he was not in the country at the time, being in America. Though Araba's relatives mostly prepared the lunch, Mrs. Grace Ayensu, who was one of President Nkrumah's main woman supporters, was cooking in the kitchen, and we had a really nice day. Araba became a frequent and much loved visitor. When she became pregnant she was vomiting badly, and I brought her to stay with us in the guest room as Ted was travelling a lot. She started vomiting blood and when we took her to hospital we discovered that she had typhoid fever, and she was put in isolation at the military hospital. I was worried for the baby but in due course she produced a beautiful little girl, Adorkwa, and she was perfect. Then Ted and Araba went to live in Lagos, Nigeria and I was given an open invitation to come and stay with them.

Breid and Joseph Amamoo lived within walking distance of the airport house. One day, when James had returned from one of his trips, I saw in the waste paper bin a ripped receipt and discovered it was for a very expensive watch. It was dated the day of his return and

I thought that it looked suspicious. I was really upset and imagined all sorts of things so I went over to Breid's and Joseph's and told Breid. She tried to calm me down. Later that evening we went over to them for drinks and Joseph, without my knowledge, mentioned it to James. (Breid had told me at one time that Joseph's nickname was The Swedru Cobra.) As we were going home in the car James really blasted me: why should I tell Joseph? So I asked, "Well, who did you buy it for?" and he said, "My mother!" So I couldn't say any more but though I watched and watched I never ever at any time, saw his mother wearing it!

There was an article in the newspaper, which said that Ghanaians only marry foreigners to get a stay and they don't really love them and when they bring them to Ghana they just take Ghanaian wives in addition. I decided that it had to be answered. James had travelled to Japan so I invited all the European wives that I knew and we discussed the letter and what to do about it. We had such a lovely time that we decided there and then to form a club: 'The European Wives of Ghanaians' Club'. They voted me president and Mrs. Glenda Butah my deputy. We drafted a reply to the letter and with Mrs. Breid Amamoo took it to the editor of the Sunday Mirror, and they published it for us. We agreed to meet once a month in each other's houses and just to provide tea and sandwiches. When James came back and saw the letter and heard about the club, he was furious! He said, "If I go to another meeting I should not return to his house, so that was the end of my meetings. They went on for a couple of months and then it petered out. Volda and John Owusu were frequent visitors and we used to go to them. They had moved to Burma Camp and Volda had transferred her poultry farm onto land that she had bought, and was building a permanent building to house the chickens, with a bank loan. She was very generous and always used to give us chicken and eggs, and I used to give her fish when I could. Joe Butah had been transferred from Takoradi and was living in the Mess so Glenda and Justin used to come and stay with us for the weekend whenever she came to Accra. After a while they moved into Juba Villas, Burma Camp, so they became regular visitors.

Breid Amamoo and Joseph were living round the corner from

us and they were kind enough to allow Mummy to swim in their swimming pool; and Hamish, Rosina and Julien used to play with Samiah and Suzie, Breid's daughters. There were always people popping in for drinks everyday as Ghana is a free society and people just visit without telling you. Almost everyday we had someone extra for lunch and the guest room was always full with somebody, coming from Kumasi or Takoradi for a few days.

When James travelled I used to go and supervise the building of the extension on our Tema house. There were two labourers and a mason: Kofi, Nketsia and Christian, and in fact James kept them on to build all the houses. Christian, the mason, was very hard-working. He liked to drink the local gin, Apeteshie, but he would start work as soon as it got light and continue working until he couldn't see anymore. Then he would stop, chop (eat heavy) and get boozed on his Apeteshie and the next morning he would be right back at work again. He was a very fast and neat mason and his work was excellent. Nketsia seemed more intelligent than the other two and he was put in charge of the stores. They all worked hard and didn't steal. By Easter 1976 the house was ready, so we bought furniture from the Boatyard and for the first time in our married life moved into our own house. James said, "That I shouldn't' tell anybody that we had moved as he wanted me to go to London for him"; so I didn't. He gave me some money and bought me a ticket and I went off to London. In the meantime he started Christian, Kofi and Nketsia on building the boys' quarters on the plot of land that we had bought at Ablemkpe, Achimota Forest, Accra. We had been allocated the plot from the Ministry of Lands when we were in Takoradi in 1970 but up till then we had been unable to build. But now he said, "That we should build a boys' quarters so that the Ministry wouldn't take the land away from us. We had bought a tipper truck from Addis Ababa and that helped with the building.

James told me that I was to go to England and find a house to buy wherever I liked, and when I had found one I was to call a friend of his in Holland and tell him the amount required for the house and furniture. I was to open a bank account and he would send me the money to buy the house. Nobody knew I was coming so I took a mini-cab and went straight to Mummy and Laraine, who were living in Southend. After two days I went to my godmother Auntie Iris, my father's sister – and Uncle Derek in Letchworth in Hertfordshire. I had always loved it there when I visited them as a child; so I decided to buy the house there. James had said that he would come on holiday and I thought that we have the sea in Ghana, and London is so dirty. At Letchworth it was all farms and countryside, and the air is so much cleaner than London. Uncle Derek and I went round all the estate agencies looking at houses, but none appealed to me. Then one day we went to one agent and they said, "We've just got a new one in but no details ready yet, but it's in the same area as you are already going so you may as well pop in and see it!" That house was 21 Blackmore, Lordship Estate – a brand new estate built on the Lordship Farm. (When I was a child I used to walk with Daddy and Uncle Derek across the farm to go to the Fox Inn at Willian, as Letchworth was a Quaker town where there were no pubs.) When I got to the house, the lady was so surprised she said, "Oh! I only put it in yesterday afternoon!" We went round the house and I knew that this was the one I wanted. We left and went round the corner and I said, "Lets go back" so we did and I told them, "I want this house. Please don't let anybody else see it!" Then uncle Derek and I went all round buying the furniture etc. for the house and Uncle and Auntie agreed to take care of the house and be there when the furniture was delivered. James came and we signed the contract and for my birthday on 10th May he bought me a brand new red Mini-Clubman, and then I took him to London Airport and he flew on a business trip to Kuwait.

I had to drive myself all the way back from London Airport to Letchworth on the A1. One thing I found was that all the road signs on the roundabouts were so far round that by the time I saw them you have missed your turning and have to go round again. After going round three or four roundabouts twice, I finally reached Uncle and Auntie in Letchworth. I then returned to Ghana and to the house in Tema.

The house in Tema was very small in comparison to all the houses that we had up till then, but it was very compact and with the air-conditioners it was really lovely, so at first I had no servants and did all the housework myself, cooking, washing etc. But when the children and I went to London for the school holidays in July, James was alone so he got somebody in to cook and clean. When the children and I got to London it was so exciting to be going to our own home. Chief Petty Officer Abban, who was the Chief Clerk in the Defence Office at the High Commission in London, came to meet us with Mummy at the airport and took us to Letchworth. Abban used to come and see us every week and if we needed anything. I just had to ring and he would come; He was a very tall, handsome young man who is really lovely/ Nothing was too much trouble for him and he has such a pleasant manner that everybody liked him: the children and Mummy. He used to call Mummy, 'Mummy' everytime time he came, and as soon as we saw him everybody was happy. My nephew Aviv came to stay with us for the holidays and Julien used to get jealous of Aviv though he loved him. Aviv started calling me Mummy as the children called me Mummy all day. I started taking them to see all the sights of London and they had great fun in Trafalgar Square with all the pigeons and they loved the horse guards' parade. Hamish, Rosina and Aviv had a photo taken at the door of 10 Downing Street but Julien refused; he didn't like being photographed and always refused to be in a photo or would pull a face and put out his tongue! Then we went to the Tower of London and the ravens fascinated them. We couldn't go down into the dungeons, as there had been a bomb there the year before which killed some school-children, so they were a bit disappointed as I had told them all about the dungeons, which I had seen on a school trip as a child. But they saw all the armour (this was before most of it was moved to Leeds Castle).

They liked Madame Tussaud's and the Planetarium. We went to St Paul's, which is my favourite cathedral in London, Westminster Abbey and the National Galleries. We had almost completed when there was a bomb (IRA) in Marks and Spencer's at Marble Arch! So we decided not to go up to London again! So the children resumed their TV watching and I did all my necessary shopping for Ghana, in Letchworth, where the shops were very good; if they didn't have what you wanted, they ordered it, for you and it arrived in a couple of days.

Roni and Laraine came to stay and we all went to Woburn Abbey for Julien's birthday on 6th August. We had lunch in the restaurant and Roni found a worm in his salad. When he complained the manager said, "That we could have the whole meal for all of us for free, so that was very nice. The children enjoyed it very much, seeing the safari park and the fun-fair and the dolphinarium. I enjoyed seeing all the beautiful china that they had in the abbey, some really beautiful pieces. When we returned home, everybody was really happy but tired. That was summer 1976.

When we returned to Ghana in September 1976, Hamish was to go to secondary school at Cape Coast: Mfanstsipim, one of the best schools in Ghana. So we had to buy all his uniforms and requirements and he had to take a chop box (tuck box) for his food which included gari, (which is made from dried cassava and delicious with milk and sugar), sardines, corned beef, tinnapa (canned mackerel in tomato sauce); and Omo soap, all of which were readily available in Ghana at that time. His cousin Freddie van Dyke was in the second year so he was assigned to take care of Hamish. Also the deputy headmaster was Mr. Kutin, who was TT Kutin's brother, so he was also keeping an eye on Hamish. We all went with Hamish – Rosina, Julien and his daddy and I. He was being very brave, as we had all heard stories of what they do to new boys. The school was beautiful, set on a hill, with white buildings with red tiled roofs, which look really lovely when the sky is blue and the sun is shining. Rosina was taking the common entrance that year so she was still at St John's with Julien. When we returned, the same workers who built the Tema extension – Christian, Kofi and Nketsia – went to our plot at Ablempke and started building the boy's quarters, so that we shouldn't lose the plot of land, which had been allocated to us in 1970 by J.G. Amamoo when he was Junior Minister for Lands and Mineral Resources. Christian was such a good mason and fast worker that in six weeks he had completed the boy's quarters. So with the money left from James's retirement from the Navy – James had retired in August 1976 and received a gratuity of twenty-eight thousand Cedis: that was a lot of money at that time – we used ten thousand for the extension at Tema, eight thousand as a deposit on a Teshie house with the Housing Corporation, and ten thousand to build the boys' quarters at Ablempke. Then James applied for a mortgage loan from the Ghana Commercial Bank HQ and we were able to complete the Ablempke house, which took seventeen months from the time of starting the foundations. James retired from the Navy into the job of Managing Director of the State Fishing Corporation, which was a political appointment, and he had a contract for five years. Abban, who was due for retirement from the Navy, was persuaded by James to come and work with him in the State Fishing Corporation at Tema.

Summer 1976

When James joined us at Letchworth we took a trip with the children. First, we took the sleeper train to Glasgow, where we stayed at the Albany Hotel in Bothwell Street, and then hired a car and went to visit all my relatives, first to Auntie Vi (Uncle Don had died) who looked after us very well and then to Uncle Tommy, Auntie Isa and my cousin Glen Anderson. Auntie Isa prepared a delicious dinner and set the table so beautifully with all her best china. Glen showed the children the Hepburn piano, which had been made by my great-grandmother's company, and he also fascinated them with his collection of precious stones. He used to scour the hills for them and Auntie Isa made them up into brooches and bracelets. Julien loved Uncle Tommy and was wearing his glasses. Uncle Tommy and Auntie Isa were Jehovah Witnesses and Auntie Isa is the gentlest and loveliest person that you could meet. They had to wait many years before they had Glen so he was a very precious child. Then, on to Cousin Irene and her husband Sam. They had two boys at that time, Scott and Kirk. They had a beautiful house at Bothwell, and they entertained us well. There is nothing like Scottish entertainment at home – you can eat till you burst. From Irene we went to her mother, Uncle Andrew and Auntie Jessie, and Irene's brother Maurice. There we had to eat again. Uncle Andrew and Maurice are both keen golfers. Then we went to my cousin Jean. (Jean's husband Roni had died the year before.) She has three children: David, Alison and wee Ronny.

Anyway, though there was a lot of sadness, she had made beautiful cakes and they had a new addition to the family – a West Highland white, puppy called Dougal. He was a lovely ball of white fluff. Jean was still looking as lovely and as young as I remembered her. I hadn't seen her since her wedding ten years before, and the children were a joy. We then went to visit my cousin Norman and Margaret in their beautiful house. They had Leslie and Lorna, who were both the same ages as Hamish and Rosina, and they always got on well together. Unfortunately, I had started with a septic finger on the train up to Scotland so at this point I had to go to the hospital. They dressed it for me but said that it wasn't ready for lancing.

After a pleasant stay in Glasgow we took a plane on to Amsterdam in Holland and stayed at the Hotel 'Europe'. The children were fascinated by the ashtrays, which were stamped on the bottom, honestly, 'Stolen from Hotel l'Europe'. Job Van-Loon, who I had met previously in Ghana and the next day went to his home in Hilversum, took us out to dinner. There I met his lovely wife Thea, who was very pregnant. They had one son, Martin, who was about three years old. They had the most beautiful house with a swimming pool so of course Hamish and Rosina wanted to swim, as well as Julien, who couldn't swim. Martin had been taught to swim from six months old because of the pool and the possible risk of an accident. Another German lady was visiting. We were sitting round the pool when suddenly Martin, not knowing that Julien couldn't swim, pushed him in the deep end of the pool. My God! I can't swim and Thea was too pregnant; and Hamish and Rosina were right down the far end of the pool. I saw Julien standing on the bottom of the pool looking up at me so the German lady, whose name I can't remember, jumped in and pulled him out. Poor Julien and poor me! What a fright! Anyway, all was well and they all dressed up and Thea took us out to a restaurant for all the children to have pancakes. All the time I was in Amsterdam my finger was worrying me, and whilst the children were on a boat trip on the canal, I went to hospital and it still wasn't ready for lancing. So I didn't really enjoy that trip and my finger was throbbing all the time. In the hotel they had a pianist playing in the bar, which was nice, and one day I was wearing a beautiful blue lace dress and he started playing 'In Her Sweet Little Alice Blue Gown'.

On my return to England I had to go to hospital once again and at last they said my finger was ready for lancing so they gave me three local anesthetic injections but still, when they started cutting, I felt it all. Anyway, it was a great relief and I had to go for dressing and my finger was not quite healed by the time I returned to Ghana. So I had to go to the State Fishing Corporation Clinic doctor, who removed the dressing and gave me an anti-biotic spray, and in no time at all it was better. All the skin dried up and it was healed and I was never so relieved in all my life.

Doris Adjei was now my good friend and came to visit me in Tema at least once a week, and then my dear Pat returned from Britain and managed to get a job with the State Fishing Corporation Clinic and they rented James's brother Joseph's house for her. I met her mother, father and sisters and brothers. Pat had many brothers who all looked very similar. Another new friend, but who had become just as dear, was Miss Pinto (Henrietta) but I always called her Miss Pinto. James also became good friends with Mr. E.M. Debrah. Teresa – Mrs. Debrah – became a good friend too and it became almost a ritual to have dinner with them on Sundays. Even Mummy joined us when she came on her visits to Ghana. Every weekend we used to go and see the progress of the house and very often I would go round buying things for it. We cannot talk about that house without mentioning the great help given by Dr. Kofi Sam and Mr. Atipoe of the Tema Steel Works – they really helped a lot. Mr. Atipoe had been at school with James and was the only Ewe that I knew him to get on with, as he was very tribalistic.

I was very happy in the Tema house. I was growing roses; I had bought a lot of roses with me from England as Harkness roses were grown at Letchworth and I had my dear Yarrow, my garden boy from Burma Camp. We took cuttings and grew our own roses and mango trees, bougainvillea and floribunda roses in the front garden. Mrs. Bernasko (Ester) gave me a lot of love grass, which doesn't grow high, and I grew a beautiful lawn, and outside the front wall I grew roses and carpet grass, and I also grew porcelain roses, which look like large wax flowers but are actually real. They originate from the Far East.

We put fairy lights all around the house under the eves so once the grass had grown we had some lovely parties on the veranda and in the garden. Volda had moved to Burma Camp so whenever we went to Accra we went to visit her and Glenda, who was also living there. Volda's poultry farm was expanding and she was always very generous with her chickens and eggs and I always tried to give her fish in return. The children loved Auntie Volda and were always ready to go to her anytime. Her house was a home and there was always lots to eat. She used to give enormous parties and invited lots of diplomats, especially the Israelis, who became very good friends of mine: Narva, Sera, Estee, Balfouria and the most special one; Ora; she was so lovely and I really loved her.

Any government function at the Castle at Osu or at the State House, or any parade at Black Star Square: we were always invited, and we used to go and visit General I. K. Acheampong, the Head of State, and his wife Faustina at their residence in Burma Camp. The house was always full of people but he always used to say to me, "Be at home", and "God's time is the best." Whenever we wanted to leave he would say, "No, stay longer" and usually he would give me an envelope with some money and he would say, "For the children." Auntie Faustie was always giving me bottles of champagne to take home. To me, Acheampong was always the most generous man and when I was at the house I used to see all sorts of people, little, ordinary people who came to him for help and he always did help them! All the old politicians used to be around him and I always warned him: "If you are in trouble, nobody will help you!"

One time when I returned from London the confusion at the airport was so terrible, that for any foreigner coming through for the first time, it was a rude shock, with custom officers taking bribes; so I told him and said that he should pay a unexpected visit, to see for himself. I told him that one Saturday, and on the following Tuesday I read in the papers that he had paid an unexpected visit to the airport. During that time the American Ambassador was Shirley Temple, the famous child star, now Mrs. Black, and I must say that she was still very lovely and always dressed so well. She didn't stay very long as there was some disagreement with the Government as far as I can remember. Her daughter married somebody from the Italian Embassy and her husband was into fishing in the Gulf.

The parties at the Castle were really lovely with lights in the gardens and all the ladies wearing beautiful, elaborate African evening dress, which only if you see can you really appreciate, with lots of gold jewellery; the men in their military uniforms – the Navy white and Air Force blue and the Army red, mess undress or in the richly woven Kente (the national dress) which is really outstanding in all different colours and designs; the Armed Forces band in dress uniform playing high-life (the Ghanaian traditional music); and the entire ambassador's and their wives, some wearing their national dress. The parties always started at 6.30pm and in the tropics at six o'clock it suddenly gets dark really quickly, like somebody has switched out the light. The night air was warm and humid, just beginning to cool down. The castle at Osu was right on the sea; so you get the occasional sea breeze, which cools everything down. You have to park your car outside, unless you are really privileged to park in the small car park at the entrance, where we parked most times. There would be lots of cars and chauffeurs dropping ambassadors and then moving off. Then the State Protocol Officer, Major Kwame, would greet us and then move off to mingle with the other guests. James and I would stay together for maybe ten minutes and then he would say, "Excuse me" after he had left me with a suitable woman friend. I normally wandered round from friendly face to friendly face, occasionally being introduced to some diplomat who had just arrived. Mostly though, all parties were the same people, and I would meet a lot of the other military wives there: Volda and Glenda and Auntie Linda Gardiner as Uncle Robert had now retired from the UN and was back in Ghana and had been appointed a minister by the government. Then I would normally go and greet Acheampong and the members of the SMC (the Supreme Military Council), who normally stood in line to receive guests. The guests usually arrive at about 7.30 and the Ghana National Anthem would be played. They would stay for about one hour and the National Anthem would be played again, and then they would leave. Depending on whether or not we were going on to dinner somewhere we would leave immediately or chat to a few remaining friends and leave by 9pm. If you tried to leave too soon you couldn't get the car out so it was better to wait a bit until the congestion at the car park settled down. One thing: at the castle it was on grass so you had to wear wedge heel sandals or shoes because if you wore stilettos your heels would constantly sink into the ground! Parties at the State House were much better as it was on concrete. Sometimes in the rainy season the parties would be held inside the Banqueting Hall, which was really large and beautiful, and I attended many large banquets there.

One tragic thing that happened during our stay in Tema was that Col. Bernasko's eldest son suddenly died of cerebral malaria. It was a big shock to me as we had just been there the previous Sunday and he had served me with a coca-cola. When I heard the news I became ill thinking of that lovely boy lying dead. Ester – Mrs. Bernasko – was pregnant and she nearly lost the baby. I went to the funeral with Doris and I got really angry with the professional wailers who kept moaning every time a new person arrived. The service was at St. George's, Burma camp, the Garrison church, where we all went. Col. Bernasko used to play the organ in church. The boy was then buried at the Military Cemetery at Osu. When I came home I was shaking with malaria fever – the shock was so great. Such a beautiful, lovely, good boy to be struck down so young!

Ester, Mrs. Bernasko, was very, very depressed for a long while. One day I decided to send some flowers to cheer her up and also a bottle of champagne so I sent the driver to deliver them. The next day somebody told me that Mrs. Bernasko had, had her baby! And I was surprised that they hadn't rung to inform us. They thought that I had sent the flowers because I knew, but I hadn't known. They called the baby, their first girl, Dorothy, which means God given. From then on she picked up and the baby was lovely.

Another friend that I made in Tema was Elsie Yaw, who was biology mistress at Tema Secondary School. She was James's cousin, and had a degree in Biology from University of Ghana, Legon. Her mother, who was called Madam, was also a lovely old lady. Elsie taught Hamish and Rosina for the Common Entrance Exam, and also some biology. She had two sons and a daughter by her first marriage. Whilst she was in Tema she had another baby, a little girl called Odette, by a man who shall be nameless as he turned out to be married. Another cousin of James was called Jemima. After some time, Elsie and Jemima had a big quarrel and were not talking. I never knew what it was about until many years later. Seemingly Jemima had introduced James to a girl friend of hers, who sank her teeth into him and never let go! Elsie had been annoyed with Jemima when she found out, because of me!

I myself was blissfully unaware at that time. I had developed a habit of not seeing things and blocking out nasty things. James used to stay out a lot saying he was looking at the building or going to Lodge meetings. I was only too happy to read my books and live the lives of my heroines and forget reality. When people came to the house he was such the devoted loving husband, calling me darling and kissing me in front of people, that everybody envied me for such a lovely life! Every Sunday after church he would take me to the Chinese restaurant for lunch either with the children or on our own. We would then visit Dr. and Mrs. Gardiner, Auntie Linda and Uncle Robert and then Charlotte and Kwame Nyame-Kumi and their daughter; then go home and rest, and go to Mr. Debrah in the evenings. Sometimes we would visit Mr. Debrah at Korforidua, where he had a farm and was breeding akrante (grass-cutters) and then we would spend the whole day there.

Mummy came to stay again and by this time the Ablempke house was finished, so we moved with Mummy. We had sold the tipper truck which we had bought when we were in Addis as part of 'Operation Last Chance' and with the money we bought some beautiful, brand new furniture from Furnart, which was a brand new furniture company and they made beautiful wooden furniture from the amazing woods which they had in Ghana. The man running it was Mr. Stephanie, an Italian, who made reproduction antique furniture. He had given Mr. Debrah a free sample and I had greatly admired it – the work was so professional and truly beautiful. At that time not many people had heard of the company and when our furniture was ready he was begging us to collect it from his storeroom. All the furniture had been designed to fit into the house:

two sitting areas in the sitting room and a magnificent bar and stools and a centre divider and other cabinets; in the dining room a table which seated twelve and the beautiful chairs to go with it, and; also a Welsh type dresser for the plates, glasses etc.

Abban brought many things for me in his luggage, which came by sea, on his return from the Embassy tour in London. I had bought dinner sets and cut glasses and a set of beautiful saucepans. He also brought a huge roll of blue velvet that I sewed into curtains for the sitting room myself using rufflette tape. We bought all our carpets in England and ordered Axminster carpets in blue – a design called Persian design. It was really beautiful and when I went to the house to supervise the laying of the carpet and awaiting the arrival of the furniture. I thought how beautiful the carpet was, that it didn't need any furniture at all; and I remember sitting on the carpet and thinking how lovely it was! The room was painted in emulsion in the lightest shade of blue; and with the sax blue of the curtains, and the carpet, which had several shades of blue, looked really exquisite. It was also fitted with, some nice cut glass lights, which Abban had chosen in London. That was another funny story: when I arrived in London James had given me a list of electrical goods which he needed for the house so I gave the list to Abban, who said that he would get them from an electrical wholesalers and have them delivered to the airport when I was leaving! Now as I am always the early bird hating to be late, we arrived at the airport about two hours ahead of the departure time. When we got to the check-in desk there was a pile of cardboard boxes on the floor with no label on them and nobody around, and we thought 'My God! What a lot of stuff to take!' We waited and waited and there was no sign of Abban's chap. Abban himself had come to collect us from Letchworth to the airport; so he went round and round and couldn't find him. Then at the last minute he arrived and when we said, "Where are the things?" he said, "There!" and pointed to those piles of boxes. There were eleven boxes all told, and the Ghana Airways people were good and put five on and they said the rest would come later as they were not heavy, just bulky and mostly all packing. But that was a palaver – when we got to Accra James was furious at all the boxes arriving. Jimmy Edwards came with James to meet us at the airport.

One morning in 1977 James had to go to work on a Saturday morning as they were drawing up a contract for something at the Continental Hotel. He told me that he would pick up his secretary, Payne, and take him to the hotel but he would not be in the office and would come home for lunch at one o'clock and then go back.

Just after James left, his niece Julie came with her mother – James's sister Elizabeth. I told them that if they wanted him, they should come back at one as he would come home for lunch. I asked if there was any message and they said no! James came home at lunchtime and I told him that they had come and he said. "Did they leave any message?" and I said no, "He finished lunch and then left and they hadn't come. At about four o'clock I heard a car and went out, to see Julie just about to drive away in her car. Having asked the watchman whether James was in. I said, "Where's your mother?" and she said, "That she had gone back to Takoradi", which is where she lives. She said, "When James comes, tell him to come to me for a message." When James came home I told him and he said, "What message could she tell her daughter, that she couldn't tell my wife? I will not go!"

The next day he had to continue drawing up the contract and he wanted the workers in Elmina paid (he was building his mother's house in Elmina) so I said that I would go with the children to Elmina to pay the workers – the same Christian, Kofi and Nketse, who had built both the Tema and Ablempke houses. When I got to Elmina his mother, Rosina Quayson, wasn't there, so I said to her sister Auntie Grace, "Where is Maame?" And she said that she had gone to Takoradi as she wasn't well. So I asked her what was wrong with her, and she called me into a corner and she said, "That she was bleeding", so I immediately imagined that she must have cancer. When I got back to Accra I told James and suggested that was the reason why Julie and Elizabeth had come, and he said: all the more reason to tell me, as it's a women's complaint!

Later in the week, Dr. Glover of Takoradi Hospital, rang James at work and said that his mother had cancer of the womb, and he wanted him to arrange a hospital in Accra for her. James went to the Military Hospital to find that Julie, who was a lawyer in 'the Legal Directorate in Burma Camp, had arranged for his mother to be admitted to an 'Other Ranks' ward. As officers' families should go to the Officers' Family Ward, He was furious. But the sister in charge of the ward, who was a personal friend, suggested that his mother would probably be happier with people around her and that she would take special care. I went to visit her with James and shortly afterwards she had an operation: a hysterectomy (removal of the womb). Her blood was very low and she needed blood transfusions to build her up first, so many people from 'the Fishing Corporation' volunteered to give their blood. After the operation she got up and was walking around but to me she didn't look too good!

When I went to Elmina I told the workers to finish quickly as I didn't think that she would last much longer. Her one dream was to have the house built so that she could have a fine funeral there and be laid in state, and it seemed that as soon as the house was ready she just gave up. The children and I went to London for the summer and as she was still in the hospital, we went to see her before we left. Three weeks later we received a telegram from James that his mother was dead and to inform his sisters Anna, Joan and Wilhelmina, who were all in London at that time. So I rang them and told them and they made their arrangements to go to Ghana for the funeral. James told us that there was no need for us to come so we stayed on in Letchworth, but of course James was not able to join us as planned. The children watched their TV and taped films to take back to Ghana. Mummy and I did a lot of shopping to take back also. Every year the situation in Ghana got worse so you had to take more and more things, even soap and toothpaste, if you wanted a good one. The Ghana-made Lux soap, which was very good, was in short supply so we were always loaded going back; with the children's allowance we had four suitcases so that was quite good! When we arrived back in Ghana we went to Elmina to lay a wreath at Maame's tomb and also went to church in the Methodist church in Elmina.

I was busy with the garden in the new house and was growing roses, jasmine, mangoes, porcelain roses, and bougainvillea in all colours. There is nothing like a display of bougainvillea in different colours in the beautiful sunshine, with all the different types like double, single and variegated.

September 1977

In September 1977, it was the twenty-fifth anniversary of the founding of 'the 'Black Star Line' (the state shipping line) so the company invited all the shipping agents from all over the world. There were many cocktail parties and lunches and dinners; and James, as the chairman, was the host.

There was a formal banquet at the State House and James and I were the hosts and sat at the head of the table. The Commissioner for transport sat next to me, and it was a very grand. I wore a, royal blue and white long dress and had my hair up in curls and ringlets. The Armed Forces band played and we danced the whole night. Then there was a party for all the workers of Black Star Line at the community centre in Accra and I presented long service awards to several workers.

After so many days of lunches, cocktails and dinners I was really tired and one day I returned from shopping in Accra, wearing only a cotton top and trousers, and kicked off my shoes and lay down on the settee in the sitting room – it had been very hot outside that day. The next minute the doorbell rang. I went to open it with no shoes on and there were the two British agent's representatives, Mr. Len Goodman and Mr. Nick Hallings-Pott. I greeted them and invited them to come in and gave them a drink.

The next minute Julien, who had just come in from school, called me. "Mummy," he said, "You've forgotten!" Daddy invited them for lunch today!" Luckily, we have lunch everyday so there always food to eat. I went into the kitchen and told the cook, Awuni (not my original Awuni), to change the tablecloth for the best one and set places for another two. I couldn't change or anything otherwise they would realise that I had forgotten. We had prepared some chicken curry for the next day so we added that to what we already had and I sent the driver to buy kenkey, a Ghanaian food, made from fermented corn, and told him to buy mangoes, oranges and bananas for sweet. The next minute the PRO for Black Star Line arrived along with Captain Techie-Menson himself: (the MD of Black Star Line). James had still not arrived by this time! Luckily we had fried a lot of fish that day so I told Awuni to make fresh pepper gravy with tomatoes, onions and fresh pepper finely ground with some small salt. Finally James arrived and we all got to the table to eat.

It was one of the loveliest lunches that I had ever given and everybody kept saying how nice the food was! Afterwards when they had all gone I said to James, "How was the lunch?" and he said, "Very nice" and I told him that I had forgotten completely about it and he was amazed. Much later I told Mr. Hallings-Pott, a lovely gentleman, that I had forgotten that day and he said that it had been an excellent lunch. So that was a laugh!

After two weeks of parties etc. all the guests departed for their various countries inviting us to visit them in return, and we promised to go!

November 1977

James asked me to accompany him on a trip to Germany for Black Star Line; there was to be a conference in Hamburg. We arrived in Hamburg and were met by Mr. Brown, the Black Star Line representative in Hamburg, and a German driver, Jan-Claus, who spoke very good English. Capt. Techie-Menson and another director, who shall remain nameless, joined us. Much to my horror, the other director was accompanied by his girlfriend (he was married and I knew his wife) and nobody seemed to be bothered. I felt quite insulted to be pushed into her company, as she was a very 'bush' Ghanaian girl. Anyway, she joined us for all the lunches, dinners etc. and even when we were given a car to take us round, took over and went round looking for a second-hand car to buy. The Black Star Line agents in Hamburg were very, very nice and took us out to a beautiful lunch in a very old and famous restaurant, where I remember having the most delicious bread, and I ate so much I almost couldn't eat any of the meal. In the evening they took us to the Hamsa Theatre for a variety show and it was lovely with jugglers and acrobats and trained dogs pushing cars – more like a circus in England – with beautiful costumes and you could eat whilst you watched. It was a very pleasant evening.

The next day we drove out of Hamburg and went to a school for training police dogs; and after touring the kennels, we saw a demonstration of the dogs finding drugs in cars, in the engine and in the doors. They almost ripped off the doors with their teeth. And people who wore special safety suits were being asked by the police to stop, and then run, and the dogs were chasing and catching them with their teeth. Because of the special safety suits, the people were unharmed. It was very enlightening and afterwards we joined the staff for a German meal of 'one pot', which was like Scotch broth and served with huge sausages. I enjoyed that very much – it was very cold as it was November and the food 'warmed the cockles of your heart'.

The managing director of the firm that handled Black Star Line ships in Hamburg, invited us to his beautiful villa outside of Hamburg. It was set on a lake, and had the most beautiful garden. It was an old thatched cottage that he had extended and had renewed the thatch so you couldn't tell the old from the new. The host's name was Alexander, and he and his wife Anna took us all out. Capt. Techie-Menson accompanied us and we had the most beautiful lunch at a local restaurant. We had pheasant, which was in season, and it was delicious. It was a large party – about twenty altogether. We returned to his house and sat around the swimming pool, though being November it was too cold to swim. Inside the house, in the cellar he had made a bar, which was just like being on a ship. After a pleasant day we returned to Hamburg very happy and tired.

The next day we flew to Paris accompanied by Mr. Brown, Capt. Techie-Menson and the unnamed director, who had disgorged his girlfriend, much to my relief. We were met by the French agent and taken to our hotel in the evening. They collected us and took us to dinner at the new Concorde Hotel. The restaurant was so high up like the Post Office Tower restaurant and as I am afraid of heights, especially with glass windows, I sat with my back to the window and didn't look down. We were joined by the Managing Director of the French agency and had a really delicious meal. The weather was very cold so I couldn't do any sightseeing apart from looking out of the window of the car.

The next day, after the men finished with the meeting, we were taken to the restaurant on the Eiffel Tower for lunch and from there back to the hotel and on to Amsterdam. In Amsterdam we were met by the Dutch agents and taken to the Hotel L'Europe again. The owner of the company came and collected us, driving himself in a very old Cadillac, and took us to the restaurant, the name of which in English means 'The Black Sheep'. I discovered that day why millionaires are millionaires: mostly because they are mean with themselves. He was so proud of keeping his Cadillac for so many years that he was expecting the Cadillac people to give him a new one free. Anyway we had a lovely lunch. By 'we' I mean James, myself, Mr. Brown, Capt. Techie-Menson and the unnamed director. When we came out it was hailing and freezing – it was still November – and the old man left us. He said, "That he must dash". He left us standing in the cold and told us that we could get a taxi across the road, and drove off.

In the evening we had a dinner and Arie Block, who was the Black Star Line agent in Rotterdam, drove over with his wife and joined Mr. and Mrs. Hausemann, the agent's representative in Amsterdam, and we had another lovely dinner. The next day the representatives from Antwerp came to Amsterdam and we had lunch with them, and then – back to London.

Mummy and I took the train to Scotland while James went to Italy with Mr. John Wilson. We were met by a representative of John's company and provided with a driver in John's own personal car. We went round visiting all the aunties, uncles and cousins and had a very pleasant time. We stayed at the Albany Hotel and invited all the uncles and aunties to have lunch and dinner with us. The final evening, John returned from Italy and we had a lovely dinner with many of the people in his company who I had entertained at one time or another when they came to Ghana. That was a lovely few days. The day we were leaving, it started snowing, and the train home was slipping on the rails, and it was so cold that we didn't get much sleep. We always travelled on the sleeper to Scotland, as you don't waste any of the day.

Whilst we were away on the trip, the children went to stay with Volda and John Owusu in Burma Camp and they had a lovely time playing with Victor and Kwaku and Allison, John's niece, who now lived with them.

On my return to Ghana I concentrated on the garden, growing different varieties of hibiscus: double and bell, and the lawn was coming on nicely. Yarrow the garden boy, who had moved with us again, was a very hardworking gardener. He used to work in Burma Camp in the morning and then come home and have lunch (I used to feed everybody in the house: watchman, driver and maid everyday except Sunday when they had the day off) but Yarrow never took the day off and if I was home would come and do the dishes for me; and get on and work in the garden. Yarrow was from Northern Togo and his family were there so he preferred to be around the house. If I looked and thought the grass needed cutting, the next minute Yarrow had done it. He kept the garden really clean and beautiful.

Abban had now returned to Ghana and was a frequent visitor to the house. Everybody was always happy to see him. The children would jump all over him and they would all whisper together and Abban would say, "Mummy, next Saturday, three o'clock I will come and take them out. Sometimes they went swimming and sometimes to the cinema or to Dan's bar for milkshakes or bumper cars – another treat.

In 1977 my dear friend Pat informed me that she was having a wedding, so when I went to London I brought back her wedding-dress and bridesmaids dresses, which her sister Mary had bought for her. She had the wedding in November and Volda, who had gone to America to do a cake-decorating course, baked and iced a beautiful wedding cake for her and didn't charge her; she just got her to get the ingredients. Miss Pinto prepared all the small-chops for the wedding and Abban was driving around helping in all sorts of ways. Mummy came to Ghana again and Pat asked Mummy to come and help her dress for the wedding.

Rosina was bridesmaid again and wore a beautiful floral dress in pastel shades, which I had brought from London. Pat's niece Grace was the other small bridesmaid, and her sister Suzy, the chief bridesmaid.

Her bridegroom was J. C. Amonoo-Mooney, who was a senior state attorney at Ho in the Volta region of Ghana. Pat made James the chairman for the wedding and so many of the State Fishing Corporation staff came to the wedding. Her father gave her away. It was held at the University of Ghana, Legon and was really grand. The weather was lovely and the sun shone. I wore a red dress with a yellow hat. On the morning of the wedding, the roses in the garden were all so beautiful that I made a bouquet for Pat: white, red, and pink and yellow; and I topped it with a tuberose and tied a beautiful blue velvet ribbon around it. Pat had ordered a bouquet from Parks and Gardens; but when she saw mine she just removed some ribbons from the Parks and Gardens one, added them to mine and used mine. It came out beautifully in the photographs.

James had a Polaroid camera so he waited outside the chapel and took a photo as soon as the newly-weds came out, and gave it to them so they could see themselves immediately. They were thrilled.

The reception was lovely. Miss Pinto excelled herself and everybody admired Volda's cake and she got lots of orders, and everybody went home very happy. The following Sunday we arranged a lunch at our house for a few selected guests of Pat and J. C. James had to travel but we went ahead and had a lovely lunch sitting on a long table outside in the front garden, which was now beautiful with the roses, tuberoses and the porcelain roses and frangipani trees in yellow; and the lawn at the front was now well grown and green through constant sprinkling.

In June 1978, Doris came and told me that she wanted to have a wedding so I said, "Okay, when I go to London in the summer I will buy you a beautiful dress," but she said, "No, she wanted to do it quickly before Kwesi changed his mind". I asked Pat if she would lend her dress to Doris and she said, "No! Then one day when Abban came to visit I asked him," What happened to your wife's wedding dress? I s it here?" and he said, "Yes" and I said, "Do you think that she would lend it to Doris?" and he said that he would ask. So, by and by, he brought his wife's wedding dress along with the diamante headdress and necklace and earrings to match. Doris was thrilled! Now Kwesi was a Catholic and very devout so Doris had to go for catechism lessons. The priest, an American, said that he wanted somebody to vouch for her so she asked me. So I went to see the priest and told him how long I had known her and what a nice girl she was. Then we went to see Volda about a cake and she was so thrilled for Doris that she again made the cake free and Doris only bought the ingredients. Miss Pinto, who was Doris's aunt, made the small-chops.

Doris used our Mercedes-Benz for the wedding and we had the reception in the garden of our house. She of course invited Abban and his wife.

I made a bouquet for Doris and it was lovely. The wedding was on the first of July. I had just had a minor operation so was not able to do much. Her grandfather Dr. Evans-Anfom was the chairman. The wedding was attended by the Knights of St. John as Kwesi was a member, and they certainly swelled the ranks. In fact we didn't know that they would all be coming so we didn't have enough glasses. Abban and Sally joined in the serving as we were short-handed as Miss Pinto hadn't brought so many of her girls as she normally did. The wedding was at the Catholic cathedral and was really splendid. The weather was beautiful and my garden looked lovely.

The reception was in the back garden, where we had built a summer house with fridges and freezers and sinks, so that all the serving could be done from there and nobody need enter the house. We also had a bathroom in the study/guest room, which opened onto the garden, so people could use the toilet without going into the house. Doris asked me to cut the cake with her, which is a tradition in Ghana that some senior female should assist the bride. She looked so beautiful. Doris is a real 'Black Beauty'. She was so happy and we were all happy for her! Her best friend Joyce was bridesmaid and wore yellow. Doris had requested me to wear my turquoise blue dress, as she loved me in that dress, and I wore a hat in organdie with flowers on it. When most of the guests had gone we all went into the house and Abban and Sally sat down and had a drink as they had been serving most of the time. It was another lovely wedding.

Soon after that James came and told me that he had spent five years with the Fishing Corporation, so he was going to hand in his resignation letter. He went to see Col. Nkegbe, who was Commissioner for Agriculture at that time, but the colonel refused to accept it! The children and I went to Letchworth for the summer as usual. James had to go to America as the Chairman of Black Star Line so he said that he would pay for me to go too. We flew on Concorde to New York and I must say that the service in the Concorde Lounge at London Heathrow airport was the best that I have ever received, with champagne, smoked salmon, chicken vol-au-vents and caviar, which I personally love. The Concorde flight, I was not so mad about, especially the landing; and the noise was so great that I thought the plane would break up and never stop.

We were met in New York by the American agents and taken to the famous Waldorf Astoria Hotel. We arrived in New York time-wise before we left London, as there was five hours difference and the flight was only three hours and thirty minutes. So we went out to lunch and in the evening we went out to dinner with the agent and his wife. The next day I was taken shopping in a chauffeur-driven Cadillac, which was really fantastic. I went to Saks Fifth Avenue and bought a lot of bedlinen and towels. At the weekend we flew to Washington to stay with Col. and Mrs. Albert and Nancy Enkansa. Albert was the Military Attaché at the Ghana Embassy in Washington. They had a beautiful house and Washington was lovely. On the Sunday morning we went to the Arlington Cemetery, where President Kennedy was buried, and we went around the Washington Memorial and saw Abraham Lincoln.

Albert suggested to James that he should buy a Ford transit van, as it was very useful for the farm and everything. We had a rice farm. So on the way from the cemetery they stopped at several used-car dealers. I didn't get out of the car as I wasn't feeling so well and I wasn't very interested. (Maybe if I had foreseen the trouble it would cause later I might have shown more interest!) Anyway, after some time they both came back delighted that they had found a van and said that I should look at the end of one line of cars, and I looked and saw the back of a grey van, and then we went home. Nancy and Albert looked after us royally and we had a lovely time in Washington. I have omitted to say that this was the middle of August and Washington was as hot and humid as Ghana. From Washington we flew to Montreal in Canada, we were met by, the Black Star Line agent, Capt. Techie-Menson and his wife Veronique. We all drove together to Ottawa and had lunch with the Ghana High Commissioner in Canada at the residency. The Canadian agents took us out to dinner and the next day Veronique and I were taken shopping by one of the wives. We then flew back to New York and were taken out to a show on Broadway and then we went to the agent's house, a beautiful old farmhouse on the Hudson River, for dinner.

Summer 1978

When we returned from our trip to America, we took the children to Hamburg at the invitation of Continental Seaways, the German agents. We were met by Mr. Norski and taken to the hotel and then on to the office to meet the owner of the company, Anne Marie, who was Swedish. She was a very generous lady. We were taken out to lunch at a Chinese restaurant near the office. The next day Anne-Marie and Mr. Norski arranged for the children and Mr. Brown's children to go for a boat ride and also visit the zoo. A young German man accompanied them, and they had really good fun. We went to Bremerhaven with Anne Marie, Mr. Norski and Mr. Brown and we had a really nice lunch there in a quaint old restaurant. The children fell in love with Hamburg and Julien started learning German from that time. In the evening we all went to the Hamsa Theatre again and after a couple of very pleasant days we returned to London. Oh, before I forget, we also visited Alexander and his wife Anna, and the children were able to swim in the pool and Alexander's grandchildren were there. We went again to the same restaurant as before and had another delicious lunch. One day the driver Jan-Claus suggested taking us somewhere but I couldn't quite understand what he meant;

he kept saying 'Der hiede'. He said that all the tourists go there and the field is all red and very pretty. So I said, "Okay, lets go there!" When we got there, much to my surprise and delight, it was hills of heather and it reminded me so much of my beloved Scotland. Jan-Claus bought me a basket made of woven heather, and a pot of honey from bees, which were fed on the heather. There were hives all over the fields. They also had black-faced sheep, who were very tall and shepherded by German shepherd dogs. All in all, a very pleasant and delightful day, which the children enjoyed very much.

Another thing that we saw on the way were beautiful thatched farmhouses with real stork nests, which I found fascinating. We returned to Hamburg and spent a very pleasant evening at Mr. Brown's house. His wife Diana was James's cousin. So after a very pleasant stay we returned to England. James had ordered a B.M.W. car, which was ready when we returned, so we took Mummy and went up to Scotland for a few days. We stayed at a hotel near Glasgow Airport at the invitation of John Wilson. We went to his house and met his wife Margaret and his children and we had a lovely dinner with them all.

My cousin Linda was living in Cambelltown so we drove over to see her. She had just had a baby boy and Auntie Vi was with her. The drive was so beautiful, driving past so many lochs and seeing all the highland cattle, which the children had not seen before. We had a lovely day with Linda, and Paul, her husband, and Auntie Vi and Linda's two boys Kevin and Alan; and then we returned to Glasgow. I rang my father, who had remarried by this time and was living in Yorkshire, to say; that we would like to visit him on the way back and he said, "Okay" and I said that Mummy was with us and he said, "That's alright." So we drove down to York on the A1 motorway and rang him to ask the final directions. He said, "That he would meet us at the local pub". We arrived at the pub and, no sign of him! I asked for him and nobody seemed to know him. So we decided to try to find the house on our own! We found the house but nobody was in. James said, "That he was leaving." As we started off, we saw Daddy walking along the road. He took us back to the house, apologised and explained that his wife was walking a friend's dog that they were looking after, and, "That she would be coming". We had a cup of tea and a chat and he showed us round the garden, where he was growing lots of vegetables, and then we decided to leave. His wife Martha had not returned so we got the feeling that she did not want to meet us. So up to the time of writing this, in 1985, I have not met my stepmother. Anyway, we had a pleasant drive down the A1 and arrived home very happy and tired.

When we got back there was a call from Volda and John. James was supposed to leave the house key with them but he had dashed to the airport and forgotten. Anyway, some water was flooding the house and was running down the stairs and out of the front door. They had managed to turn the water off from the mains, but thought it was best for James to return. When James returned to Ghana he was met on the aircraft steps by the Managing Director of Ghana Airways and told, "Oh, James, it was announced today that you have been sacked and there is to be a board of enquiry into your term in office as Managing Director of the State Fishing Corporation." As you can imagine, he was absolutely shocked. He rang me in London and told me. I was very, very sorry for him!

The children and I returned to Ghana and this time Rosina was going to secondary school at Cape Coast: Wesley Girls, so we all took her to school. The State Fishing Corporation probe started in November 1978 and before it started there was an unfortunate newspaper story of which there was no grain of truth. The Ford transit van, which James and Albert had bought in Washington, arrived in Ghana and somebody (I know who and he knows who, but I will not name him) splashed the headlines. 'A Disco on Wheels'. Of course it attracted big interest but sorry to disappoint everybody – there never was a disco on wheels, only a Ford transit van which had bucket seats and the normal radio cassette player, which all American cars had at that time! The next thing: the Government had said, "That it had seized the disco on wheels". When in actual fact it was still with James, parked at the Teshie house in the garage, because it hadn't been licensed yet! I told James that I would go with Cdr. Butah to see Gen. Hamidu and explain the whole thing, But James said, "If you go there, don't come back to my house." So I didn't go!

He told his brother-in-law to drive it to the Special Branch. He drove it there and parked it and nobody took a blind bit of notice of it at all. He waited and saw the director of Special Branch and they were all jumping, 'where is it?' and they were all disappointed. They made my brother-in-law drive it to the M.I. (Military Intelligence) annex and there it stayed. When the newspapers finally published a denial it was in some small remote corner at the back where nobody reads, so the damage was done and the vehicle was never returned! James always blamed me for allowing the van to be shipped but I said that he should not have bought it, as there was no need for it at that time!

James employed a barrister, Mr. Peter Swaniker; and a lawyer, Mr. Jonah Lamptey, to help him during the probe. The probe sat for six months and after each day people from the Fishing Corporation would come and literally keep wake over the day's proceedings. One man who was a very faithful friend was Mr. Steve Boateng; Abban had gone to London to do a short course, though he was back by May of 1979. Commander and Mrs. Butah were also good friends; they used to come to us or invite us to their home in Burma Camp almost every other evening. James started drinking heavily and Glenda and Joe, who also enjoyed drinking, drank with him. I have never been a drinker – only the occasional champagne or the odd glass of wine, so I mostly drank minerals or my tea.

James spent many evenings out. He said that he was in conference with the lawyers discussing the day's affairs. The probe went on and on over Christmas up till April and James was still drinking heavily. I had always believed James when he said that he had done nothing wrong; he had; only worked very hard to bring the Fishing Corporation up so that it could sell fish to the people very cheaply, so I was not worried. James started praying all the time when he had never done that before, though he had always come to church with us at St. George's, Burma Camp.

One day we had a lot of visitors in the house and Jimmy Edwards came with Nana Tawiah, who lived near Jimmy. They went into the study and when later some of the visitors wanted to leave, I found the door locked. I thought it odd but saw off the visitors anyway. In

April, when the probe finished, James had got liver trouble from all the drinking so he decided to go to London to see doctors and have a rest. The children and I would join him in July when the schools closed. So on 11th May he left Ghana on Swissair for London! On 15th May 1979 I was sitting in Rosina's bedroom sewing red velvet curtains for the Teshie house. Now Teshie is a house that I have not mentioned much as I was so fed up with building by this time; apart from in the beginning before the boys' quarters were built, when I used to cook for the workers every day and I bought kenkey and made fish stew for them. When the boy's quarters were completed I bought a cooker for them at Kingsway Stores and we put a fridge/freezer in the house for them and I made sure that they were supplied with rice, fish and gari and they did their own cooking. After that I did not bother much with the building of the house.

Anyway, it was now finished and James said that he wanted to make it a guest house for the business associates he hoped to make through the consultancy business which he wanted to set up once the probe was all in the past. So on 15th May, as I was sewing the curtains, the phone rang and it was Ama Opuni. She said that there was something happening at Burma Camp and that she had collected the children from school and that Julien was with her! Julien was now at 'Morning Star School' having left St Johns because the children had started taunting him about his daddy chopping Ghana's money during the probe, and he had broken down crying and refused to go back to that school again! So he was now at Morning Star and used to have lunch at Ama's with all the boys. Ama had four boys. After a while people rang to say that it was all over. Seemingly, Flt-Lt. Rawlings had tried to take over the Air Force station and had arrested some fellow Air Force officers and locked them up for a few hours. Then it was all over and Rawlings was put on trial for treason!

Flt-Lt. Jerry Rawlings was only 33 years old in 1979. He was a half-caste, his father being Scottish. I didn't know it at that time but he was to shatter the small orderly life that I had made for myself; and make me come face to face with reality and a lot of other people as well! On Sunday 27th May Doris and I went to the

Teshie house to hang the curtains and make the place habitable, as James had invited Joe Ifill, the Black Star Line, driver in London, to Ghana for a holiday, with his wife Pat. Joe, a West Indian, had worked for Black Star Line for many years and had never been to Ghana. They were to arrive on 3rd June. Doris and I were quite dusty so I sent the driver William to the Palm Court Chinese Restaurant to buy some take-away. The driver came back and said that they wouldn't give him the food. So Doris and I jumped in the car and went to Palm Court to eat there. Whilst we were there I saw Lt. Dennis, who I had not seen for some time. I said, "Dennis, don't you love me anymore? I haven't seen you for ages," and he said, "No, Madam, I was in Takoradi and have been having some problems!" On Friday 1st June it was my fifteenth wedding anniversary, so Joe Butah and Glenda took me to the Stop Over restaurant at the airport as James was still in London. When we were going in, Col. Felli called us and he said to me, "Where is my brother?" and I said, "He's in London" so he said, "That we should have a drink with him," so we did. When we were leaving after having a lovely dinner; he called out to us, "Goodnight!" That was the last time I would see him alive, though I didn't know it at that moment! On Sunday 3rd we had to go to the airport to meet Joe and Pat Ifill and we thought that James was coming with them; though I thought that if he couldn't be with me on our wedding anniversary I didn't see why he should bother coming now, three days later!

The plane was delayed so we came back to Burma Camp. Glenda didn't have a maid so I took my maid Mary to look after Glenda's children: Justin, Rhian and Suzanne. The plane finally arrived about midnight, but, no James! Anyway we welcomed Pat and Ifill, and James had sent a lot of food with them, including smoked salmon, caviar and smoked cheese. We took Pat and Ifill to Glenda's house at Burma Camp for a drink before taking them to Teeshie. We were telling Joe how difficult things were in Ghana and how you couldn't get a lot of things and Joe said, "Never mind! There might be a miracle tomorrow!" 'Famous last words!' Then we drove them to Teshie and settled them in the house. We then returned to Burma Camp; it was about three o'clock in the morning on 4th June 1979!

Glenda said, "Do you want to come in?" and I said, "No, I'll just collect Mary and go as I'm really tired." When we left Burma Camp it was deathly quiet! The lull before the storm! We met only one military jeep speeding from the military hospital; then we got home and I went straight to bed.

Now I normally wake at 5.30am and always listen to the six o'clock news, but because I had been so late I overslept a bit. I was awoken by Nketsia. (Nketsia was one of the workers who worked on the houses. He had been so good and honest and hardworking that when I discovered that he had O-levels, I got James to let him join the Navy, and after he had completed his basic training and was posted to Navy Headquarters, Burma Camp as a writer, was now living in the boys' quarters and was always around to do odd jobs.) Nketsia was banging on the door and shouting, "Madam! Madam! There's been a coup!" So I put the radio on and they were playing military music, which they normally do when there's been a coup. So Nketsia asked: "Should he go to work?" and I said, "Yes, he should go as normal; it has nothing to do with other ranks."

Then I worried about Pat and Joe at Teshie. I rang lawyer Lamptey and asked him to go and collect them from Teshie on the Labadi road and bring them to the house. I must say that he was very calm and brave and I greatly admired him! Joe was really scared as there was shooting going on all around, even a tank firing on the Achimota road really close to the house, and helicopters flying around really close. Rawlings was flying a jet all around and flying really low; at least we all thought that it was Rawlings! Rawlings came on the radio and made an announcement that 'the Armed Forces Revolutionary Council' had taken over the country. He, was shouting quite wildly at times. Then later, General Odartey-Wellington came on and said that they the government had regained control! Then Rawlings was back; it was a terrible time! I was so worried about Glenda and the children. The baby Suzanne was only four months old at the time. I kept trying to get through to Burma Camp as I knew that they must restore communications soon as they needed them for themselves.

On the third day I got through and got Glenda, who started crying and so did I. "She said that the soldiers had been there so many times and they had taken Joe Butah away, and that she and the children had been lying under the table for three days with shooting going on all around them all night and day! There was a knock on her door, and she was really scared and I said, "I will hang on" and then she said, "That it was Nketsia!" So I spoke to him and told him to try and bring her out of Burma Camp and if he couldn't, to stay there with her. Luckily Nketsia had been issued with a gun, so he said to Glenda, "Can you drive?" and she said, "Yes!" It was raining heavily so he decided that they had a good chance of getting through! He put the children in the back and sat in the front with his gun out of the window. Instead of passing the main road they went out the back past Kingsway Stores and out down the back roads. Because it was raining heavily the soldiers were sheltering, and as they passed any soldiers Nketsia shouted, "Action! Action!" And so they were able to escape. When Glenda reached me it was still raining and the car was full of water! She was crying and so was I, with relief. I gave her a large whisky and she started to tell of her ordeal; also Justin and Rhian, I must say that Julien, Justin and Rhian seemed to think that the whole thing was a great lark! Anyway, they were safe, or were they? That night they announced that so many wanted men were on the run and Commander Boham, James, was one!

Then I was afraid they would come to the house looking for him; so I decided to write a letter informing the A.F.R.C. (Armed Forces Revolutionary Council) that he had left the country on 11th May and not returned. The next day we all: Pat and Joe, Julien and myself (Hamish and Rosina were in boarding school at Cape Coast) with Glenda, Justin, Rhian and baby Suzanne went to the British High Commission. This was about four days after the coup and we hadn't left the house up to that time. We saw the High Commissioner, Mr. James Mellon, who happened to come from Glasgow, the same as me! I asked for someone to come with me to Burma Camp and deliver the letter to say that James was not in the country. We went in a British High Commission car: myself, and Mr. Calder and Mr. Harrison of the British High Commission. When we reached Burma Camp nobody seemed to know where we should go! But just then Col. Vivien, the British Military Attaché, came along and he said, "That he would deliver the message." So we returned home. We were told not to go out, so we stayed home. We had plenty of food and the children watched the video. Abban came and told me not to go out. He brought us bread and tomatoes. It was announced that all our assets were frozen, including the children's. Julien said, "Mummy, touch me. I'm frozen," and was giggling. Mummy rang from London and I told her over and over again, "Tell James not to come!"

We had been able to trace where Joe was held and Nketsia went to see him, as did Fritz, a military policeman who lived in Glenda's boy's quarters. He used to come everyday absolutely drunk and terrify us all with his gun, apart from Julien and Justin who were fascinated by the gun. One day we were up in my bedroom and he climbed the ladder that we used to reach the water tanks, and knocked on the window; you can imagine how terrified we all were! By 12th June I decided to bring Hamish and Rosina from school and try to leave the country. Abban came frequently to deliver letters to the airport to send to London, and bring bread and tomatoes. One day Fritz came and decided that he wanted the Sirocco, Mrs. Butah's car; we didn't know what to do! But just then Abban arrived and I told him what was happening. he told Fritz, "I'm Chief Petty Officer Abban and I have a Sirocco. Where do you want to go?" So he took him away.

Pat and Joe went to Cape Coast to collect Hamish and Rosina; I sent letters to their respective headmistress and headmaster requesting that they be allowed to leave. It was a good chance for Pat and Joe to see a bit of the countryside – it had not been a very good holiday for them. There was the odd shooting heard all over at any time of the day or night, and the soldiers were just looting at random! We decided to paint the Union Jack and stick it on the doors! Can you imagine, not one of us could remember how to do it! We looked through magazines and finally found a tiny flag for a British Airways advert, and we finally drew one, well at least Hamish did; he had arrived from school by this time. So we put the flag up on the front and back doors. But one thing: God was very good to us and was protecting us as no soldiers ever came near the house apart from Nketsia and Fritz.

One day we were all in the back garden and a navy jeep arrived at the back and we were all alarmed! But it was a couple of Petty Officers from the Navy HQ making sure that we were all right! Mr. Calder and Mr. Harrison used to pop in occasionally and they said that they were patrolling all British houses to make sure everybody was safe. One day Joan Bruce-Konnuah, who lived opposite the back of the house, came over. She had never visited before though I had been to her house a couple of times as she was a friend of both Bried and Volda. She was English and her husband had been a minister during Busia's time and had been arrested with Joseph. She said, "Girl! I've been through it all! Let me take some things to my house for safekeeping." Glenda and Nketsia urged me to send some things; although I felt all along that our house was very safe! So we removed some of the things to her house.

Then we decided to try to leave the country; at least if I could only get the children out! I arranged first for Capt. Techie-Menson to come and take Joe and Pat, as Joe was working for Black Star Line, so he did. I gave Pat my jewellery to take to London for me, and Glenda also gave her something very important to take, and I was most grateful to Pat and everything was delivered safely! It was announced that Steve Opimpah had been made Navy Commander, so I rang him to see what he could do about getting Joe Butah released. He asked, "For my number" and I gave it to him. I also told him that Glenda and the children were with me. The next morning, very early, he rang and asked to speak to Glenda. He told her that my house was not safe and that she should leave immediately and return to Burma Camp! Glenda told me this and then, then to my amazement, packed immediately and left within ten minutes. I had just put breakfast on the table and I said, "Eat first!" and she said, "No! I have to go!" and she left. She never even suggested that we come with her! I was very hurt at her abrupt departure!

Joe's Mercedes-Benz had been taken to Military Police HQ so it was quite safe. Also, somebody had taken his amplifier for safekeeping. I had also written several petitions on James's behalf and sent them to Rawlings through Ms. Elizabeth Ohene, who was editor of the *Graphic* daily newspaper, having been appointed by Rawlings. From the time that it was announced that our assets had been frozen, people were coming and giving me money. I was so grateful for their kindnesses. Abban was still coming constantly. There was never anything going on between us; he was just a very reliable and true friend in need, collecting letters to send to London. I sent the children to the airport, with Joan Bruce-Konnuah, to try to get on a British Caledonia flight; we felt that if they went with Joan, people would think that they were her children and it would not draw attention to them. But unfortunately at that time there had been an accident with the D.C. 10s and they were all grounded, so they were using smaller planes and they were unable to get a seat! Now another problem: the Teshie house was empty and the tenant in the Tema house was leaving at the end of June! So in addition to the other problems I had two empty houses on my hands. I went round and round like a mad woman. Everybody was too scared to touch them because of James's name. Eventually I was able to rent both, at least to have somebody occupy them! I was also able to move James's Mercedes-Benz out and put it in a safe place – at great personal risk and also to the person who then concealed it! I must say that I am forever grateful, to all the dear friends who helped me! My dear sister Doris was of course coming to see me; and Miss Pinto, dear soul, gave me one hundred cedis, which to her was like 'the Widow's Mite' and I really cried on receipt of that. Another friend Mr. Addoo and his wife brought me five hundred cedis. At last, Joe Butah was released and he came home with his head shaved. He put on one of his golf caps to cover it up! Anyway, he was safe and well and it was lovely to see him. There was an announcement on the radio and television that James had been fined five hundred thousand cedis – something to do with some engine breaking down. In the Fishing Corporation, report they said that his assets were confiscated by the State. I now decided that we had all better try and leave; we went to the airport several days and couldn't get a flight. Then somebody told me that U.T.A. were sending a big plane. I went to the U.T.A. Manager (a really kind and sympathetic man) and he said that the children would have to get French visas because they had Ghanaian passports. I went dashing to the French Embassy and explained the situation. They were absolutely marvellous. The young lady in charge of the visas filled in all the forms for me and I had the visas within one hour. I dashed back to the U.T.A. office, only to hear the manager tell the man in front of me, "I'm sorry, I was expecting a big plane, but it's only a small one so I can't accommodate even my own passengers!" Then I knew it was hopeless and I broke down and cried in the Manager's office. He didn't know what to do with me and said, "Madam, I'm so sorry" and I said, "Oh I know its not your fault. Thank you very much for all your help." Everyday we went to the airport and saw the same people, mostly Lebanese, all trying to leave Ghana, but no luck!

On Friday 15th June, in the evening, we had a small meeting of friends and we decided to try again the next morning. Kwesi Opuni was there and he was going to come to the airport with us. Then Joe and Glenda came and Joe offered to go to the airport with us too. Kwesi Opuni said, "Do you think that's wise, Joe?" Glenda called me aside and said, "Valerie, please let Joe go to the airport with you! It will make him feel a man again, as all the imprisonment and brutality of the soldiers has unmanned him!" I said, "Okay" so it was agreed that we would meet Joe at the airport; he would try to speak to one of the Ghana Airways people to get us all on the plane. The next morning I listened to the six o'clock news – and no new shocks. I left Nketsia in charge of the house. Doris came and went to the airport with us. I saw one of my Ghana Airways friends and she said that she was going to try for us. I tried to keep out of the way and not be conspicuous. I told the children to take only some underwear and one dress as I didn't want the soldiers stopping us because we had too much!

I was sitting somewhere when my driver, Martei, came to say, "Madam! They say that they have shot Gen. Acheampong and Utuka this morning!" My blood froze as I was sitting there in shock! I saw the soldiers go up to Commander Butah and at gunpoint order him out from behind the Ghana Airways desk! The next moment they came over to me and said, "Madam, come with us." By this time we were outside the airport entrance with an audience of hundreds, as is always the case when Ghana Airways leaves for London, especially on Saturday. They said, "Madam, come with us!" and I said, "I am a British subject and you have no right to take me anywhere." (In Ghana, even if you are married to a Ghanaian, you can't have dual nationality.) One of them said, "Your husband had been chopping Ghana's money!" and I said, "My husband has done nothing wrong and he has worked very hard for this country!" There were about twelve soldiers and three Flying officers: Okai-Quaye and two others. They all had AK-47 rifles and I remember one of the officers had a pistol in his belt. They put me in a white Peugeot caravan with five of them with guns, and the children in Commander Butah's car with one soldier! They took us to Arakan barracks, where they had set up their headquarters. I told them that Lord Carrington (the then British Foreign Secretary) had recognised their regime and if they did anything to me they would be in trouble. On the way to Arakan they said, "We'll take her to Dennis" (who had been put in charge of Military Intelligence) and I sighed a sigh of relief, as Dennis, was the same Dennis that I had met with Doris only the week before at the Chinese restaurant!

When I had been arrested I told Doris to go to the British High Commission and inform them. When we got to Arakan they said, "Madam, may we have your passport?" and I said, "I'm sorry, but this passport is the property of the British Government and you have no right to take it!" They said, "Madam, you are being difficult," and I repeated my sentence. They went in to Dennis, who came out after a while and he told them to take me home and that he would come to the house later. The children were all transferred to the Peugeot and we all had to squeeze in the back bucket seat! Then we drove with Commander Butah in his car to the Air Force station and I said, "What are we coming to do here?" They said, "That they were going to lock Commander Butah up." I then started crying; up till then I had been cool, calm, and collected! They said, "Madam, why are you crying? We are not going to do anything to you." I said, "I am crying because you are going to lock my friend's husband up." Then they took me towards Juba Villas and I said, "Where are you going?" They said, " We are taking you home," and I said, "I don't live in Burma Camp; my husband retired in 1976." They said, "Where do you live?" and I said, "At Ablempke." They said, "Oh yes, Commander has a mansion there!" and I said, "The next time you go to the Air Force base look well at the house opposite the entrance (where Col. Techie-Menson was staying). It's exactly the same plan as our house!" On the way to the house they were saying that life is hard for them in Ghana and I agreed with them that things were bad. When we reached the house Nketsia came out in his uniform. When they saw him they were happy and asked who was he? When I said that I had left him in charge of the house they were very happy and just dropped us in front of the house and didn't even come into the house!

There was Doris. I said, "What happened? I said that you should go to the British High Commission." She said, "I didn't know where it was, so I decided to come and ask Mrs. Bruce-Konuah, and then I saw you coming!" Just then Ted Bernasko turned up so I sent him to inform Mr. Calder and Mr. Harrison. They came as soon as they could and when I was relating the story to them they asked, "Madam, did they have guns?" and I said, "No!" and Hamish said, "Mummy, they all had guns!" and I didn't see any of them. (Living in the military camp the soldiers all carried guns from time to time so it was normal to me to see them with guns.) They had taken the children's Ghanaian passports and all our Ghana Airways tickets. Abban came that evening to see what had happened? And Glenda came too and was very angry with me because Joe had been re-arrested and was being held at the Air Force station guardroom. Mr. Calder and Mr. Harrison said, "That they would try through Lt. Dennis and General Hamidu to get permission for us to leave the country. In the meantime the A.F.R.C. Government had made it compulsory for everybody to get an exit permit to leave the country. In England, so many people who had witnessed my arrest had rung to inform Mummy; and Mummy had got on to the Foreign Office and had also gone to see the local M.P. Mr. Ian Stuart, about getting me out of Ghana. She had been asked to avoid any publicity, otherwise, they could make up some trumped up charge against me to keep me there! Glenda now came back to visit me. Joe had been sent to the Nsawam prison, where they were keeping most of the officers, who had held Government posts. There was a terrible petrol shortage and the driver had to queue for three days sometimes, so we had to pool our rations so Glenda could go and visit Joe at the prison. I accompanied Glenda to Nsawam prison to take provisions to Joe. It was so horrible at the prison – we weren't allowed to see him, just leave the provisions. Up till that time nobody had been allowed to see any of the prisoners. I went with Glenda to prison HQ. to try to get a pass for her to see him, but no luck!

One day when I was collecting Glenda and the children from Burma Camp we heard that the students were demonstrating in favour of the A.F.R.C. Government, so we passed through a back road coming out at Air Force Mess and found ourselves bang in the middle of the march. The boys thought that we were Lebanese and they said, "Are you being deported?" and Glenda said, "No! But she would like to be!" We had to drive slowly through the crowd until we got to Military Hospital. Then we were able to beat a fast retreat!

As James had been sacked from the Fishing Corporation we were lucky that we were staying in our own house; and the drivers, watchmen and maid were all paid by us. So life was not disrupted so much for the children, in that we didn't have to leave the house. So many of our friends who had been living in Burma Camp had to leave all their belongings and seek shelter with friends in town. In the midst of trouble you have to count your blessings! James at least was not in Ghana, but though I didn't know it was actually in Israel, where my brother-in law Roni had taken him to his mother. So I didn't have to worry about him. We were all well and I had taken responsibility for both Glenda and myself. Abban came most evenings to check that we were okay. His brother-in-law was Lt. Dennis and he was able to get the children's passports and tickets back for me! But in the meantime I had got British passports for the children from the Consular Section of the British High Commission through Mr. Harrison, who produced the passports overnight. Here, I would like to say a big thank you to all the staff at the British High Commission, who deserve great praise for their achievements. In a crisis the Foreign Office staff, at home and abroad, are excellent! All our vaccinations were up-to-date so we had no problem about them. One day Admiral Hansen and Auntie Lily came to see if we were all right. Whilst we were talking their driver came to say, "Some soldiers are prowling round with a gun!" So we were all scared but then it turned out to be only Nketsiah. Another time I was awoken in the middle of the night by shouting! I thought: "My God! The soldiers have come now!" My heart started beating like a drum, but when I went out from my bedroom it turned out to be thieves and I said, "Only thieves!" and went back to sleep quite happily! It was only the next morning when I got up and saw how they had removed the louver windows and tried to break the bars that I got quite a shock! But never mind, it wasn't soldiers, which was our main worry; and the thieves didn't get anything that time!

We kept checking with Mr. Calder and Mr. Harrison. Now the children and I were booked to go on our annual summer holiday to London on 27th July as Julien's school was closing very late. (Julien's school, Morning Star was one of the only ones who really gave value for money and didn't close early for lack of funds!) On the 25th Mr. Calder rang and asked if we could come to the British High Commission as soon as possible. I said, "that we would be there by 11am". We all went: Glenda and her children, Hamish, Rosina and Julien. We went in the VW combi, which was the safest form of transport as it didn't attract too much attention as there were still roadblocks all over the place and you could be stopped and searched at any time, anywhere! On the way we passed a lunatic from the mental hospital. I wanted to give him some money and had only a fifty cedis note. I said, "Never mind, we need luck!" Glenda said, "I think that you must be as mad as him!" When we got to the High Commission Mr. Calder said, "That he had met Lt. Dennis the night before at the castle and he had given him the pass for us to leave the country!" How we all cheered! So we arranged to leave on the scheduled flight, as we were already booked. Mr. Calder and Mr. Harrison said that, "They would come and collect us and take us to the airport." I had hoarded a jerry can of five gallons of petrol so we could be mobile to get to the airport, so I decided to give it to them as a gesture of thanks! Unfortunately Abban didn't come for a couple of days and his phone was not working so we had to leave without telling him that we were actually leaving, although I knew that Dennis would have told him about the pass. Glenda came to the house to see us off, as she didn't want to come to the airport. All the food left in the store I shared out between Nketsia, Yarrow the garden boy, the drivers and the maid Mary. I told them not to sell it as there would be a shortage of food as they had been selling all the stocks in the shops. I was also able to give them all two months pay each, and the rest of the money in my hand I gave to Glenda. It was a few thousand cedis! There were tears in her eyes as we left and poor Joe was still locked up in Nsawam prison!

We got to the airport, checked in all our baggage, and passed through customs, health, etc. At the last post before we went through there were four soldiers with guns. They examined the pass and said there was no stamp on it; unless we had the stamp they would not allow us to pass. Mr. Calder waited with us, and Mr. Harrison dashed back to get Dennis at the castle. In the meantime all the passengers were passing through and we were terrified in case we missed the flight. As we were standing there the Roman Catholic Archbishop of Sunyani, Father Owusu, who used to be the Armed Forces Chaplain, and had been our neighbour in 1967, appeared. "He asked me, Valerie, what's happening?" and I told him. He held my hands and said, "I will pray for you for all to go well!" He blessed all the children and then departed. I felt a great calm after he left and the next minute Mr. Harrison was back with the pass duly stamped. We were able to get on the plane; Mr. Calder and Mr. Harrison saw us right to the steps of the plane. I thanked them both very much for all their help and asked them to continue to help Mrs. Butah!

Now at last we were on board sitting in the plane. I told the children not to tell anybody who they were until we were at least three hours out from Accra, then with any problems we would be bound to go to London. Some soldiers came on the plane checking tickets and then "Thank God!" the door closed and we were on our way to London. Now I had been holding myself, the children and Mrs. Butah up, and I was ready to collapse in someone's arms. Mrs. Butah, whose father was a Welsh miner, had a habit of swearing and as a relief from all the tension I started swearing too! Even she got surprised when she heard me. I don't drink, except for my occasional champagne, or smoke, so it was my only way to reduce the tension.

Chapter Nine

BRITAIN
1979-1981

When we reached London I shot off the plane and didn't feel safe until I saw my first British policeman at the airport; there is nothing so comforting as the sight of a British policeman; there is nothing quite like them anywhere else in the world! Then, much to the children's disgust and I think my relief, I started swearing – eff. this and eff. that and this bastard and that bastard! We went through customs and collected our baggage. I was looking forward to seeing Mummy and Laraine and James. When we collected our baggage and wheeled it out there was nobody there to meet us. We looked round and round and then we saw Joe Ifill, the Black Star Line driver. He said, "Come and ring your brother!" I said, "I have no brother! Where is my mother?" He said, "She's in Letchworth!" So I rang Mummy, I said, "Mummy, why didn't you come?" and she said, "I'm sorry, darling. James said that we shouldn't come! Isn't he there?" and I said, "No!" We got in the car and drove to Pat and Ifill's flat, where Pat was waiting with James. When James came out, he had been drinking all day and with a slurred voice greeted us as if nothing at all had happened!

I think after all I had gone through and how I had defended him by writing petitions and speaking up to the soldiers on his behalf; he just killed any last feeling that I had for him. In the car on the way home he started on about my sister, how they were all staying in the house, and how if my brother-in-law was still there, what he was going to do! I was too shocked even to reply. When I reached the house and saw Mummy and Laraine I started crying and so did they; Laraine had cooked a roast dinner of lamb for me, one of my favourites, and wanted us to eat! The next minute James started shouting on Laraine and I shouted, "Stop it! I don't need this! Don't you know what I've been through?" I said to Mummy, "Please give me some of your sleeping tablets." I took two mogadon, and normally one makes me sleep till midday the next day! But I was so tense that it seemed to have no effect at all! Everything I told James that had happened in Ghana, he said, "My people would not do that!" It was as if I was telling lies! The children got into watching their TV and playing with Aviv. Roni and Laraine were going back to Israel, so after a couple of days they went to stay with a friend in Wembley. James refused to take me to the airport to see them off and in fact left the house and wrote a letter saying that he thought it was better that we got a divorce! I said, "Mummy, please give me some of your sleeping tablets." I was going to see Laraine and Roni off at the airport and then go to Auntie Dorry and Uncle Steve – lifelong friends of Mummy and Daddy. I went to Wembley and saw Laraine and Roni off and then took a mini-cab straight to Auntie Dorry's. I said, "I don't want to talk." Please just give me a bed, tell me where the tea is and give me some bread and marmalade. I want to sleep, drink tea, and sleep again." This I did for three days. Then 6th August was Julien's birthday so I wanted to be there for him. When I got back I discovered that James had come back to collect his things and when he found that I had gone he had stayed. Now when I came back he was accusing me of having been with a man; which as you know was not true! Then we were trying to get schools for the children. I said, "That the children should go to state schools. He said, "That I can't love my children if I want them to go to state schools." So we went to several boarding schools for interviews and eventually the boys got into St. Christopher's, Letchworth; and Rosina into St. Frances College, Letchworth, which was a convent school run by nuns. It was now that I began to suspect that James must have taken so much money; as how could he ever imagine sending the children to those schools without money?

I was still sleeping with him and he wanted sex every night; but I was like a dummy with no feelings left for him. He kept nagging me night and day and I used to cry all the time. I was on the pill and my blood pressure was so high, that the doctor advised that either my husband should have a vasectomy or I should be sterilized. He said, "That a vasectomy was easier." but James refused to do it! So the doctor made an appointment for me to see a gynaecologist to have the sterilization done privately, as it would have taken too long on the National Health. Within two weeks, the doctor had arranged everything; he told me not to have any sex from the time of my last period until after the operation. He also informed me that he would do a D & C. at the same time as the sterilization; to make sure that there was no pregnancy. I also had to stop taking the pill!

Now James started on about: "Don't I need his permission? before I have the operation?" I said, "The doctor didn't mention anything about that!" He would get up in the morning and start drinking by nine o'clock without eating any breakfast; and nag me all day long and I would start crying and he would say, "Crocodile tears!" and almost all night he would go on and on. The doctor had prescribed tranquilizers for him but he wouldn't take them! The day I went to have the operation in November, he took me to the hospital, still moaning about the consent letter. We met the doctor before the operation and there and then he asked James to sign the consent to the operation, and he signed like a lamb, without a cheep! I was given a private room and told that as soon as I came round from the anesthetic, I could go home. The nurses were marvellous to me. I myself was feeling very desperate and depressed. When I was being wheeled into the theatre I thought I would be quite happy to go now!

I awoke to nurses patting my arm and an oxygen mask on my face and the nurses calling my name, "Valerie! Valerie! Wake up!" I felt absolutely terrible – really sick and weak. It appears that I almost got my wish, and nearly didn't wake up! I wasn't allowed to go home and was kept in until the next day Mummy told me later that when she had come, I was as white as the sheet and she was really worried!

I had two wounds: one on my navel and one on my left side below my bikini line. The wound was dressed and I had to go back and have the stitches removed in seven days. As soon as the stitches, were removed James was worrying me for sex, and he had his way and the wound on my navel came open again! Mummy went to the chemist and got an antibiotic spray at my request, and Mummy dressed the wound again and sprayed it, and after a few days, it healed!

Life continued. Everyday James was drinking and nagging me. One night just before Christmas, 1979, at about two o'clock in the morning, he got up and said, "That he was leaving and not coming back!" By this time I had no feelings left. He packed a few things and I asked him, "How am I going to pay the children's school fees?" and he told me, "You can go and whore yourself to pay the school fees!" He went to Mummy and told her that he was leaving, then he went to Rosina, and then slammed the door and left! I went to Mummy and asked her to give me one of her sleeping tablets. I didn't cry or anything – he had made me cry so much that the tears had dried up! The next morning at 7am, he was back and he came and took some more things. Then he took my Mini-car. That made me see red, so I went to the police! They were very sympathetic but there wasn't much that I could do! They said that I could charge him with stealing my car! But I felt that I couldn't do that so they said that they could put out a missing persons bulletin. They couldn't force him to come back, but they could ask him. It was Christmas so we put up the Christmas tree and decorations and I organised the Christmas lunch. We wrapped our presents and put them under the tree. I had bought some silk shirts for James so I wrapped them and put them with the rest of the presents. On Christmas Eve, he rang and said, "That he was going to take the children out Christmas shopping. He passed the police station to inform them that he was coming back. He wasn't in the house ten minutes when he started shouting on me (I have to stress here that I never ever shouted back) and he reduced me to tears again. Just then the police arrived and they said, "They had just come to make sure he was going to keep the peace", and he said, "That he would!"

Well, as you can imagine, it was not a very pleasant Christmas, though I tried to dress up and pretend that all was well! After Christmas I decided that I had, had enough. I went to see a solicitor about getting a divorce and started divorce proceedings. In January 1980 there was an article in the *West Africa* magazine stating that James had been abducted in America and taken to Ghana. I was so annoyed at this nonsense that I drafted a response and sent it to the editor, and it was published on 18th February 1980.

A full transcript of my letter:

LETTERS to the Editor: West Africa Magazine.
18th February 1980, page 310.

No 'Disco on Wheels'.

Sir: An article which appeared in the Ghanaian Punch of 20th December, 1979, which refers to an 'abduction bid' of my husband, Commander James Boham GN. Retired, by Ghanaian naval personnel in New York is totally untrue. My husband has never been near America since the June 4th 'revolution'.

My husband retired six years ago from the Ghana Navy, and was managing director of the State Fishing Corporation from December 1973, until September 1978, when he was sacked by Akuffo and Amedume, and since that time has held no post at all.

He sat through the State Fishing Corporation probe, without being paid. At that time we had a ten-acre rice farm from the Ministry of Agriculture at Asutsuare, and that is how we managed to live. When the probe finished my husband had problems with his liver, and on 11th May 1979, he left Ghana by Swissair.

On 4th June my husband was still out of the country, with no intentions of returning at that time, as I was due to join him along with the children, in England for our annual holiday with my mother, as I am British. Therefore, my husband has never been on the run, and, in all fairness, his name should be removed from the wanted list.

He is a very heart-broken man, having worked hard to make the State Fishing Corporation succeed in bringing cheap fish to the people. He also looked after the workers and provided them with a clinic, free food and free transport. The workers at sea also had an incentive to produce more fish by a bonus system. Unfortunately it was Ghana's lack of foreign exchange for spare parts, which caused difficulties for him.

I am sorry to disappoint the people of Ghana but there never has been a 'disco on wheels', about which there was so much publicity. The idea came out of the head of Mr. Vincent Assiesah, former PRO of SFC, as he wanted to discredit my husband. This article about 'Boham in abduction bid' is presumably also from the mind of Mr. Vincent Assiesah and his associates. The vehicle in question is a Ford transit van, with bucket seats instead of bench seats. There is no disco.

I wish Ghanaians would stop listening to foolish lies and rumours, and become united under all tribes and try to bring the country back to the beautiful place that it was in 1964, when I first arrived. It is only by hard work and sacrifice that this can be achieved.

The politicians of today should take a look back at the history since Nkrumah, and not make the same mistakes again. They should look to the welfare of the innocent people involved in all the governments that have passed, and remember that if they do not act wisely now and sort out all the problems, they may be in the same boat later.

To the soldiers of the Ghana Armed Forces I would say that when I arrived in Ghana in 1964, the Ghana Armed Forces was a wonderful unit of trained men, who had helped their sister country of Congo in time of war. Might I make a plea to the soldiers of today, to reconstruct and make the Ghana Armed Forces something to be proud of once again.

    London.   Valerie Boham (Mrs.)

In February 1980 I was in the house with Mummy, when we had an unexpected visitor – an old friend, who we shall call Leigh. He had just come from Ghana and he was going to do a degree at London University. I told him that I had started divorce proceedings and I told him all that James had done! He said, "Madam, I beg you, stop this divorce! People in Ghana will say it's because he's in trouble, that's why you're leaving him. I will talk to him to try to improve things!" I agreed and rang the solicitor and told her to stop the divorce proceedings! That was one of the biggest mistakes of my life! The situation got worse. He then started accusing me of going with Leigh! He said, "I should be ashamed of myself, going with him." At that moment James was a retired Commander and Leigh was also retired. Up to that point James had always been praising Leigh: how he should have been an officer, that he had more officer-like qualities than even some officers. Now all had changed and Leigh became a mere sailor and I was disgusting, going with him!

    I hadn't seen Leigh for some time and he met me one evening on my way home from work. (I have omitted to mention that I had gone back to work with 'the International Telephone Exchange' at Judd Street, King's Cross, starting in March 1980.) I met Leigh unexpectedly at King's Cross Station. He asked me how things were and I said, "Terrible! Now he's accusing me of going with you!" And with a beautiful twinkle in his eyes he said, "What are you going to do about that?" I replied, with a naughty twinkle in mine, "I think that I am going to go with you!" I don't know who was more surprised, him or me! James had travelled to South America, and was due back on Saturday. It was the Easter weekend so I said to him, "It will have to be tomorrow, Good Friday, as I have the day off!" So I arranged to meet him at 3pm on Good Friday at King's Cross Station. I also arranged to go out with my new friend Annette (who I had met at work; she was a very young girl from Barbados, only twenty at this time) for lunch. I left home at 10am and met

Annette at 11am; I took her to lunch at the Mount Royal Hotel in Oxford Street. I wore my brand new Royal Stewart tartan kilt with a lace jabot blouse and a matching waistcoat and my short dark brown fur jacket. It was quite nippy that day though the sun was shining. We did some window-shopping and then I walked Annette to the Underground. I then went to meet Leigh. I waited and waited and he didn't come! I rang his house and he said, "That he wasn't coming!" I told him, "If you don't come, I will go with the first man that approaches me on the station!" He said, "Okay! I will come!" When he arrived we took a taxi and tried to find a hotel. As it was a bank holiday all the hotels were full; so we went to three or four before we got a room. Leigh apologised, "That wasn't very nice!" I didn't care – once I had made up my mind, that was that! I don't even remember the name of the hotel.

Sometimes in life a person is lucky to experience a really magic love affair. And though at that precise moment I was not aware, this was mine! I will describe my love: he is black and very tall and slim, with the most beautiful twinkling eyes I have ever seen and a beautiful smile, flashing white teeth. He is also a lovely person; anybody you mention him too, says, "Oh he's lovely!" For so many years he was a very loyal friend who I had grown to rely on. Anything I needed, he would always be able to do, and with such willingness it was truly lovely to see. He used to take my children out: to cinema, sometimes swimming, or to have a hamburger. He would laugh and play with them and they were always happy with him.

When he was in the Embassy in London he would visit Mummy and if she had any problems she would ring him and he would be there! Now was the magic moment when he told me that he loved me and he had always loved me, and I realised that I also had always loved him but had not been aware! He was content to remain in the background of my life to be around me; but he never made any advances at any time because he was an honourable man and James had been his senior officer, and he never ever imagined that things would go wrong with James and I, and that I would contemplate divorce!

That first time in that awful hotel room was magic! When I undressed he asked me, "If he could look at me" and I said, "Yes!" And he stood and looked at me as if I was the most beautiful person in the world; he made me feel wonderful. His kisses are the only kisses that I ever want in the world. As a lover he was so romantic, telling me that I was so pretty and over and over again how much he loved me. After all the agony of the previous months I was floating on air! I was so happy; I was so in love, so wonderfully in love. It was not lust, as our affair was more of a spiritual thing than sexual. He took me to the station and waited until the train left. How terrible it is to say goodbye to your lover; I was really happy, walking on air with stars in my eyes!

I reached home and Mummy said, "That James had been ringing the whole day from South America and was really angry and wanted to know where I had been. I was too happy to care about all of his nonsense. I went to sleep and for the first of many occasions dreamed of my love! Nothing could bring me down from my cloud of perfect happiness! James came back the next day but I just got myself ready for work. I had changed my hair to blond again and cut it very short, so I used to do it every Sunday. On Monday, when I got to work, Annette said to me, "Mrs. Boham, I hate your husband" and I said, "Why?" She said, "That he had rung her up, and she unwittingly told him the time that I left her. I told her not to worry – James had searched my work diary to get her number. Leigh rang me at work and everybody thought that he was my husband (as I didn't give James the number because he would have been ringing me and nagging me about something).

Leigh would ring me and tell me he loved me and then sometimes when I left work and went down the subway to cross the road, there was a certain telephone box and sometimes he would pop out laughing and surprise me. I never knew when he would be there. Then we would go to St. Pancras Station and have a coffee together; then he would see me back to King's Cross and we would kiss in a secluded part of the tunnel between St Pancras and King's Cross stations. His kisses were so beautiful and I never wanted to leave. Then I would go and get the train home. He used to time, the time it took for me to get home and I would just enter the house and he would ring, "Darling, Darling, I love you, I love you so much. Do you know how much I love you?" I would reply, "I love you too! And yes, I know how much you love me!" Now Leigh, unfortunately, was married. He had told Mummy how much he loved me when he was in the Embassy but Mummy had not told me; and he said, "That he went to a party and he met this girl and she wasn't very happy as she had just failed her nursing exams so he was trying to cheer her up and he took her home. He said, "When she saw him all alone in that three bed-roomed house she decided to move in with him. Her aunt came from Ghana and saw the situation and the next moment she said, "That the girl was pregnant, and the Aunt said, "They must get married! So Leigh decided to marry the girl!

So they arranged a big wedding; and the one thing that had always puzzled me was revealed to me. Leigh had always been such a good family friend, always visiting and helping out in so many ways; and when he got married, we were all in London: James, myself, and the children. But he never invited us to the wedding! He came one week, visiting as normal and the next week when he came he said, "That he had got married!" We were all amazed and said, "How could you get married and not invite us?" He now told me, "That he couldn't bear for me to be at the wedding because he loved me!" After the wedding there turned out to be no baby! This was the first of many attempts to come; always she would say that, "She was pregnant!" and always nothing would come!

Much to my sorrow, I had just had the operation the previous November, otherwise, I would have got pregnant for Leigh immediately! After a couple of years Leigh had a baby with a girl and at this time his son was eight months old. He had wanted to give the baby to his wife but the girl refused so he had his wife and a mortgage on the house and the girl and the baby to keep! James, in a fit of jealousy, had told me about the baby; but it made no difference to me. Rather, I was happy that Leigh should have a child, as he was so good with my children that he deserved to be a father. When I was on early shift I used to ring him from the station at 6am before his wife, who was a nurse at the mental hospital, and worked nights, got home. I would ring him and then get the train and go to work. At work he would ring me when he went to college; and then he would ring me in the evenings. If James was in I would let him answer the phone, then Leigh wouldn't put any money in! If I answered, he knew that I was alone. Mummy had gone to Israel to Laraine, as Laraine was having baby Amanda. As I briefly mentioned before, when I filed for divorce I applied for a job with the International Telephone Exchange and had started work in March. I had spent ten days in Israel with Laraine, before I started work, and Laraine was pregnant at that time; it was the only time I saw her pregnant, as I had been in Ghana when she was expecting Aviv. So from Good Friday, which was in April, till June I was floating on air. Leigh and I had made love physically only twice and it had been heavenly; but there was never any opportunity for more and I was satisfied with Leigh's kissing! When I got home I was still sleeping with James, but now; I used to imagine it was Leigh and I didn't mind so much! All my dreams were of him and my first thoughts in the morning were of him.

One day he decided that he had better come and visit us in the house, but we both found it such an ordeal that we couldn't face it again. When he came we went to the children's schools, and the children all came running to him; he loved them so! And they all loved him too and I loved him more because of the way he loved my children! In June, James surprised me. He said, "That he had bought me a ticket to go to Ghana," just for a few days; to see if I could see Justice Abban, who was dealing with (The Armed Forces Revolutionary Council) convicts' appeals. James had been given a ten-year sentence in absentia. I told Leigh, and the night before I left we met at St. Pancras and I gave him a token and I asked him to give me something and he said, "That he had nothing with him." So I said, "Okay! Give me anything that you have in your pocket!" so he gave me a coin! He came to see me off at Finsbury Park Station, as it was so hard to say goodbye. He was looking lovely he had been somewhere special at college that day and was wearing a new dark suit and he really looked smart.

So I went to Ghana and stayed with Glenda and Joe at Burma

Camp. The children were really happy to see me and every morning they all came into bed with me. Our house was in a sorry state, all dusty and empty. Many things had been taken, by James's brother-in-law and sister, and his Fanti wife (though I didn't really know about her at that time,) only that somebody had rung Mummy in England and told her that James had another wife; Mummy had told her that she couldn't be another wife as I was the only legal wife!) It was really sad to visit the house in that condition; my dear Yarrow the garden boy was there and his wife had just had another baby. I gave him some money as he wanted to send his wife home and he was from Northern Togo. It was lovely to be in Ghana, and Joe took me to see lawyers Swaniker and Lamptey. We went to see a few people about James's case; but everybody said, "That nothing could be done at that time!"

When I got back to London and rang Leigh, he said, "That he had been thinking while I was away." He said, "That he loved my children and he didn't want me to lose them so he felt that we should stop!" I agreed as it was also affecting his studies, and I wanted him to do really well, to prove to the world that my love was capable of so much more! It was very hard not to ring him or see him and I used to long for him all the time! Anyway, I made up my mind to concentrate on James and the children; but things were no better and I was so unhappy! The funny thing was that James had accused me of going with Leigh before the affair began, but whilst it was on – from April to June 1980, he never said a word! Then suddenly again, when nothing was going on, he started accusing me again. He went on and on almost all night! Then one night I broke down and I said, "Yes I love him, I would like to marry him; but I don't know if that would be possible!" He stormed out of the house and went to Leigh's house in London. Leigh rang me and said, "What happened? He came here shouting and in front of my wife and my brother and his wife accused me of having an affair with you!" I said, "I'm sorry, but he kept nagging me and I broke down!" He said, "Please speak to my wife. I have told her that it's not true!" I spoke to his wife and told her that it was not true; and that because of the coup and everything, James was not normal.

So we continued. Life was miserable. My only pleasure was going to work; I really enjoyed my work. James started coming to meet me and that was hell! He would be smoking all the way and have the radio blaring and he would be nagging me all the way home! When I went home on the train from King's Cross, I would sit in a non-smoking compartment and close my eyes until I got to Stevenage, and it was absolutely peaceful. By the time I got home I was perfectly relaxed. He used to come and sit from 3pm when I was off at 4.30pm.

Wendy Gibbons

When I was working at International one of the girls there was called Wendy Gibbons. She was a Londoner born and bred and was separated from her husband, also called Jim, and lived somewhere near Elephant and Castle with her mother. One day when I went up for tea she was sitting at the table with some holiday brochures and she had them opened at a page for Israel. She said, "That she would love to go to Israel as her dad was Jewish though she wasn't, as her mother wasn't." (You can only be Jewish if your mother is a Jew.) The flight was £88 including five days at a hotel in Tel-Aviv. I said, "Why don't you come with me; that flight is so cheap and I was going to my sister anyway." So she agreed and went to find out about the flight. When she came back she was disappointed, for the winter week break that we had coming – first week in December – she couldn't get the hotel. So I said, "Look, if you don't mind sleeping on the settee, you can come to my sister with me."

"Are you sure," she said. I said, "Yes. Anyway, come with me and I will ring my sister now to make sure." So I rang Laraine and she said, "Yes, of course!" so Wendy arranged the tickets. Wendy had never flown before or been out of England, so she had to get a passport and everything. We got a pay rise back-dated for six months so we were well able to pay the fare and have plenty of spending money. Wendy had three children like me, two boys and a girl, though they were slightly older than mine as she was three years older than me.

She came to spend the night with me in Letchworth as the flight was early in the morning with Monarch Airlines from Luton. When we left it was frosty and cold. Wendy was really excited. We stayed for ten days and Roni, Laraine, Aviv and baby Amanda came to meet us. Laraine got on well with Wendy, as I knew she would. Wendy and I paid for a two-day guided tour of Israel and we went to Bethlehem, Jerusalem and visited all the holy places: the Mount of Olives, and the tombs of Jesus and David; and I was amazed at Hebron at the Tombs of the Patriarchs of Abraham, Isaac and Jacob. Their bones had been carried in the wilderness, and they rested in the catacombs. You read about them in the Bible but you never expect to see their actual tombs.

The coach driver took a fancy to Wendy and offered her a hundred camels if she would marry him. She was laughing and so happy. When we got to Jerusalem there was a night out on the town with the group; but I decided to ring Ora and Rami, my Israeli friends from Ghana, as on my last visit I spent two days staying with them and they had treated me so well. They had taken me to see, 'The Messiah' played by the Israeli Philharmonic Orchestra in an open-air theatre and it was amazing. So I thought that I must at least see them this time.

When I rang them they said, "That Ora's mother was not well so Ora was taking turns with her sister to watch her. So we arranged that Rami would meet me at the hotel and Ora's son would come and pick us and take us to Ora's mother to see Ora. Wendy met Rami and we sat in the foyer of the hotel waiting for Ora's son, and Wendy left with the group for a night on the town in Jerusalem. Ora's son, who was in the Israeli Army, came in a military jeep and took us to Ora's mother. Ora came out to us in the car for a little and we had a long chat about all that had happened since we last met; and then Rami dropped me back at the hotel. Wendy hadn't come back by the time I got there so I got into bed. She soon came in and had, had a lovely time and was really happy. When we got back to Tel-Aviv we booked another day trip to the Dead Sea, but the morning we were due to go I got a runny tummy in the night so I was too weak to go. Wendy wanted to cancel going but I insisted that she went so we sent Aviv, who was now ten years, with her and she had a nice day. I had been to the Dead Sea the first time I came, with Laraine and Roni, so I wasn't really missing anything. The baby Amanda was beautiful with blond hair and blue eyes. Laraine though, was looking tired. I loved Israel – the weather, and the food; everything was so fresh. We used to go and have a lamb shawarma and a fresh fruit punch – you choose your own fruit and they made it fresh for you, lovely! All along the sea front you would find little open-air bars. I slept in the room with Aviv and he was so happy that I was with him. Aviv is a lovely boy and I really love him, and he's now a typical Israeli boy, only they speak English in the house.

After a lovely ten days we returned and James met us at the airport at Luton. Now Wendy had transferred from Garrick Exchange to Wren House so I didn't see her so much. One day just before Christmas she came over and gave me a bottle of Oil of Ulay with a white rose in a Christmas pack. I didn't have a present for her, but I said that I would give her one after Christmas. She had just had her hair done and was looking lovely. She told me that she had made a man friend at Wren House who used to see her home safely. She had given him the little wooden cross made of olive wood which the bus driver had given her as a souvenir in Israel. She asked if I could give her another one, as I had bought several, so I said that I would. The first week in January I went into work and one of the girls, who was also the union rep, said to me, "That she had heard that something had happened to Wendy; could I find out?" So I said, "Yes, I will call her mother!" As soon as I rang Wendy's mother she started to tell me the most dreadful story; in fact I sat listening with tears streaming down my face. Wendy's estranged husband had come to the mother's flat after following Wendy home from work and taken a brick and smashed the glass door down and started beating Wendy with the brick. When her mother had tried to stop him he had thrown her into the bathroom, causing bruising and cracked ribs, and then he had taken Wendy out onto the pavement and bashed her brains out. Her mother said that her brains were all over the pavement and he tried to pull her eyes out. When I heard how her brains were out I knew that Wendy was dead. The union rep rang the hospital and they said that they had operated and she was on machines to keep her alive! Some of the girls said, "They were going to visit her" but I said, "I wouldn't go and I wanted to remember her happy, the way that she had been when we came back from Israel. When the girls came back they were all, ill and had to go home. I rang Wendy's mother and told her that I would not be going to the hospital. She understood and said, "That she and Wendy's sister all thank me for taking Wendy to Israel and making her so happy! When I told Laraine she was so sorry but she said, "That she had, had a funny dream. There was a photograph of her, Wendy and me; and Wendy had no head in the photo. Wendy was kept on the machines until September when they were switched off. I rang the hospital and the nurse told me that when they were bathing her there was no response so she had been clinically dead from that first day. Because she was kept alive her husband was charged with manslaughter and got only ten years!

James was still meeting me, waiting outside for hours. When the girls went out to buy cigarettes they would all come in laughing! "Your husband's waiting for you again!" Sometimes I would pretend that I hadn't seen him and make for the Underground. In November 1980, when we were in bed, he suddenly punched me in the middle of my spine and I screamed. Mummy came running. She knocked on the door and asked, "If I was alright?" I said, "Yes", though I wasn't; I got terrible pain in my neck! I got him to take me to a private physiotherapist. He was moaning about the expense, but I wanted the best treatment. He had jarred my spine and they had to pull my legs and my head and twist my neck. It was very painful, and the physiotherapist was surprised that I was still at work as people with much less than that didn't go to work! The children were in the boarding school so luckily they were not part of all this. The only place where I was happy was at work and I never wanted to go home!

In December 1980, James said, "Joe Butah   rriving from Ghana. Do you want to come and meet him?" I sai   'es!" as the last time

I saw him was when he came to the airport with me and was arrested. So we went to the airport at Heathrow. Glenda was supposed to come from Wales to meet him but she wasn't there! When we got there, Joe arrived and we took him to have a drink at the airport bar. He had bought a bottle of whiskey duty free so they opened it and started drinking straight away. James by now was drinking everyday; he would start at nine in the morning without eating breakfast. Suddenly Glenda appeared. She said, "That they had a puncture on the motorway from Wales!" She asked me to come with her to the ladies. When we got there she asked me, "What's this I hear about you having an affair with Leigh?" I said, "I don't know what you are talking about; I haven't seen him for months!" I felt: if James wanted to stay with me as his wife then he didn't need anybody knowing about any affair, especially as it was over! When we got back to the men Glenda said, "Well, James! I've spoken to Valerie and she says that this affair with Leigh is not true!" So he said to me, "But didn't you tell me that you loved him?" And I said, "Yes! But I just wanted to hurt you!" because, as I said before, I didn't think that I had to say it in public when it was all over anyway! The next minute James punched me across the face and broke my tooth. I took the broken bit and put it in Joe's hand and said, "Don't you see? Now he's broken my tooth!" I started crying and said, "I can't go home with him now!" so Joe talked to him and I calmed down a bit. James said, "That he had to see Mr. Lamptey's wife on the way home". I sat in the car and refused to go in, my face was swollen with tears and bruised and I needed more time to calm down. When we got home I didn't tell Mummy what had happened, I washed my face and freshened my lipstick and I didn't look too bad, though the tip of my tooth was all rough from the broken bit.

Joe and Glenda said, "That they would come and stay with us after Christmas to try to sort things out!" We had a very miserable Christmas. Mummy went to her friend Auntie Dorrie; and we just watched television mostly. We had our usual dinner of turkey and all the trimmings. I bought the children headphone radios, which was the latest thing at that time! On New Year's weekend Glenda and Joe and the three children Justin, Rhian and Suzanne came. It was lovely to see the children, and Hamish, Rosina and Julien all made a big fuss of them.

Then we sat down and Joe asked about the problems and I gave my case and James gave his. Joe said, "That James wanted me to stop work and try again and the children should leave boarding school and come home". and they said that I should agree that Mummy should be found somewhere else, to give us all a chance. Mummy at this time had now gone to Laraine in Tel-Aviv. We went to the Council to try and find somewhere for Mummy to go but there was nowhere available. I wrote to Mummy in Israel at James's instigation, that we didn't want her to come back and live with us, as we were trying to sort ourselves out! I had to put in two week's notice at work, so I put in my notice. The council had just let us know that a flat-let was available at 'The Biggin' in Hitchin for Mummy. On the Friday of the first week of my notice, I came home from work tired and with a slight headache. I sat down on the settee for a five-minute rest. The only other being in the house was Sheba my Siamese cat, who was so happy to see me home that she was prowling and howling round the room, flicking her tail. James started shouting the minute he walked in the door and I said, "Oh please stop shouting, I've got a headache!" The next minute, he started punching me, and punching me. I put my arm up to protect my face and he went on and on punching me; I was screaming! and screaming! Eventually, I fell on the floor and whilst I was lying on the floor he kicked me in the ribs. Then I lay quite still as if I was dead. He stopped and went and got himself a drink, and then another and another. I just lay there on the floor! Eventually, in a drunken stupor, he got up and switched out the lights and went upstairs to bed! After a while I managed to pull a cushion off the settee and I just lay on the floor; I was beaten and aching all over my body. I dragged myself up and got to the downstairs loo and washed my face. My eyes were bright red with crying and it made my green eyes ever more brilliant! I didn't know what to do. Should I go and tell somebody? I couldn't believe it had actually happened to me! It was so humiliating; even as a child I was hardly smacked, let alone beaten (and by a trained military man!). Mummy always punished us by stopping us watching television and that worked wonders. I thought: what to do? If I phoned, the police. James would be in trouble; and he was already in trouble in Ghana and because of my children I didn't want him in trouble in England. So though I didn't know it at the time; I sacrificed so much for myself by not reporting him at that moment!

The next minute he came down and my arm was so badly bruised that even my hand was hanging limp. I really thought he had broken it! I thought "Oh my God! My hand is broken and I can't even go to hospital!" He pulled my arm and I screamed in pain. He patted me and he said, "You're a bad girl, come to bed!" I had taken four Anadins but was still throbbing all over and when I got to bed he said, "Let me play love with my wife to make her feel better!" I was in no condition to protest. I lay on the bed and he jumped on me and had his way; I lay there throbbing all over and felt like a sack of potatoes or an old lady of ninety and I thought: God, it would be better to be a prostitute than go through all this; at least you get paid for it! For me that was the absolute end of everything! I can honestly say, in fact, put my hand on the Bible and say, that in the seventeen years since Hamish was conceived in 1963 until 1980 when I fell in love with Leigh. I had never looked at or thought about another man. I was a devoted, faithful, loyal, dutiful wife; thinking only of my husband and children, wanting only the best for us all as a family!

The next morning, when he sobered up and saw my bruises, he got worried. He said, "Shall I take you to the doctor?" I thought: he doesn't even realise what that would mean as it would be reported to the police!

My whole right arm was bruised from shoulder to hand and my back was turning yellow, blue, red. My front was all bruised; my left leg was also bruised, though I don't know how; my head had swollen in the night and now the swelling had moved down, so my whole face was puffed. My head was full of blood (lucky my hair was short!), as the Masonic signet ring, which I had bought him in Israel, had cut my head in many places! I washed my hair and the blood was running in the water. Luckily it was Saturday and I didn't have to go to work. I was allowed four days off work without a certificate, so I got him to ring on Monday to say that I had fallen over and bumped my head. We had very heavy snow at that time and everywhere was icy and slippery. On Friday, which was my last day I had to go to work; the girls gave me a beautiful vase of Irish china and a big card, which everybody had signed. I had to take them for drinks at the pub, which was the only time that I had gone there!

My close friends were Annette, Jackie and Carol. One girl asked me why I didn't come in the last few days and I said, "I fell down!" She laughingly said, "Come on, we all know your husband beat you!" I thought: My God! You don't know how right you are! James came to meet me with Kwame Asante and we went to Ken Appiah-Minka's house. James had promised to take me to 'The Talk of the Town' nightclub for dinner; but there was a thick fog and I didn't really feel up to it, so I said, "Let's just go home!" So that was the end of my job at International, where I was so happy.

When we reached home Rosina was waiting in the garage, so it was just as well that we came home; we didn't know that she had an exit from school that weekend. Hamish and Julien popped in on Sunday but I didn't tell the children about the beating. Later, Mummy told me, "That Hamish told her, that he had seen the bruises on my arm!" The next couple of weeks I was like a zombie; I just didn't know what to do? I was so afraid of James, though he was being really nice; as I think he really scared himself when he saw my bruises. He said, "That he wanted me to go to Ghana again for him! He had given Power of Attorney to his nephew Joseph McLean-Arthur to do his appeal against his ten-year sentence in absentia; and Joseph, who was an engineer with the Fishing Corporation, had gone to Las Palmas, on a vessel which was on charter, so was not there to attend the hearing. I would have gone to the moon, or anywhere, to get away from him!

A few days before I left, Mummy came back from Israel and James sent a mini-cab to meet her and booked her into the Broadway Hotel in Letchworth. I was in no condition to protest. We packed her things and I thought how terrible to be packing Mummy's things (though she would be safer away from him!).

Top: At a lunch at Volda's house, Burma camp with Rosemary Anoff, Dr. Anoff's wife, 1977.
Bottom: Rosina playing her piano in the Accra house, 1977.

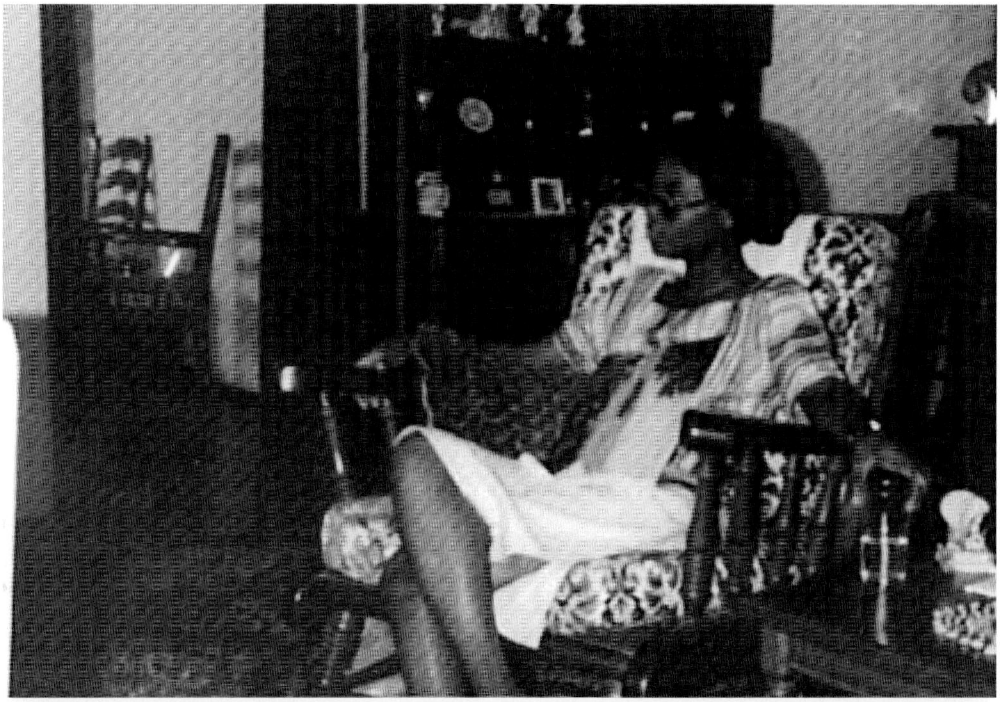

Top: My dear Agatha sitting in the sitting room of the Accra house.
Bottom: James and me before going to a reception at The Castle Osu, Accra, Ghana.

Top Left: Julien and me at Doris's wedding reception held in the garden at the Accra house.
Top Right: Doris, Joyce, Sally and me at Doris's wedding.
Bottom: Group photo of Doris's wedding, 1977.

Family group, 1977, at the Letchworth House, Hertfordshire, England, the last photo of us all taken together..

Top: James and me at a lunch for Black Star Line Agents around the world, Accra, 1977.
Bottom: With Johnny and the girls, Lizzie, Peggy, Tawiah and Ago and their cousin Tina, with Auntie's baby, Johnny, faithful political supporter, also Chris Lamptey, Lizzie's then boyfriend, Accra, 1982.

My favourite photograph of the children taken in Takoradi, Hamish, Rosina and Julien.

Top: Uncle David, Commodore Hansen with President Nkrumah inspecting the Ghana Navy Guard of Honour, Accra, 1964.
Bottom: President Kwame Nkrumah with General Ankrah and General Steve Otu on board GNV Kromatse 1964.

Top: GNV Kromantse, 1964, James on the bridge.
Bottom: Ekua, Teneriffe, 1994. Photo by Domingo.

Chapter Ten

GHANA
1981–1984

On 11th March 1981 I left for Ghana. James had rang Jonah Lamptey to meet me; he didn't want Glenda and Joe to know that I was coming! I didn't know why? But he used to get funny like that at times. Kwame Asante was on the flight and I saw him but we didn't travel together. It was a pleasant flight and Kwame came to assist me with my baggage. There were some Q-movement chaps and they collected my baggage with me and sorted out customs, and once I had seen Jonah, Kwame left me. I got to the house about four o'clock in the morning. I was of course very tired, and the house was terribly dirty, dusty and mouldy. The sheets on the bed were smelly and musty, but I was so tired I just switched on the air-conditioner and slept! I sent Nketsia to ring Ama Opuni to say that I had arrived. When I got up I started cleaning and unpacking things and generally trying to make the house look like home again!

I discovered so many things had been stolen, by who I don't truly know up to this day, but all of the drawers in the bedroom were empty as if it was a new married quarter! I had only bought three dresses and three pairs of trousers and six tops, thinking that I would find some things in Ghana! Only a few of my very old dresses were there; almost all of my Ghanaian cloths were gone. The only ones left were the ones that I had sewed into long dresses.

I remember James complaining when I made them, saying that I was wasting good cloth! But now, I was lucky that I had done that, otherwise, they would have gone too! All the sheets, towels, ornaments gone; in the kitchen, all the pans, cutlery the house had been really stripped! Anyway I thought that 'there is no use crying over spilt milk'. I just arranged what was left and washed my old dresses with Zoflora disinfectant, which I had brought from London, which made everything smell nice again. All the TVs, videos and electronic equipment was gone; there was no music or radio in the house. I was lucky to meet the air-conditioners!

The curtains, carpets and chairs were in the sitting room and the bed in the bedroom so I managed with them. After having a fully equipped house it was like camping in the house. Still I could cook and sleep, though there was no water to bath in and I had to use a bucket and a cup, just like in India. As I am fairly adept at that it wasn't so much of a problem! There was no water in the whole area. Ama Opuni came to pick me in the afternoon and took me to her house to have some fu-fu, (which is a Ghanaian speciality prepared by pounding plantain and cassava or just yam and coco yam with a little water). It becomes like a dough, which you break bits off and swallow with some soup, light soup or abenkwa or groundnut soup. It is delicious and I love it.) In the evening she said, "That she had to go and see somebody in town" so I agreed to accompany her to see how the town was! When Ama finished I asked her to pass Doris's house so I could surprise her! When we got there Kwesi was in and Nana and Brigitte, but no Doris! I said, "Where is she?" and he said, "I don't know. She's normally here by now!" We waited a while and when she still didn't come we left. On the way Ama said, "That she would buy me some kelewele, which is chopped ripe plantain fried with ginger and pepper delicious! I wanted her to take me straight home but she insisted I go back to her house. When we got there Doris was sitting on the chair! She said, "That she had been thinking of me and decided to visit my house to see if Nketsia had any news of me, and when she got there she was told that I had come, and that Ama had taken me to her house, so she had come and was sitting waiting for us to come back! So whilst we had been waiting in Doris's house, she had been waiting in Ama's house! So that is my beautiful twin sister Doris!

The next few days I was very busy getting the house in order and trying to get my car on the road; I had bought a brand new battery with me from London and four new tyres and a jack, just as well as the old tyres had been changed and the jack was missing and also the wheel spanner. My neighbour Mrs. Pat Atepe was a great help to me and her driver brought me a driver, a lovely boy called Prosper, who was also a mechanic. I went to Burma Camp on 13th March as it was Mrs. Butah's birthday and I wanted to surprise her! I don't know who got more of a surprise. My clock was on her wall, my two pouffes in the sitting room, and my ornaments on the divider. And when the boy passed with the washing, my brand new sheets, which I had bought when I went to America and had never used, were on the pile of washing. She was having a birthday party and my best tablecloth, which Miss. Pinto's daughter had brought me from Italy, was on the table along with a lot of my crockery. My freezer and washing machine were in use in the kitchen, and the icemaker as well. I was so shocked that I couldn't say a word and I left. Pat had driven me in her car. Joe said, "That he would bring me a TV and a video as they had the TV, video and all the films in their bedroom. Also, my spare velvet cushion covers were on their chairs. I told them that I had come that day and that I was in the house.

The next day Pat took me to the Water and Sewerage Corporation, HQ, to get a tanker of water. The tanker came and filled the tanks and then we found that they were leaking and all the water ran away. I had to get the fitters to come and weld them and resurface them before we could get the tanker again. The tanks were repaired and the tanker came again and the tanker driver stepped on the connecting pipe so all the water flowed right down the hill. So we started again and fixed the pipe and filled the tanks; and eventually I was able to have a bath! Jonah Lamptey had taken the battery to have acid put in it and to charge it, so I was mobile again. By now I had scrubbed the kitchen and the bathroom with Flash; and dusted, washed and polished the sitting room, so the house was not looking too bad. James had sent some paint through the Ghana Airways girls, so I was able to paint the sitting room, kitchen, dining room and my bedroom. We took our time to slowly do the rest of the house. The garden was dry and dead and there was not much that I could do about it; as Yarrow the garden boy had died the year before, just after I visited. I decided just to keep the grass down but not to paint the outside of the house or do too much with the garden as people notice things and talk, and I wanted them to see the house looking dilapidated and say: look at that house looking so shabby when it used to be so nice!

Another lovely surprise: Miss Pinto appeared. She said, "That she had come with her brother-in-law and just passed the house to see it and saw the car and decided to come in. So that was truly a lovely surprise! Also Mr. Steve Boateng, who had been with the Fishing Corporation, came to see me. When he saw the house he said, "Yes, now it looks like your house again!"

I went with Jonah to see Mr. Swaniker about James's case. Everybody was afraid to handle the cases, as they had put a transitional provision in the new Ghana Constitution that nobody could alter the sentences as they stood. And the Liman government was afraid, anyway. We had got a date for court to be heard. As James's nephew had the Power of Attorney and had instigated the case, I could not actually do anything!

I used to sleep at 7pm and get up at 5.30am. After all the nagging and tension from James in the last few months; suddenly I felt free. I was very lonely and unhappy but free of James's constant nagging! My ticket expired after one month. James was sending me food parcels through Ghana Airways and as I was on my own I wasn't actually using very much. Mary, Nketsiah's wife, was pregnant with her first child, so I sent her to the midwife and she had a beautiful baby boy. They decided to call him Julien, after my youngest son, as Nketsiah and Julien had always been great friends. I brought Mary into the house and put her in Rosina's bedroom so I could help her by taking care of the baby whilst she had some decent sleep. The week after the baby was born we had an out-dooring ceremony in the house (a traditional naming ceremony). Nketsiah's father came and named him and a few friends of Nketsiah popped in. I gave them one thousand cedis from all of us for the baby. The next week he was circumcised so we had to give him extra-special attention. Then I had a letter from James, who was furious that I had brought Mary into the house and I must send her back to the boy's quarters immediately. I called Nketsiah and told him and he agreed that Mary was well enough to go back to the boy's quarters. I still looked after the baby for her whenever she needed to rest or go to the market, and the little boy became very special to me. He used to call me Madam.

I started visiting old friends, Auntie Linda and Uncle Robert Gardiner. I always went to Auntie Linda at any odd time I had and often joined them for lunch, and normally I tried to be there to have tea with Auntie Linda. Another good tea buddy was Rear-Admiral David Hansen (Uncle David) and Auntie Lily, who really gave me great support and understanding. Auntie Lily had gone through her own divorce and almost everything that had been done to me had been done to her also. Then I would go to Burma Camp and visit Joe and Glenda and I was always most welcome to join them for lunch. Joe normally went to golf in the afternoon so I would stay with Glenda and the children. Then in Tema there were Volda and John Owusu, who had now retired from the Armed Forces. They were living in their own house in Tema, which was built to the same plan as ours as James, had given them the plan. Volda was running the poultry farm and was building a restaurant on the site near the farm, to be called 'Calypso Inn'. After all the tension in England it was so nice to get peace and quiet to be able to think; I used to burn incense and meditate, mostly for peace for all! I used to sleep at 7pm so I told people not to visit after that time. I did a lot of reading, Mr. Boateng was a regular visitor and I was able to talk a lot to him. Basically, in my heart of hearts, I was longing to see Leigh again, but I realised that it was impossible. I was able to cast him out of my mind for days and then something would trigger it off and I was longing for him again. I used to look at the blue skies, the lovely flowers and the sunshine and think: if only he could be here too!

At Easter time James sent Julien on holidays, Hamish was preparing for his O-levels and Rosina was going to France with the school. Julien and I had a nice time together, though he wasn't very happy to see Glenda and Joe using our things, and he went home to tell his daddy! We went to court with James's appeal and it was adjourned again. I had paid for a ticket for Joseph to come back from Las Palmas but he arrived too late for the hearing. I read the Bible through from cover to cover, continued with my meditation and prayers, and early to bed, early to rise. After Julien returned to England James came to Lome, Togo and I went to stay with him in a hotel. He also came to Ghana even though he was wanted, and stayed in the house for our seventeenth wedding anniversary. I'm afraid I didn't love him anymore and I was afraid of him because of the beating.

Lagos-Araba

At last I finally made it to visit my dear Araba in Lagos. From Lome James wanted to drive though to Nigeria but when we got to the Benin border they wouldn't let me pass as I had a British passport and no visa. So I had to return to Accra. James went by air to Lagos direct. I went by air from Accra. On the plane I met a nice young lady who knew Araba so when we arrived and there was no Ted, Araba or James, they gave me a lift to Araba's house at Surelere, Lagos. Araba's mum and the children were there and they were really excited, and Araba now had a little boy called Ato as well, who was really charming and became my special buddy. I spent four days with Araba and Ted in Lagos and she couldn't do enough for me, and her mother was so nice too. Then I returned to Accra.

James went to stay with TT, who was also in exile, in Abidjan, and I went too. I loved Abidjan and it was lovely and, very French, though very expensive. James had business problems with TT and went to stay with Akwasi-Kuma and eventually stayed with Jim Addo. One time when I went James was so nasty to me that even Jim said, "Leave her alone", and "Don't mind him, Sweetheart!" He was still drinking a lot and I found that I couldn't stay with him; all I wanted was to get back to Ghana and my solitary peace! He got so angry and said, "What are you going for?" I made so many excuses as to why I had to go! At the airport he wouldn't help me get a seat and Col. Abrefa, also in exile, had to help me. Even when I went through the barrier he didn't kiss me or say goodbye. As I sat in the departure lounge I looked up and saw him scowling down at me and I thought, "Oh God, there must be more in life than this! The man is in trouble and I should stay with him and I can't!" The next day, Monday, I went to Tema as James had given me a letter for Mr. Boateng, When I got to Mr. Boateng's he said, "Leigh's here!" My heart missed a beat and started pumping. I said, "When did he come?" and he said, "Friday, I wanted to bring him to you but I knew that you were in Abidjan." When I left there I said, "Oh God, if he is here, I must see him!" Ten minutes later, going along the Teshie Road Prosper, the driver said to me, "Madam, somebody is flashing us to stop!" When I looked, it was Leigh. I got out of the car and walked towards him and he got out of his and walked towards me. When we were close he stood and looked at me and looked into my eyes, and time stood still! I looked at my love and I was full of joy! Then he said, "Now I've seen you, now I'm happy!" and he went to leave and I said, "I must see you!" and he said, "We can't! Everybody knows that you have divorced James and are married to me!" James's sisters had been spreading the rumours.

Once I had seen my love, the fire was burning fiercely. I had no thoughts but of him; he is so handsome and lovely and has the most delightful laugh! Mr. Boateng came and I forced him to bring Leigh to me in the house, then to go and leave him there and not come back! Then, my love was there in the house with me; my heart was bursting with happiness! After a few minutes Mr. Boateng left. Then Leigh said to me, "You blew it. Why did you betray me?" I said, "I didn't betray you. I told James I loved you because he forced me! I don't think that's betraying." The next minute he grabbed me in his arms and was kissing me. He said, "Darling, I love you so much. Do you know how much I love you?" and I said, "Yes, I love you so much too!" He said, "I've missed you so much!" and I said, "I've missed you so much too!"

I told him how James had beaten me, and he said, "Why didn't he come and beat me?" We talked and talked and kissed and cuddled for hours without thinking. Then Leigh said, "Where is Boateng? He's not coming. is he?" and I said, "No! I want you to stay with me! Nobody is in the house! Nobody will know!" He said, "No, Darling, not in this house!" I begged and pleaded with him to stay and he begged to be allowed to go. So at four o'clock in the morning I allowed him to go. We arranged to meet at Mr. Boateng's house the next day! That night, my dreams had become reality and I was so happy, to have seen the light shining in his eyes, to remember his wonderful kisses and just to know that he was near; and that he still loved me in spite of all the problems! The next day I went to Mr. Boateng's house and we sent my driver for petrol, and Mr. Boateng went in his car to collect Leigh and bring him to his house.

At the beginning Mr. Boateng would stay and talk, but suddenly Leigh and I would be lost to the world, only looking at each other. Sometimes Leigh would say, "Why me?" He could never understand how I loved him! And I would say, "Because you are you!" We were innocently and blissfully happy. The whole time he was around I couldn't eat at all and would go the whole day without food or drink. I only needed to see him and I was satisfied! He used to worry and try to get me to eat a biscuit or something. He had to return to London, as he was still doing his degree and was working on a project for that, about ECOWAS, the West African Economic Community. So he went, and I settled down a bit.

Then the children came for the summer holidays: Hamish, Rosina and Julien. In no time at all they had found all their friends and the house would be full. They would go to Sammy Dontoh's house. Sammy was Hamish's classmate and his brothers and sister were all the children's friends. Julien had always been much older than his age so he got on well with them too! After the children had been for a few weeks Mr. Boateng came one night when I was ready for bed. He said, "That Leigh had come!" So I said, "Okay, I will come to Tema tomorrow!" I saw Leigh and then came home. Leigh stayed for a few days and then went back to London, saying. "That he would return soon!" I was so happy with the children and their friends. They had a terrible habit of seeing one another off home. When one was leaving they would all go to see him off and then they would all come back again and they could go on all day until late in the night!

One day Hamish slept at Sammy's and I was really worried as I was leaving with Rosina at five o'clock in the morning to see James in Abidjan. I sent Prosper to bring him home before I left for the airport. Hamish, said, "That he was sorry, he just fell asleep;" and that was when I said, "I was so worried. Pease let me know in future that you are safe!" Rosina and I went to Abidjan and stayed with Jim Addo again. It wasn't a pleasant time and Rosina complained that her daddy had searched her suitcase and she was really mad! When we returned, Mr. Boateng came as usual one night and said, "That Leigh had come back." My heart stopped beating for a moment and then started pumping frantically. I told him that I was worried about the children because they hadn't come home, so he said, "That he would go and bring them in his car." Only Rosina came back. She said, "That the others would come later. Rosina and I were in the bedroom when the phone rang. It was Leigh! That was the only time that he had rang me in Ghana! I was so excited but I couldn't talk because of Rosina, so I said, "That I would go downstairs to speak. I put the phone down and rushed to the door and she said, "Mummy, you have cut it off!" and I said, "Never mind, he'll ring again!" I went down and picked up the phone in the study and he was still there. He explained, "That he was delayed because his wife had thought that she was pregnant again and she wasn't and she was crying all the time and all upset, so he couldn't leave her, and so he had to stay with her longer than he intended. He said, "That she had said, "That she knew that he would leave her one day and that she would go, and that she was just waiting for something! When he asked her, "What was that something?" she wouldn't say! He said, "He thought that it was a car, as he had promised to buy her a car!" He said, "That I was his cross and he would have to bear it!" I said, "I love you!" and he said, "I love you too!" We arranged to meet at Mr. Boateng's house the next day. I told him to find somewhere for us to go!

That night, I couldn't sleep. I was so excited and I kept thinking about what Leigh had said, and what his wife had said, so in the end, at about two o'clock in the morning, I sat down and wrote a long letter to his wife. I told her that I loved him and he loved me and that I wanted her to leave him for me! I didn't want anything but him. So we would leave the house in London for her. I told her that she hadn't been able to have a baby for him. Maybe the chemistry wasn't right between them and she would be able to have a baby with someone else. (I have seen this happen to another friend and the marriage broke up, and the next thing: she was pregnant with someone else, and this was in the days before fertility clinics.)

I decided that I would take the letter to the airport, as I had to go and see Charlotte and her children off. If I saw Leigh I would give it to him and if not I would give it to Charlotte to post in London! I didn't see Leigh so I gave it to Charlotte. Then I went to Mr. Boateng's. I had told the children that I was going to Lome with Mr. Boateng. I sent the driver home and said, "That I would drive myself home. In Mr. Boateng's I said to him," That I've done something really terrible today!" He said to me, "Where have you been?" and I said, "I went to the airport!" and he said to me, "Have you written to Leigh's wife?" I was amazed that he knew. He said, "That he would go and get the letter back" and I said, "That's not possible as the plane has left by now!" Then I started crying bitterly but what was done was done! I said, "That I would tell Leigh!" Mr. Boateng went and collected him and he came. I was so excited and hadn't eaten all day as usual. Leigh drove my car and went back to his flat to collect cheese and biscuits for me to eat, but I couldn't. I said, "Where are we going?" and he said, "You will see when we get there!" He also said, looking at me so lovingly, "Tonight, you're mine! No James! Nor my wife! Nobody else! You're mine!" He held my hand all the time he was driving. After a while I realised that we were going to Akosombo. When we got there Leigh went to the reception to book a room and then he came and collected me, and after ordering some drinks we started kissing, and after one year and three months we made beautiful love. It was so wonderful I was in dreamland. After a while I slept and woke up to see Leigh sitting up looking at me. He said, "Am I dreaming? I dream of you so much. I can't believe that you are here!" I said, "I am real. Let me pinch you to make sure!"

We left at about four o'clock in the morning. When we were going, as we got almost Michel Camp. I said, "Darling, I've done something terrible, will you forgive me?" He said, "Yes" and I said, "No, this is really bad. Don't just say 'yes'!" He said, "Okay, I forgive you!" He was holding my hand all the way that he was driving and his hand neither tightened nor loosened. I said, "I've written to your wife!" and he said, "Oh yes?" I said, "Yes, it's true! I have written to her!" and he said, "Tell me it isn't true, Darling!" and I said, "Well, I can tell you that it isn't true, but it is!" He said, "Okay, tell me what you have written so I can know how to deal with it!" He continued, "You don't know her. She's really vicious and she could even make a copy and send it to James!" So he would have to go back to London immediately!" I dropped him at Military Hospital, and went home. When I got there Hamish was sitting on the settee. He said, "Mummy, we know that you didn't go to Lome with Mr. Boateng!" I said, "Oh!" He said, "That Rosina was listening on the phone and heard me arrange to meet Leigh. So I said, "Yes, it's true! I love him, and would like to marry him!" After a silence Hamish said, "Anyway! He's okay!" I then went up and told Rosina. "I also told them not to tell their daddy as he would kill me!" I went to Ghana Airways office to get a seat for Pat on the plane and met Leigh there! He said, "That he had rung his wife and she had received the letter and all she would say was Hmm! Ahm! Hmm! So he was also leaving on that flight." Mr. Boateng came and asked, "If I would go to the airport?" and I said, "No, I will not go! He will be running away from me and I will not be there!" That was 5th September 1981.

In the evening the phone rang and it was James. He was very brusque and asked, "If I went to the airport?" and I said, "No!" As soon as I put the phone down I realised that he had been at the airport and he must have seen Leigh arriving and put two and two together. That if I was in Ghana and Leigh was there, I must also have seen him! When Leigh left he said, "That he would be back in three weeks!" The children left Ghana to return to England to go back to school on 8th September 1981. They were very happy and had, had a lovely holiday. Doris made Rosina a Ghanaian dress and Elsie, my inherited daughter, plaited Rosina's hair. Sammy, Robert, Ebo, Moses, and all their friends came to see them off at the airport; and Mr. Boateng. I made them promise not to tell Daddy about

Leigh. I made the mistake of not telling Julien anything as I felt that at 13 he was too young!

When I was on my own again and had time to think I realised that, regardless of what happened between Leigh and myself, I could not return to England as James's wife! Elsie went to London and got deported immediately on arrival as they said, "That she was "coming to work!" So she came to stay with me until she could make other arrangements to get a teaching job in Nigeria. She had completed her first degree at the University of Ghana, Legon. We had a lovely time together and she gave me a lot of good advice. I started painting again and, funny thing, I seemed to do nothing but abstracts.

No word came from Leigh and he didn't come either! After a lot of thought, on 13th October 1981, I wrote a letter to James telling him that I could not return to him as his wife; as I didn't love him anymore or like him or respect him because of the beating, and I had found out that he had, had a Fanti wife since 1975. By African customary rights he had built her a house and bought her a car and sent her to London several times. She had been in London when he beat me and had just returned to Ghana at that time. (I do know her name but will not mention it.). I said that we had come to a crossroads and that we should go our separate routes. I asked him to give me a divorce on the breakdown of the marriage and do it nicely and quietly for the sake of the children. I also sent a copy to Leigh so that he would be aware of what I was doing! In the meantime I spent my days painting, meditating and visiting friends; Auntie Linda, Auntie Lily, Miss Pinto, Pat, Volda, Glenda and Doris, and sleeping early and getting up early. In a tropical early morning before it gets too hot it is so beautiful to enjoy, watching the birds of so many beautiful colours and the flowers and just smelling the air. The bougainvillea was always out and I had planted so many colours, which were all over the back wall and now very mature and just cascading over the wall.

James had ordered his sister Joan to return the tipper truck, that he had bought in her name, as for two years he had received no money from her! I had to borrow forty thousand Cedis from Mr. Brenya to repair the truck, as it was broken down when Joan returned it. I had to buy a new starter and battery and tyres, all at kalbuli prices (black market prices). For three months I sat at the Firestone offices to get new tyres but all the tyres were being sent to Burma Camp for cocoa evacuation. Eventually I got the new tyres. The next thing was that I got a letter from a lawyer in London saying that James was filing for divorce on the grounds of my adultery with Leigh! I went to Auntie Lily and she decided to go and see a lawyer that she knew. (Auntie Lily's father had been a lawyer, and her ex-husband was now a Judge, so she had good connections legally.) That was lawyer Tagoe. A few days later two men came to the door and served me with divorce papers from the High Court in Ghana, and the lawyer was lawyer Tagoe! So I went to Auntie Lily and said, "That we can't go to Tagoe now! and she said, "Why?" and I explained. Auntie Lily took me to another lawyer friend of hers, Ofusu-Armaah, who was a professor of Law, at the Law School in the University of Ghana. He had also been head of Special Branch during Busia's time and was imprisoned by Acheampong for an alleged attempted coup. I told him my story and I liked him very much and he agreed to handle my case! I told him that I loved Leigh but I was not going to admit adultery. As the saying goes, 'He who is without sin should cast the first stone!' And James, with his multitude of sins, was casting it! So we agreed to deny adultery. I received that letter in November. I had heard nothing from Leigh up till that time. In December I was with Auntie Linda and I sent the driver to open the postbox. He came back with a letter posted in Edgware! I knew that it was from Leigh and I was so happy; but not so when I read it. It was a lawyer's letter from Mr. & Mrs. Leigh, saying that I had an infatuation and obsession with Leigh and he wanted nothing more to do with me and I shouldn't write to him again. I knew that it was because of the letter that I had written to his wife! She had forced him to send it, otherwise; she would send the letter to James. Auntie Linda was very upset for me, I myself was stunned but I had gambled and lost. When Mr. Boateng came I said, "Steve, you saw Leigh with me. Do you think that I deserve this?" He said, "No! But his wife forced him!" After that letter I became quite desperate and so depressed. On Christmas Day Uncle David and Auntie Lily came to me. We had turkey and roast potatoes and we had a nice time.

One thing about the divorce case: when I had sent my letter to James I had asked for the Tema house on the breakdown of the marriage; but as he had been insulting me by suing me for adultery I now wanted the Ablempke house, where I was now living. I received a visit from James's sister Joan and his cousin Kofi Mills, the very vultures that I would have expected to grab everything, if James had died. They said to me, "If you are told to leave here, will you go?" so I said, "When I was arrested by twelve armed soldiers I was not afraid! So if you want a fight, I am ready!" They said, "Oh No!" so I said, "I'm just telling you before you start!" I never saw them again. One night I had a visitor and when he was leaving the gate was closed and I said to the watchman, Who closed the gate?" and he said, "Nketsiah" so I went and got my key to the padlock and found that it had been changed. I called Nketsiah and he had said to my visitor, "I'm Able-Seaman Nketsiah and I don't want to see you in this house again!" I told him to open the gate, which he did, and I said that I would speak to him in the morning! The next morning I called him and he said "That he was just trying to save my marriage!" I said, "Look, not even my mother or father can tell me what to do! If I wanted to have twenty men in the house for one week it's nobody's business!" (Not that I would!) I told him that I wanted him to leave the house and the boy's quarters! He went and got his father to come and beg for him; and because of poor Mary, who was crying, and the baby, I couldn't push it. Though, I never said that they could stay I didn't push their going either! But! I knew that I had an enemy in the camp!

On the morning of 31st December 1981, I listened to the news at six o'clock to make sure that there hadn't been a coup! Since 4th June this had always been my practice. The news was about this politician here! and that politician there! I left the house at 7.30 and went to the airport to see if there were any letters. The airport was deserted: no planes, no people! I was surprised. Then I saw two men walking across the tarmac. One said to the other, "Has there been any announcement yet?" I thought: announcement! What announcement? I had to go and collect a bag of rice from Ministry of Agric, which was for Doris and I, at the State Farms side. So we drove past Flagstaff House, Army HQ. All the soldiers were wearing tin hats and were heavily armed with sandbags banked. I said to Prosper the driver, "I wonder what's going on?" Anyway, we went to buy a gallon of engine oil from the HQ of GHIP and then on to collect the rice. We passed through the Ministry of Agric to see Doris. Then we arrived at a shop at Tudu. I was sitting with the owner of the shop when we heard a lot of shouting and cheering outside. When we went outside they were shouting "Rawlings is back!" We switched on the car radio and there, sure enough was Rawlings, shouting again! They had made a coup that morning! I suddenly realised that I was celebrating as this meant that there was no hope of James getting the amnesty, that they were all hoping Liman would give on the 6th March Independence Day celebrations. I said to myself, "Oh God! What has James done to me to make me turn so much against him?"

From there I went to James's cousin Elisabeth Shepard, who runs a small hotel, 'Via Veneto'. She had run out of gas and was expecting guests to dinner and she wanted to cook some chicken. So I offered to take them home and cook them for her and bring them back when they were ready. Lizzie came home with me. When the chickens were ready I took her back to the hotel. She wanted me to stay for dinner but I said, "No!" When I got home it was about 5.30pm and I met Doris and Mary and her children. Mary was the Commissioner's secretary in the Ministry of Agric. Her husband was an army colonel, and they lived at Teshie in The Barracks. They said that there was so much fighting at Teshie so they had to run away. So Doris said, "Valerie is on her own. You can go to her!" So she had brought her to me. The next minute, on the radio they announced a 6pm! Curfew. So Doris couldn't go home. We managed to ring a neighbour to inform her husband Kwesi and the children that she was okay and was with me, but couldn't get home. I was quite happy as it meant that I could see in the New Year with Doris. We were sitting talking until almost midnight when the most terrible shooting started; guns were going off all around! In fact, some sounded right outside the house! We drank a toast to the New Year and wished one another Happy New Year for

1982 and went to bed. The guns were still shooting, with sometimes silence and then a few shots here and there!

On the TV and radio the next day they announced the New Government. I had a couple of friends who were part of it. It was so nice not to have to worry that you were part of the coup. People in Ghana were getting so used to military coups and roadblocks that the attitude was: hurry up and get on with it and let us struggle to survive in our daily lives. As always after a coup, the petrol dries up so everybody becomes housebound for a while. Uncle David and Auntie Lily came to see if I was all right and I rang Glenda in Burma Camp, who was all right this time. When I rang Uncle Robert Gardiner and Auntie Linda, they said, "That there had been a lot of shooting at Military Hospital roundabout, near their house. They said, "That a whole lorry of soldiers had been blown up and there was blood all over the place!" Uncle Robert told me, "Not to go out!" which I didn't. There was a problem with my VW Sirocco car and I sent it to the workshop owned by the Lebanese man. The driver and the fitter were testing it when soldiers stopped them. (The driver, a new one called William, had been taken to Burma Camp during the 1979 coup and badly beaten) so when they said, "That they wanted the car he just gave it to them and ran! Everybody condemned him but I didn't; as it's only if you have been arrested by soldiers before that you know what it's all about! He came back to report that the car had been seized! The Lebanese man's cousin was a member of the Motorcycle Police and he went round to him and they went round and were able to trace the car to the Air Force station, so they arranged for me to go and collect it!

So I went through all the soldiers with their guns cocked and walls of sandbags, and all so nervous and insecure! The Station Commander, Wing Commander Kelly, gave me the keys and I said to him, "I would like some letter so I can show to any soldiers that this car is clear!" So he said, "That I would have to go to Revolutionary HQ at Gondar Barracks." So we went right into the HQ of the battlefront. We had to put our hands up at each point and explain what we were doing there! There were walls of sandbags everywhere. As we were crossing a soldier came up to me and said, "Madam! The Army

Commander is calling you!" It took me a few minutes to realise who the Army Commander was. And there he was, Brigadier Arnold Quainoo! He said, "Valerie, what are you doing here?" He was with Brigadier Nunoo-Mensah, who was a member of the Government of the PNDC (Provisional National Defence Council). They were both very nice to me and Arnold said, "That we should wait in his office whilst he called somebody to prepare the letter for me. There were several naval officers around that knew me and they all came to say hallo. It was a Sunday so there was not much work going on. Arnold offered me a beer but I don't drink beer and he promised me a bottle of champagne: which I haven't received as yet! Then the letter was prepared, which said that the owner of the vehicle had been cleared by the PNDC HQ and was free, to move freely around! And for that I was very grateful; as we were frequently, stopped by soldiers at roadblocks; so all I did was show them the letter and most said, "Correct!" and were very impressed and let us pass!

The divorce was at a standstill at this point, but one thing we discovered: the Head of Chambers, at Ofusu-Armaah's chambers, was lawyer Bossman, and he had been one of the lawyers dealing with AFRC cases. He said, "That as far as he remembered, all James's properties had been forfeit to the state, so he looked through his files and found the relevant documents. So I made an appeal through Ofusu-Armaah for the house to be released to the children and me. We had to apply to the Confiscated Assets Committee; which was doing brisk business again because of all the MP's cars and houses they had just confiscated.

Auntie Lily came with me and there were some really wild and rough soldiers there! But I was lucky, I put on a Ghanaian cloth and plaited my hair nicely, and one of the roughest looking soldiers, who seemed about six feet four came to me and said, "What do you want, Sweetheart?" So we explained my mission and he took me into an office and we started the ball rolling. It took several months before we actually received our letter of allocation. In the meantime James had got me to rent out the Teshie house, and early one morning the tenant came to say that the soldiers had come in the night and asked if he was from Social Security Bank, and when he had said, "No!"

he was told that he had to report to the State House, Confiscated Assets Committee with the landlord! So I went again with Auntie Lily. (God bless her for all her support in times of trouble!) When we got there they said that the house had been confiscated in 1979 and allocated to Social Security Bank. I told them that, I had not been in the country and was not aware of the confiscation. They believed me; but said, "That I must pay the rent I had received back to the Government. They gave me three months to pay. Luckily, I had put that money in the bank and had not used it, so was able to pay it back within the stipulated time! They then gave me a receipt and I was clear, or so I thought.

One day I came home and there had been a whole crowd of soldiers who had spoken to Adjoah, my housekeeper. She said, "That they had been very nasty, and said, "That I must report to State House again!" Just prior to this I had heard that James's sister Elizabeth had said, "That they were going to cancel my residence permit." (Being married to a Ghanaian gave you no rights of residence and you had to get a residence permit.) So I had gone to see Nunoo-Mensah, a PNDC member and he had sent me to see, Mr. Johnny Hansen, who was the Secretary for the Interior (or Home Secretary). I said to Uncle David Hansen, "Do you know Johnny Hansen?" and he said, "He's my brother. I will take you to him." We had gone and arranged about getting a residence permit in my own right, which we had done. (I have omitted to mention that I had started, (with Auntie Lily's help, a nursery school in the house, called First Step Nursery;) so I had applied for an immigrant quota for the school and filled it myself, so that headache was over! Johnny Hansen had invited me, Uncle David and Auntie Lily, who was also his cousin, to his official residence for drinks. He and I had become friends. This was May 1982. I had received no word from Leigh and as I wanted to leave him free to do his university course, I tried to put him out of my mind. Sometimes, I was successful; and then other days would come when I would long to see him, or I would see somebody who would remind me of him somehow. One day I was really startled: somebody called me and when I turned round I could have sworn that it was him! I thought that I was going mad at that time! Mr. Boateng was still a constant visitor and a very good friend and brother, but he was never at any time my lover. He used to tell me of his girlfriends and I would tell him of my adventures. He also encouraged me with the school as he also had a school in Tema. A lot of James's so called best friends, often turned up and tried it on with me. But I told them all the same thing, "I don't need lovers, you know. I need friends! So lets not spoil a beautiful friendship!" I will not mention any names but some of them tried more than once! One funny one: somebody known to me since 1964 when I first arrived in Takoradi, arrived in a big white Cadillac and in a white suit to say that he had been in love with me since that time, but didn't say anything because of James; I just told him the same thing: I need friends and not lovers, and he went on his way. I gave them only water to drink and kept them on the veranda outside!

Johnny Hansen was nine years older than me but I found a lot of strength in him and he was very nice too! I told him all about Leigh (not by name) and the divorce. He said, "I like you so much!" which was preferable to those who kept saying I love you when basically they meant I lust you! I got to know and like him before I discovered that he was a totally devoted socialist, a Ghanaian equivalent of Tony Benn! He even had his own political party 'The People's Revolutionary Party'. I was in India at that time and hadn't really heard about him. A very nice person and I was very happy and comfortable with him. He was of course very busy, but he used to ring me everyday, and the most delightful thing about him is his voice! On the telephone or addressing a rally he has the most charismatic voice! Anyway, when the soldiers came to the house and said I should report; I called him and he sent one of his aides and his police bodyguard with me to the State House. I took photocopies of the receipt for the repayment of the rent and the letter allocating the house to the children and me, which I showed to the soldier in charge and said, "If they want any more information, they should contact The Confiscated Assets Committee, who have finished with me!" James was always under the misapprehension, that I used Johnny to get me the house. It was not so! I had started and completed the proceedings before I met Johnny, and Johnny is a very honest lawyer;

who stuck by his socialist principles and never took a bribe from anyone whilst in office, or did anything wrong!

The loveliest thing from my friendship with Johnny was that I acquired four beautiful grown-up daughters! Johnny had twins of 21 and two other girls of 19 and 20. I got on very well with them and at Christmas of 1982 they gathered round the table and said, "Auntie Ekua (my Ghanaian name), Daddy has had many girlfriends but we didn't like them, but we like you and we would like Daddy to marry you when your divorce comes through!" I thought that was one of the loveliest compliments that I could receive. They were all very lovely, and like the sisters in *Little Women,* used to share all their clothes, etc. I love them and still to this day they are my treasured daughters even though now they are all 'big women'. We all got on so well I told them, "Even if I am not with your daddy, I will always be there for you wherever I am! and you will always be welcome to come to me, anytime, anywhere!"

They had never known their mother as Johnny had taken them all himself when they were very small. Their mother was a West Indian from Jamaica, but they had not seen her since the youngest, Ago, was six months, and they had lost all trace of her.

Let me describe them for you: Lizzie (Akwele, which means first born twin in Ga) was the elder twin and really beautiful. The only trouble with her is that she is shy with people that she doesn't know. She has a wonderful sense of fashion (taking after her grandmother Harriet, who was a dress-designer) and she is very generous and she gives herself. She would make somebody a lovely wife, as she is a good cook and a great little homemaker, arranging things with beautiful taste. Peggy (Akukor, the second twin) is also beautiful but different to Lizzie, she's much stronger and could lead and control the others. She also has a great flair for fashion and they all used to spend hours dressing and doing their hair, like any normal young ladies. They were not identical twins but you could see that they were sisters. The Gas, the tribe from Accra, has a special bond with twins and they even have a festival to celebrate twins. Frances (Tawiah, which means follow twins) was taller and slightly darker than the twins. She was much more sensitive and could easily end up in tears. Then Matilde, Ago, (Ago, which means after twins and after Tawiah) follows Tawiah. Matilde, a mischievous little elf, who was slimmer and the tallest of all! She would make a beautiful model as she looks like Iman. Her and Tawiah used to argue and she would reduce Tawiah to tears; then the next minute they would be best of friends again! So that was my instant family. God had separated me from my own children and I missed them so much, and gave me four beautiful girls who had never known their mother to fill my aching heart. Hamish my eldest son used to write to me very often but Rosina and Julien hardly at all! At times it used to upset me so much not to hear from them, as I had tried very hard to be a good mother to them. It was only because I didn't want to report their daddy about the beating that I had to leave them and stay away so long. I did think that they would be safe with him, as I knew that he loved them, and they were in the boarding schools as well.

As I mentioned earlier, I had started a nursery school in the house with the help of Auntie Lily. I employed three teachers and I had about fifty children registered though they didn't all come everyday. I cannot tell you how much I gained from those children spiritually. They fed me with great love. I loved them all and they all loved their white woman teacher. They came at 7.30am and left by 1pm, so apart from the times when I had to go round to find food and things I was with them everyday. I used to do 'round and round the garden like a teddy bear' with them and tickle the palms of their hands and under their arms. They would all queue up for me to do it to them and then break into peals of laughter. They were from age two up till six years. We used to teach them nursery rhymes; and the older ones the alphabet, numbers and how to write their names.

My friendship with Johnny had been had been very discreet and quiet. I only went to his official residence but saw no official visitors, always being in the upstairs study, and he came to me or we went to Uncle David and Auntie Lily. Johnny was told that because my husband was a wanted man, he should not be seen with me! So in March 1983, Johnny said to me. "Get dressed. We are going to the castle for a party!" So I dressed up in a beautiful yellow lace caftan, which I had made, and had my hair set in ringlets. One thing that Johnny had forgotten was that he was deputising for the Foreign Minister, who was travelling; so that night he was both Interior Minister and Foreign Minister. So as soon as we arrived he was whisked off to greet the Diplomatic guests. Myself, not being a stranger to Diplomatic functions, and being followed around by Johnny's policeman bodyguard (who was so proud to be guarding me), found some friends and acquaintances to talk too! There were many officers there too. Including the Army Commander, Arnold Quainoo. He said that I was looking lovely. The Air Force Commander too when he saw me said, "Oh! Where's your husband?" and I said, "Shh! I'm not with him any more, I am with Johnny!" I had a lovely evening and Johnny came to find me when it was time to go. I had enjoyed being back in society from which I had been excluded for four years!" The next day, Johnny took me to the Spanish Ambassador's residence. It was to say farewell to the British High Commissioner, Mr. Mellor, who was the same one who had helped me during the 1979 coup. As Johnny had always gone to parties alone! Everybody was very curious about me! I wore a white lace Ghanaian dress with a slit skirt and a Nigerian style top, and I tied a turban on my head and wore my pearl earrings, the only ones left of my jewellery. The American Ambassador was the most curious; I told him that my name was Valerie, and nothing more! Through a mix-up at the table I ended up the chief lady guest, next in line to the British High Commissioner's wife. I sat on the left hand of the Spanish Ambassador, with the American Ambassador at my left. They were very interested that I had a nursery school and I didn't tell them much else than that! Johnny later told me that the American Ambassador had asked him "Where did you get that beautiful woman?" From then on I went to all receptions and dinners with Johnny: the Egyptians, the Australians, the Canadians, the Hungarians, Czechoslovakians. I had a lovely time as I really seem to thrive in the International Diplomatic set, as I have always had a fascination for all things foreign. The Chinese Ambassador's wife became a good friend though she couldn't speak a word of English and we did all our talking through her interpreter, who was really fluent in English and so charming that you didn't feel that you were not actually talking directly to the Ambassador's wife. I also picked up a few words in Mandarin. But my real darling was the Hungarian Ambassador's wife, who was so lovely, and we used to go to the Hungarians very often. We also went to the Indians, and the Ethiopians. The Ethiopian Ambassador was married to a Swedish lady who was also lovely. The Yugoslavian Ambassador and his wife were also good friends of Johnny. The wife was a poet and a mystic, and she gave me one of her books to read. Johnny had never had a hostess before and I arranged lunches in Johnny's own house and we entertained: the Indians, Ethiopians, Yugoslavs, Czechoslovakians and Hungarians for formal lunches. We gave them Ghanaian food. The girls dressed up and helped me serve the food and I taught them how to set the table etc. and Johnny was very happy!

One day when I went to visit Johnny in the official house, I found a gentleman sitting in the chair, who looked very much like Johnny with the white beard, though slightly darker than Johnny's. He introduced himself as Emmanuel, Dr. Hansen. He was Johnny's cousin and had come on a visit from England. He was a Professor, at Durham University, where he taught Political Studies. He was very nice and we got on instantly. He was a vegetarian and a diabetic so I arranged and cooked him many special dishes. Johnny was practising French and he said to me, "Etes vous Anglais?" and I replied, "Non, je suis Ecossaise!" Emmanuel thought that was great and from then on he called me Ecossaise (which means Scottish).

One day I was at home and Adjoa my housekeeper said, "Madam! Uncle Johnny's got a new post!" I said, "No! as I have just left him, and he didn't say anything. I think that it is Uncle Emmanuel!" And sure enough they had made Emmanuel 'the 'Secretary to the Cabinet' for the Government. Poor Emmanuel! He hadn't been able to tell his wife Elaine, who was English and was in London with their children Mameanna and Ashia (now known as Ashia Hansen, who broke the world record for the triple jump in 1998, and won many more honours besides). Another time I was with Johnny in the house and Emmanuel came in with a paper. He said, "Oh! your husband's in the paper, making a coup!" I laughed and said, "Oh yes?" He said, "You think I'm joking? See!" And when I looked in the middle pages, sure enough, there was James's name along with Jim Addoo and others! I must state that, that was the first time that

I knew of that, and I certainly didn't denounce him to the Ghana Government. As James later alleged! I didn't even know what he was up to at that time and didn't even care, as long as he finished with the divorce, which seemed to be at a complete standstill! I had to get a lawyer in England by post, as James was concentrating on the case there, as he couldn't come to Ghana at all.

One of the most delightful people that I met through Johnny was his father, Frank Gilbert Hansen. He was 87 years old when I met him, and a perfect gentleman of the old school; he used to wear top hat and tails when he was a young man. He lived on his own in a nice little bungalow and he did his own cooking, washing and cleaning. His mind was so sharp and he was up-to-date on all subjects so it was a pleasure to converse with him. He had a lovely collection of books locked up in a beautiful cabinet, and one day when I went with Johnny I asked if I could borrow some? And he said, "Yes, certainly, I should come and help myself!" When we got outside Johnny said to me, "The old man likes you; he never lends his books to anyone!" The old man used to make the most delicious Melba toast and I asked Johnny to ask him if he would teach me how to make it. (The old man used to make the toast for the girls to take to school with them and everybody called it 'Grandpa's Toast'.) He said, "Yes, but I should buy him one bottle of gin, whiskey and brandy!" He later said, "That he was joking about that!" I made a special trip to see the old man and he taught me how to make the toast. Then I made some myself at home and sent it to him, to taste and approve. He wrote me a 'Certificate of Toast Making' in his beautiful copperplate handwriting, which would put many a youngster to shame. I enjoyed many delightful days of conversation with him. Johnny's mother Harriet Hansen was also a very interesting lady. A very devout Jehovah Witness; she was a dress designer, milliner and caterer, having trained in Edinburgh, Scotland. She was always trying to make new recipes using cassava and beans and other ingredients. She used to make cakes and sell them to Kingsway Stores. She was very professional, very eager, and enthusiastic, and a bit overpowering times. The old man and she did not get along and they had split up many years before, but were still married.

In 1982/83 Ghana had a severe drought, and people were hoarding food, so what there was became very expensive; and people couldn't live on their salaries. The nursery had been doing well and I was able to pay the staff and run the house and the car, but things now became extremely difficult. There was a severe petrol shortage and it was rationed and you had to have coupons. Even with the coupons, sometimes you had to queue for three days! In June 1983 Johnny told the Government. That he couldn't work with them anymore, and he was removed from office. He was going to a Peace conference in Prague and as he was going to be away for six weeks, he asked me to stay with the girls in his own house. I did and it was a wonderful opportunity to really get to know the girls and their cousin Tina, Johnny's sister's daughter. We all got on really well; I took my video there and we watched films and we saved our petrol coupons so we could go out, and we really enjoyed ourselves. Johnny spent longer than expected and when he came back I stayed with him in the house and tried to find someone to rent my house. I enjoyed Johnny's company and we were both very comfortable together; he would read his political books and I would read mine, mostly biographies and historical novels.

The lawyer in England wrote asking if I would agree to the divorce on two years separation; and thinking that James was at last relenting, I agreed! Then all the happy atmosphere in the house was changed by Johnny's sister Clara, who was Mrs. Boham and married to a distant cousin of James's who worked with the railways. She had been in England and when she returned and saw how happy the girls were with me, and me in Johnny's house, caused trouble between the girls and me. I was trying to protect them all but she used it against me! So our beautiful harmonious life was disrupted. I had brought a lot of things to Johnny's house and created a home; which was not so before, and I fed Johnny for almost a year, as he did not receive any salary and could not continue with his legal work whilst in office. All of this, Johnny himself acknowledges; but I think that his sister thought that he was giving me money though that was not the case as I supported myself! Johnny himself supported me against his sister; but, like I said, the atmosphere was not the same!

One day in February, we were going to Tema Fishing Harbour to get fish and when we reached the Nungua police barrier and turned the corner, a white Peugeot car was also turning coming from Tema. When I looked, there was my love, Leigh, sitting in the car. He looked at me and smiled! I made out that I hadn't seen him; but my heart stopped beating again! When I got to the harbour, I met Doris and Mary, who were also there to collect fish. I told Doris that I had seen Leigh on the way coming. She said, "Are you sure?" and I said, "Yes!" Then I was in dreamland again. When we were returning to Accra, Johnny said, "That he would call in at his office on the way home. Then again I saw Leigh. He turned the corner and he put his head out of the window, waving to me, and I waved back! I was so shattered. All the old feelings came back; he looked so handsome and lovely. When I got home and Johnny had left to go back to the office. I sat down and cried, "How could he come to Ghana and not come and find me? Mr. Boateng knew where I was!" The next day, I met Mr. Boateng, who was on his way to the Ashanti region. I said, "I saw him!" He said, "I know. He told me!" I told him that I loved him even more if that were possible and I must see him!" He said, "He's going to London tonight!" I told Mr. Boateng that I had just received word, that I had got the Decree Nisi, and the Absolute should be through in six weeks and that I would go to London by April! I was so shattered that I couldn't eat for a week.

The next surprise was that one day, I was sitting in the house with Johnny's mother and who should walk in the door but my beloved Hamish; my darling, lovely Hamish! I was so happy. He had grown so much. James had sent him to Mr. Brenya, and Mr. Brenya had sent him to me! But the wicked thing that James did! All the time that Hamish had wanted to come James wouldn't let him; but; when he knew that I would have to come to London to finish things. He sent Hamish to Ghana so that he could not be in London to give me the help that I would need! When I was leaving I asked Hamish, "Where do you want to stay?" and he said with Uncle Johnny as he liked him!" So I told him, "That I was not sure if I would come back here!" He said, "It didn't matter, he would stay with uncle Johnny as he liked him!" Johnny's twin daughters had also left for London two weeks before I left.

Chapter Eleven

BRITAIN
1984-1985

So, thinking that I was at last a free woman, I came to London to sort out the settlement. I decided the whole thing in a rush, so Mummy didn't even know that I was coming, just that I would be coming sometime! When I got to London Airport my first thought was of Leigh, but I didn't have his new phone number, and I decided that I mustn't contact him till all was absolutely over. I took the Underground to King's Cross Station, and then the train to Hitchin in Hertfordshire, where Mummy was staying, and got there, by Noon. Mummy was staying in 'The Biggin', which was built in 1568 and is four hundred years old. It used to be a place where the monks stayed before the dissolution of the monasteries. It is on the river and there are ducks swimming around; it was very pretty. I arrived on 1st May 1984 and it was very hot, the sun was shining and all the blossoms were out! I was so pleased to see Mummy, but I was also very shocked as she had aged a great deal; and she had had a bout of flu and was very weak and could hardly walk, only very slowly! She was happy to see me and had rushed out to buy so many things which she knew that I liked. I got her Complan and started to feed her up and slowly she improved. I also met Mrs. Proctor, who had helped Mummy so much in the difficult time when she first moved in. The Biggin should be a museum and people should not live there! So Mummy and I arranged to see the lawyer and I met her for the first time. From her letters I had pictured her as being fair; and she was, and I liked her. But I got a shock.

I was not free, as I had imagined! The Absolute would only be given with the settlement and James was fighting all the way! In Ghana, on Good Friday, I had slaughtered a sheep; but it was not over yet, this long, terrible divorce battle! From the lawyers I went to Rosina's school to see her. She came down the stairs, saw Mummy and then saw me and rushed over and held me tight; she was so pleased to see me. She took us up to her room and her friends all came in: Nouha, Pretty and all. We had a lovely chat and then I said, "That I was going to see Julien!" I went to Julien's room and he was sleeping. He woke up and sat up, looked at me and rubbed his eyes, then he hugged me and said, approvingly, "You're looking good!" We had a long chat and then he rang a cab and we went back to Hitchin.

In August we went up to Scotland to see Auntie Vi. She had just had another operation on her ankle for the arthritis. The weather was marvellous and we didn't go anywhere, just sat in the garden for ten days. Norman, my cousin, and Margaret his wife came with their two children, Leslie and Lorna; and Uncle Andrew and Auntie Jessie and my cousin Maurice; and my cousin Jean looking as lovely as ever. After a few days' peace in a real home once again, in my hometown, eating my sliced sausage and soft rolls, and the lovely round pies; and listening to the lovely accent, which always seemed to rejuvenate me; we returned to Hitchin and trouble! One of the old biddies in the place, (who had no joy left in her life,) decided to cause trouble and report me: Mummy was not supposed to have visitors in the place, but my sister Laraine had stayed for six months and there was no trouble. We got a letter from the landlords saying that I must leave! I had nowhere to go. The funny thing I discovered is that the more you have in life, the more people want to do for you or give you free! But when you are really in need, nobody wants to know! I went to the solicitor and told her what had happened and I also told her that I intended to go back to the house in Letchworth as I was part-owner of the house. James had changed the locks. I went to the police and they advised me that I was also entitled to change the locks and move in! So I went to the builders and got them to come and change them. I also put locks on all the bedroom doors. I didn't break in; I got in with a key! How I got that key? I will not disclose in order to protect the innocent! Mummy and I went to 21 Blackmore, Lordship Estate, Letchworth at 2pm. We met nobody in the house! We had no idea, whether James was in the country or in Nigeria? When we got to the house we saw some bags with Lagos tags on them and then we saw the previous day's newspaper on the kitchen table, after the builders had finished. They assured me that nobody could get in! Mummy and I sat and waited; we had no idea whether James would come or not! We made tea and waited, scared stiff! At about 10pm we went and lay down on the bed fully clothed. At 11.45 we heard a car and saw James and two women get out. He came and found the porch door locked! The next thing I saw was him, breaking the porch door with a hammer! Where he got it from I don't know, maybe the car? I dialed 999 and said, That somebody was breaking in! The next thing we heard was the front door smash. Luckily I had put a lock on the bedroom door. I put a chair against it and called the police again. They said, "That a car was on the way and should at the house by now! The next minute James was smashing the bedroom door! I said, "James! I have called the police and they are coming!" He went down the stairs; I think the police had then arrived. After a while I started banging on the door and shouting, "Help! Police!" as I didn't want to come out if they were not there! They called out to me and I opened the door and went downstairs. In the kitchen I saw two police, one male and one female; also James and two Ghanaian women. I said, "I am the owner of this house and I have every right to be here!" The policeman asked, "If I could wait upstairs and he would come," so I did! They spoke to James and then they came up. I told them about the divorce and the fact that I had to leave Mummy's place and had nowhere to go! (I also told them that I had consulted the police and been told that I had every right to change the locks.) They asked James, "If he would leave!" and he said, "No!" They told him that I had as much right to stay there as him! He said, "That I could stay but Mummy should go!" The policeman told him that as he had his guests, I was also entitled to have whoever

I wanted in the house! Then whatever he said to the policeman, the policeman said, "Madam, if you have anywhere that you can stay, I advise you to leave! As I cannot guarantee your safety!" If a policeman tells you that in England you would be a fool to ignore it! I asked them if they would wait for me until a cab came. And so at 1.30am I left the house back to The Biggin. Absolutely shattered!

First thing in the morning Mummy and I went to the lawyer to get an injunction to get me back in the house. The lawyer's relation had just died and she couldn't come to court! She had just briefed a barrister who was not really conversant with the case! So we arranged to meet at the court before the hearing. Unfortunately, James's lawyer produced a letter, I had written to Rosina, which had stolen from her, saying that I was living with Johnny as his wife! That letter completely stumped me! They said, "That he, James, would agree to me staying in the house with him but they could not put him out! I said, "If that was the case then I couldn't go there as there was no way that an injunction could help me when he was drunk!" The barrister said to me, "How do you know that he is still drinking?" and I said, "When I went to the house there was an empty bottle of Remy Martin and a full bottle of vodka and many empty beer cans in the rubbish!" So an injunction was made that he should not molest me and I should not molest him! (big joke!) and I was back at square one with nowhere to go!

I decided to put my pride in my pocket and go and see my godmother, Auntie Iris, my father's sister. James had caused trouble between us, (his motto was divide and rule!) but I thought that in the circumstances 'blood would be thicker than water!' We went to see her and asked if I could stay there, and showed her the letter from Mummy's landlords, the Hitchin Trust', a charitable organisation. Saying that they would evict Mummy as well if I didn't leave! Now since Uncle Derek had died, Auntie Iris had got a new man friend in her life who was younger than her; so I don't know her reason, But she said, "No!" She said that her family would be angry with her if she helped me, and that she needed the room for her plants!

Christmas 1984

I had kept in contact with Bried Amamoo by letter and she was in London and had just moved to a new house in Dollis Hill. She had written to invite Mummy and me to come on Christmas Day for dinner. Also, one time when I visited Jimmy and Betty Prempeh, John Owusu had been there and had given me their new address at Cricklewood. I told Rosina that we – Mummy and I – would be staying at Annette's at Christmas as Annette had gone to Barbados, and she was welcome to come any time that she liked. So just before Christmas she arrived. She said, "That her daddy had rang from Lagos and been nasty to her on the phone so she decided to leave before he came back. On Christmas Day at about 11am, Volda rang and invited us all for lunch. I told her that we had already been invited to Bried's for the evening so if we came, we couldn't eat very much. So John came and took us to their house. Rosina, Mummy and I: we had a lovely time. Jimmy and Betty came with Annabel their daughter, and Volda's brother Louis. We then got a mini-cab and went to Bried and Joseph's. There were Samia and Suzie, Bried's daughters, now very lovely sophisticated young ladies just having finished school and now both at Buckingham University. Samia's boyfriend Edrich was also there as his parents were Dutch diplomats and were away at the time. Breid made a beautiful table with lovely glasses, wine, and everything was perfect and we had a lovely evening.

I then suggested to Rosina that as the first of January was her daddy's birthday and she had spent Christmas with me, she should go and spend New Years Day with her Daddy. So she agreed and left the Friday after Christmas. We were quite amazed on Sunday evening to find her back. She said, "That the whole two days she was there her Daddy didn't talk to her and so on Sunday she had told Julien that she was leaving and her daddy didn't even take her to the station!" On New Year's Eve Mummy and I were invited to a friend of mine and his wife's at Chalk Hill Estate. Freddy Green was Auntie Lizzie of Via Veneto Hotel in Accra's nephew, and I had met him in Ghana when he was there on a visit, and somebody had given him my number. (I later found out that it was Jimmy) and he had rung me and invited Mummy and me home to meet his wife; whose name was Gem and who is a West Indian from Jamaica, a lovely tall lady. They had two boys with the lovely names Gavin and Jason. Freddy's father was Scottish and it was his mother who was related to Auntie Lizzie. Rosina at first didn't want to come as she didn't know them, but Freddy persuaded her to come and she liked Gem and had a lovely time playing all the video films that she liked, even when I wanted to leave! She didn't want to come! Gem prepared us a lovely meal and we had a very enjoyable day. We returned home just before midnight on New Year's Day 1985 and we all drank ginger wine and had shortbread, which is a very Scottish, thing, and toasted ourselves 'Happy New Year'. In the morning my darling Leigh rang and, wished me, "Happy New Year, Darling. I hope all your dreams come true!" I couldn't talk as Rosina was there! So Rosina stayed until just before Annette returned. I had promised Annette that I would meet her at Gatwick Airport with her boots, coat and scarf as she had left wearing only a light linen suit. The day that she was due to return I looked out of the window and got a big shock: thick snow, really thick, had fallen in the night; but I had to go to Gatwick to meet her, as she had no coat! Rosina, Mummy and I got the bus to Kilburn Park Station and then the Underground to Victoria. At Victoria there were hardly any trains running and they kept repeating, "Unless your journey is absolutely necessary, please don't travel!" The Gatwick Express was delayed and there were so many people waiting on the platform. Anyway, we waited and eventually got on the train, which was standing room only, just like the Underground. When we got to the Gatwick Station there were so many people standing on the escalator with suitcases that people started falling on top of one another, so they had to stop the escalator. We discovered that the airport was closed but we decided to wait. We tried to find something to eat but all we could find was a sticky bun and a cup of tea as there were thousands of people there! Eventually, after three hours, the airport was open and Annette's flight came in; most of the passengers came out and there was no Annette! What was happening? Suddenly she came rushing out! She had been stopped by customs and had been caught with eight bottles of rum that she hadn't declared! Annette asked me to come in with her to the customs, which I did; but the customs people asked me to leave. Rosina and Mummy waited for what seemed ages then my name, Ms Valerie Brown, was called over the tannoy and would I please go to the information desk! One customs officer informed me that they were going to fine Annette ninety pounds so asked if I could pay it? I only had twenty pounds so Rosina offered to pay with a cheque; but Annette declined so she was fined only forty pounds but allowed only one bottle of rum! So finally she was out! It was still snowing and freezing. Rosina left us at Gatwick to return to Thornton Heath, where she was staying and studying at Croydon College. Mummy, Annette and I went to Victoria. Annette rang her dad, a black cab driver, and he picked us to Annette's flat. We had a cup of tea whilst we waited for him and then he took us to Annette's flat where we collected our things, and he dropped us at Kings Cross Station where we got our train back to Hitchin and 'The Biggin'. The snow was thick on the ground and it was freezing. The next week I went up to spend the weekend with Annette, to hear all about her trip; and her grandmother, who was ninety years old and had brought Annette up until she was twelve when Annette returned to England with her sister Margaret.

Just before Christmas I had sent a Christmas card to Leigh with Annette's phone number and nothing else. I told her that if his wife rang she would say that she knew nothing about it! And if Leigh himself rang she should give him Mummy's number at 'The Biggin'. He had called me and also he had rung on New Years Day as I mentioned before, but I couldn't speak to him because Rosina was there! Now at Annette's he came one night and picked me in his white Mercedes-Benz car, and we parked somewhere and then he was saying, "Is it really you, Darling? I have missed you so!" and I said, "Yes! And I have missed you too!" and then he said, "Oh God! how much I love you!" And then we were lost in a wonderful embrace and such wonderful kisses and we went on and on for hours. Because he had somebody staying at his house at the time and Annette only had a bedsit, we were not able to make love fully, but his kisses meant the whole world to me. He took me back to Annette's and promised to come and take me to Hitchin the following evening. He came the following day and took me back to Hitchin and then told me that he was going to Ghana the following week. I was devastated and happy at the same time; happy because I had seen him, and devastated because we never seemed to be in the same continent at the same time! His wife was staying in England and that gave me consolation, as neither of us could have him, while he was in Ghana. I could talk to him when I could get through. We talked more than any married couple living together and I told him all my problems and he told me all his hopes and dreams. He was worried because I had nowhere to stay but was unable to help with that. So after a long kissing session he left me at The Biggin with Mummy and drove away. Mummy had asked many friends of hers from the church if they had a room for me to stay, but to no avail. One even told mummy that I was far too attractive and she couldn't trust her husband with me! So once more I went back to my Auntie Iris, my godmother! (but she was no fairy godmother!) She was not prepared to help even though she had three bedrooms and it was only her, and her boyfriend; she was not prepared to help when I was in dire trouble! So I thanked her and we left, as she was desperate that we should leave before her man got home! From a child I had always loved Auntie Iris and had bought the house in Letchworth because of her; but because James had caused trouble, which I was not a part of, she could only kick me when I was down! I suppose it's because she never had a child of her own, so she didn't have the maternal instinct! I know that if Uncle Derek had been alive, He would never have turned me out, Whatever had happened in the past! I said to Mummy, "Never mind!" At least she can't say, "If you had come to me I would have taken you in." So, what to do now? Just then I had a call from Frank Okyne, the Managing Director of Ghana Airways. He was inviting me to come and help him do some shopping for his wife so I packed my bags and left Mummy's and went to meet him in his hotel. He took me to his cousin's place for dinner and then dropped me at Annette's at Kilburn Park. Annette had another friend staying with her so the next day, Frank collected me and took me to Rosina's at Thornton Heath. Rosina was then nineteen years old, my lovely daughter. I stayed with her a couple of days but my lawyer advised that if I remained with her I would cut her off from her daddy, which would not be fair on her. Johnny had a good friend who was also John Owusu's brother (cousin, there is no distinction in Ghana, a cousin is a brother and your grandmother's sister is also your grandmother) - Jimmy Prempeh, and his wife Betty. I rang them and they said, "That I should come and stay with them!" They were buying a house and I could have a room in the house! So I went to stay with them and baby Annabel. They looked after me well, making me fu-fu and ground rice, my favourites. On 27th February 1985 I moved into a room at their house at Craven Park! It was the very first time in my life that I had ever rented a room and stayed on my own! There were four other rooms, and they were rented by Betty's cousin Joe, and Jimmy's brother Addo, and Ester his niece. Later, another Ghanaian couple called Joe and Bea came and joined us! We all got on very well in the house.

When we went to court in November, James's lawyer said, "That they would be bringing an affidavit! It took until May before he brought it! and it was full of all sorts of lies! He said, "That he had been sending me one hundred pounds sterling a week, whilst I was in Ghana, which was not true; and I used the money to build Leigh's house, which was not true, apart from once arranging one hundred bags of cement for Leigh, for which he paid! I don't even know where Leigh's house is even up to this day! It's somewhere in Nungua, so he told me, but I've never been there! So how I could have been building it, I don't know! After a lot of investigation I prepared a reply affidavit and we are now awaiting a reply to that! Mummy came to stay with me here and Rosina came and stayed a couple of nights. Julien also visited a couple of times. They always came when James was not in the country but as soon as he was back they stopped coming, as if they were afraid that he would know or something! It's really sad and painful to know that you have children and yet not see them! Some days I got so depressed, if I started thinking about them, especially Julien. I remember when he was younger he wouldn't let me breathe; he was with me every minute, glued to me like an extra limb! Mummy! Mummy! Mummy! Up until he was two I never had a full night's sleep! He was always up calling Mummy! Mummy! Mummy! I used to be so tired; I would just get him off to sleep and crawl back to bed and he would be up again! After all that, he now doesn't want to know me! I ring and ring the place where he is staying, but as they are friends of James's and I have not been invited there, I don't go there. So I try and ring and send the occasional note and hope that he will ring me or come and visit me; but his time is only for his friends. He says that, "He doesn't want to be involved in the divorce! He doesn't realise that as the only child under age he is totally involved! As I wasn't in the country when the Decree Nisi was granted, even though his daddy was not in the country either, he was granted custody, and I was supposed to have reasonable access, which his daddy did not grant! That is why I am condemned to sit it out to the bitter end in this shabby room, with no heating apart from my own electric convector heater or a gas cylinder fire that is too expensive to run. Even in my parents' home at Charlton we always had constant gas heating as my father worked for SEGAS, so got a discount. People, including James's cousin Hector, used to come to our house to get warm!

Betty, the landlord's wife, said, "That she was going to church and would I accompany her?" So I agreed. We went to a church at Surrey Square, south London: The Church of the Lord, Aladura. It is an African Pentecostal Church. I loved the atmosphere – so happy, not anything funny at all. It is a pure Christian church but with a very friendly, feeling. I loved the singing and, for the first time in a long while, felt uplifted! So Betty and I started going every two weeks or once a month when Betty, who is a theatre sister and works nights, had her free Sunday. We used to go with Annabel, who also enjoyed it so much and would be clapping. They got a new church at Caledonian Road near King's Cross, and we started gong there. The Primate of the church, Dr. Adejobi, came from Nigeria for the inauguration of the new church. Betty and I met him and he invited us to his house. Mummy was visiting me at the time and came with us to the church, though she felt that it was too noisy for her as everybody claps their hands when they sing. One Sunday I wanted to go to church and Mummy and I went over to collect Betty. But Betty was ill so she couldn't come.

Mummy said, "That she didn't want to wait for the bus to the Underground station so we should get a mini-cab. So we went to the mini-cab office, as Betty's phone wasn't working. I got in the cab and I could see that the driver was an African, so I asked, "Where do you come from?" and he said, "Ghana!" I said, "I lived in Ghana for twenty years!" and we started talking. He said to me, "Where are you going?" so I said, "The tube station!" He said, "No, when you get to the tube station you will take the train somewhere?" I said, "I can't afford to take you where I am going." He said, "This is my car and my petrol and I will take you anywhere you want to go, without charging you!" I couldn't believe my ears, after so many knocks, so I said, "I'm going to Caledonian Road." So he took us there and then he said, "What time do you close?" and I was amazed again. He said, "That he would come and collect us and take us home!" On the way coming home we were talking and discovered that we had mutual friends; he had recognised me as he used to be with the Ghana Foreign Service. He was doing a Doctorate of Law at London University, and he showed me his university identity card for the Law Faculty. When we got home we invited him in for a cup of tea, and by this time we had discovered that his name was Sam. He was quite shocked to see where I was living, We had a nice long chat and then he went on his way. He said, "That anywhere I want to go I must let him know and he would take me!" I couldn't believe such kindness! When he was gone I had a little weep, because nobody had shown me such kindness for a long time, and I was truly fed-up waiting for buses in the freezing winds! Mummy too was amazed! The next Friday he rang and asked me, "If I was going to church on Sunday?" I was very surprised and grateful, as I probably would not have rung him! He duly collected Mummy and me, and took us to collect Betty on the way, and came back and collected us afterwards! Now Mummy was going home to Hitchin immediately after the church so I asked Sam to take us to King's Cross Station. We all went and had a cup of tea and a sandwich in the buffet and then Sam said, "That he didn't like the idea of Mummy going on the train alone, so he would drive her to Hitchin!" Well, we were totally overwhelmed again. So we dropped

Betty at a convenient bus stop, as she had to get home for Annabel, and took Mummy to The Biggin, in Hitchin.

On the way back I told Sam all about my divorce, and he said, "That he would like to see the affidavit as he had specialised in Family Law for his Masters!" So when we reached the house I gave him all the affidavits I had and he took them home to study and to give me any advice that he could. He also said, "That he was prepared to see my lawyer and answer any questions about Ghana she may have." In the meantime we were drawing up another affidavit as when we went to court the previous November James's lawyer had said, "That they would be bringing another affidavit, which had not materialised until April–May. I had written to Mr. Brenya, Mr. Boateng and Leigh to refute certain allegations that James had made, but received no replies; so I was not sure if the letters had reached their targets, as the post in Ghana was not hundred percent reliable! So we decided to go ahead without them in the hope that we may receive something from them at a later date. Sam happened to have been born on the same day as me, 10th May 1943, so was one year older than me. We found that we had many interests in common. He was seriously studying; he would even study all night and then spend the whole morning in the Law Library. Sometimes I wouldn't see him for days and then he would pop in for a cup of tea; and he would come and take me to Betty's every two weeks to go to church. As Betty was a night nurse (theatre sister) at Charing Cross Hospital, so she worked one week on and one week off. So the week that she worked I didn't go to church as it was quite far and I wasn't too happy going on my own as Betty had taken me there. One Sunday when I went there I met an old friend from 1963. James Armaah, Kwesi Armaah's brother (Kwesi Armaah had been Ghana's Ambassador to London in the sixties) and Daniel Blay-Afful's cousin. (We had our engagement party in his house in London and he later married James's niece Julie.) So that was a pleasant surprise!

At Christmas time, December 1984, I had written a letter to my French penfriend Guy as I had heard from Mummy that his parents had both died within a couple of months of each other. I received a pleasant letter back, so I wrote and told him about how

I got pregnant with Hamish and had to get married. (I had previously told him that I was married but not the reason why!) I then told him about the divorce. One day I was sitting in my room on a Saturday night waiting for '*Dynasty*' to come on, when the phone rang and a voice said, "Valerie?" I said, "Yes!" and he said, "It's Guy!" I said, "Guy! where are you?" and he said, "I'm in Tahiti!" So we talked for about half an hour. He told me of his wife and children – he had three. He said, "That he would come to France for a holiday and would like us to meet once again!" So that was a lovely surprise and certainly lifted my spirits. Life was pretty boring, just waiting for the settlement to be over, mostly reading, writing and sleeping. Also I did a lot of praying, meditation and fasting. One thing with Rosina and Julien: when their daddy was out of the country they would come to me, but when he was in England they deserted me! I was really sad and used to cry a lot thinking of them. It was only faithful Hamish, who used to write about every five days, unless he was studying hard for his exams! Hamish said, "That he was really happy in Ghana," and I was really happy for him, because his daddy had made him lose all confidence in himself and he was now regaining his real nature. One thing that Rosina and Julien don't realise is that their daddy will only want them and give them money until this divorce is over, so that I get as little as possible! But when it's over and one of his Ghanaian women gets her claws on him and gets herself pregnant, he will ditch them like a ton of bricks! Not that he would want to, but the woman would want all the money for herself, her child and her family!

But I put all my trust in 'God;' he will not put me to shame! I make no plans for the future until all is over and I'm truly free!! Life begins at forty, so they say, so I am just beginning to walk right now! I hope that the mistakes and sufferings of the last forty years will make me wiser and more able to begin the new life; which will start as soon as I am free? I hope to be alive, fit and well at eighty years, so I can write a book about the next forty years and that I will not make the same mistakes! Who knows? But God! Lets wait and see!

Keith Miller 1985

Mummy rang me to say that my Auntie Edie, my father's stepsister, had rung her to tell her that my cousin Roderick Miller had died of a heart attack. I wrote a sympathy card to Uncle bill and Auntie Freda, and a note to say that I would like to see Keith again; as I wouldn't like to hear that he had died and I had not seen him for years, after all the time that we spent together as children. I put my number in the note and a few days later Keith rang, and we arranged for him to come and see me. He arrived and I think that he was pleasantly surprised to see that I was not fat and forty. He, also, was not looking too bad! He worked in a casino so worked nights. We had a good laugh talking about old times. He could always make me laugh as he was full of fun – do you remember this? and do you remember that? Keith had also had to get married almost the same time as me, and he had three daughters, and was also divorced. He had, had a vasectomy about the same time that I was sterilized and he told me his experience of that! very painful!

I was telling him about how James was keeping the children from me and he said, "Lets go and see your daughter now!" So he drove me over to Croyden to see Rosina. She was very pleased to see us, as were all the students in the house. They made us tea and invited us to go to a party with them. We refused and we drove around a bit and then Keith took me home and we had another cup of tea and then he said, "Your bed's so comfortable, I think I'll have a kip there!" so I said, "Okay! No problem!" We had so many memories to share and we had got up to a lot of mischief together as children. One funny thing that he told me: he said, "That he was about 18 years old and he went to the pub at the top of the road, with his brother Rod, and this boy came in and he was talking about this girl who was so free and easy, and he was just waiting for her parents to go out, to go and have a bit! Keith said, "Oh yeh! What's her name?" and the boy said, "Valerie Brown!" So Keith thought: My God! I'll wait and have it out with her. So he waited and the girl came, and it wasn't me, but another Valerie Brown who lived in the flats at the top of the road! Keith said, "Boy! was I relieved!" So Keith re-entered my life, though we didn't see much of each other as he was working all night and I used to sleep early; and when he had some time off he used to spend it with his daughters, he was very close too.

Rodney Mulliner 1985

One day in June, I was watching BBC1 on a Sunday evening and a new programme was coming on: an Australian film '*For the Term of His Natural Life*' and the actors' names were rolling, when I saw the name Rod Mulliner. I thought: it can't be! But yes it was! And there was my dear Rodney, after twenty years. He played an English officer who was really bad to the prisoners. It was lovely to see him after more than twenty years, looking so well and acting really well. After that, I saw him in a couple of other Australian films. Later I saw 'Mulliner Castings' on several Australian programmes and wondered if that was him? Mummy was soon on the phone and asking me, "Did I see Rodney?" Mummy had always loved Rodney. He used to doff his hat to her and say, "Good morning, Mrs. Brown." He always wore his hat and his coat like a cloak, and had an Elvis quiff, which he used to drop over his face when he wanted. He was like some great Shakespearean actor and he was only 19 years then! Good luck to him in all he undertakes!

July 1985

The latest crisis! I rang Rosina on Wednesday, as I had waited for her to come for over six weeks. As she was on holidays she had gone to stay with Auntie Volda for a week, and then back home to Daddy in Letchworth and then back to Auntie Volda. When I asked her why she hadn't rung me, she said, "No particular reason!" That hurt a lot! Then she said, "Julien's going to America on Friday!" just like that, as if it was a casual school-friend or something, not my baby, my youngest son! I said, "Where is he?" She said, "That she didn't know the number of the place where he was staying!" I put the phone down and my stomach started turning. I felt a pain, where, I can't say.

But a pain! In the heart I suspect! Annette had gone to Italy with her Italian friend Christina, so I was going to stay at her place, to watch it for her until she got back.

I watched the last episode of 'Dallas' for the current season (in which Bobby died!) and then Sam came to take me to Annette's. He had a new car that day, a lovely cream one. I told him that I wasn't feeling well, and what Rosina had said. On the way to Annette's, I started feeling hot and shivery and then I realised that I was going to vomit. Sam wanted to take me to the hospital. I said, "Yes!" then "No!" We had to stop the car for me to vomit by the roadside. After that I felt better, though very weak and shaky. I told Sam to take me to Annette's as I had some Andrews liver salts there! I took some and went to sleep immediately! The next morning I was still shaky. I rang my solicitor, Mrs. Diane Burleigh, and told her that Julien would be leaving the country on Friday without my having been informed. James was going against the custody order. I was granted reasonable access but I had had none; as I couldn't visit him in the house in Letchworth. The friends that he stayed with during the week in Mill Hill, London, were friends of James's and I had never been invited there, though I had rung Julien several times there and they knew who was calling but never acknowledged me! So I had no access to my son and James had been pumping him full of stories – of how I stole all his things in Ghana and how I had denounced him to the Government of Ghana – that were never true! The custody order said, "That Julien should not be taken out of the country without the consent of both parents and I had not even been informed officially. Previously, on my birthday, 10th May 1985, Julien, Rosina, Mummy and I had all gone to see a film together: 'Falling in Love' with Robert de Niro and Meryl Streep, and then for a pizza at Leicester Square. Then their daddy had insisted they came to him for that weekend, knowing it was my birthday. But they had beaten him, by coming to lunch with me and then going on to him. So we all parted about 5pm. Mummy coming home with me and Rosina going straight to King's Cross and Julien going to pick up his things from the house where he was staying. Whilst we were having a cup of tea Julien said, (in front of Mummy and Rosina), "Mummy, do you know that Rosina tells everything! She told Daddy I was going to America and not coming back!" He asked me if she had told me, and though she had, I said, "No!" but asked him, "Are you going to America and not coming back?" and he said, "Yes!" I said nothing. I didn't think that he could get the money to go even if he really meant it! A few weeks later Rosina said, "Mummy, Daddy's bought Julien the ticket to go to America!" but I still imagined that Julien would come and see me to tell me himself! I rang him and he said, "Nothing!" I sent him a card inviting him to come and stay with me a couple of days when he finished his O- Levels; but as my room is pretty miserable and I had no money to spend on him, the prospect was not very interesting, so I heard no more. The solicitor said, "That she would ring the immigration at the airport but as Julien was now over 16 he could take himself out of the country; though James was in breach of the custody order for buying the ticket and not asking me through my solicitor for my permission! I told Rosina that I was on my own at Annette's and she could come to me, but she didn't come! On Saturday I rang Rosina to ask if Julien went and she said, "Yes!" and she had seen him on Thursday before he left. On Tuesday afternoon at about 5pm I had a very abusive call from Volda, saying that James had rang Rosina and blasted her for telling me that Julien was going. I tried to explain my point of view but she was not interested. I told her that when I had needed a friend she had not been there for me, and put the phone down on her. (I know that if John had tried to take Kwaku out of the country like that, she would have made the biggest stink). 'A Friend in Need is a Friend Indeed!' I was really upset! She accused me of holding up the divorce! It is not me! and never has been me! James is sitting pretty in the house, flying off to Nigeria and the house is empty and I am suffering in one miserable room with nothing of my own in a most unpleasant neighbourhood. Even as a child I hadn't lived like that! I only pray to God that it will be over soon and he will not put me to shame! Luckily. before Volda rang I had taken a dose of milk of magnesia, so my stomach was quite settled. I sat and wrote a short note to Volda and posted it immediately. Then at nine o'clock Rosina rang. She said, "What are you trying to do to me?" She was so abusive that I put the phone down on her! She rang again and I said, "If I had reported your daddy when he beat me up, I would not be in this situation now and neither would you!" and put the phone down again and took it off the hook! I asked Annette's neighbour, George, to come and sit with me for a while, as I needed somebody to talk too and complain to. After a while I calmed down and was able to get some sleep! If supposed friends cannot help, they should not hinder!

The immigration people were supposed to let the solicitor know whether they had apprehended Julien and let us know his destination, but so far we have heard nothing. Julien just wants to get away from the whole situation; it's not only me he's rejecting, he's rejecting his father too as every time he goes home his father has different women in the house and that's not pleasant for the children. Even one time when Rosina went somebody was sleeping in her bed! I asked the solicitor, "Can't we get this case to court, and over and finished with?" She said, "That without the valuation on the house in Ghana the court would throw her out of court! Personally I can't see of what interest is that house, as it is worthless to me here as you can't get any money out of Ghana and the roof needs repairs, and so many other problems, as it has not been lived in for over two years. When I rang Mrs. Burleigh she said, "That Ofusu-Armaah, my lawyer in Ghana, had rung her," so she gave me his telephone number and I rang him. He said, "That he had been unable to get the valuation on the house as every time they had been there, they had not met anybody there to let them in!" I told him to contact Johnny, and he said, "That he would write straight away to Harry Sawyer, who was going to do the valuation, and ask him to contact Johnny!" I also wrote to Johnny to tell him to contact Harry Sawyer.

Annette rang me on 15th August and told me that she had a problem and asked if I could come over so I said, "Yes!" She said, "That I should stay for the weekend with her and I wondered what it was all about? I was soon to discover that it was not really her problem, but mine!

The day after she returned from Italy, when I had returned home, a letter arrived addressed to me! She recognised Rosina's writing as

Rosina had sent her a postcard before! She suspected that something was wrong, so she had opened it! She told me that the letter was really, really bad, and she didn't know what to do? So she had rung Rosina and asked her to come and see her. She had tried to get through to her but to no avail! She told her, that I was not like Rosina had made out! Annette knew that I was still very upset about Julien leaving the country like that without telling me or seeing me! So she kept the letter until she felt that I was ready for it! She had wanted to tear it up, but as it was not her letter felt that she couldn't do that! So she asked me if I was ready to read it? And I said, "Yes!" as she had prepared me for the letter, it was not such a shock as if I had opened it and read it myself in the first place! Well, Annette was not wrong – it was a very terrible letter using language that nobody should ever write to their mother, especially somebody who had been to a convent school! Rosina had said, "That her daddy had not made her write the letter; but all the poison in it was from his evil mind (probably with Volda's assistance). She had been completely brainwashed by him, even though she was not aware! She says that I don't know her, but judging by her letter she definitely does not know or appreciate me!

The next day I went out and looked for a card to send to her. I got one that said, Good Luck! and I wrote: "Rosina darling, I forgive you and feel very sorry for you, as you must be very unhappy! Lots of love, Mummy." She would not hear from me again until she had apologised for her mistaken thoughts about me; but I hope that this divorce can be finally settled so we can all be happy once again! That very morning I had received a lovely letter from Hamish, still in Ghana, telling me how lovely I was, and what a lovely mother I am and how much he loved me. He had sent me a lovely photo of himself, 'To The Person Dearest to him in all The World'. It was as if the two of them, Hamish and Rosina, were writing of totally different people! Hamish also hoped that Julien would contact one of us, so that we would not lose contact with him! At least that was a wonderful consolation to my battered mother's heart!

Whilst I was at Annette's after she had given me the letter I remained there for a few days as at least there I could have a nice shower; whilst at Craven Park I had to share the bathroom with so many others! The phone rang and it was Ofusu-Armaah (my Ghanaian lawyer) ringing from Germany. I told him all about Rosina's letter and how upset I was, and he said, "That I am so lovely and most people don't know how nice I am." which I thought was a lovely compliment! He said, "That he would be passing through London in September and would definitely see me!"

After a few days with Annette when I had calmed down, I returned to Craven Park to await Guy's call! I got myself all prepared to go to Paris at a moment's notice! It was really sad to think of the entire family split up! Hamish in Ghana! Myself in this miserable room at Craven Park! Rosina with her Auntie Volda! And Julien in America somewhere! And their daddy miserable in Lagos or Letchworth! I will be so happy to get a flat or apartment to call home, where the children will feel free to come to whenever they like! As they are now all grown -up I do not expect us to be all together at one time as we were before. But I would love to be able to put Mummy in a comfortable place so she could spend the rest of her days in comfort and peace and tranquility; to repay her for always being there for me when needed and being so understanding and loving. Whatever I have done, and though giving her opinion, never forcing me into anything!

Guy – Paris 1985

Guy rang from Paris and I arranged a flight that he paid for, and went to Paris for three days. Then he was flying on to Geneva before returning to Tahiti. It was the middle of August and Paris was very hot and sunny. He met me at the airport and we went to his parent's flat at Cergy, Pont-Oise. We had not seen one another for over twenty years but he looked just the same as he did when he was 18. We went to Montmartre and the Sacre Coeur, my favourite place in Paris, and had lunch in the square, with all the artist's painting all around us. We then went to Versailles and walked in the beautiful gardens. We didn't go inside as we had done that before many years ago. Guy took me to a restaurant near the house, called Au-Weekend and we had a lovely meal and he said, "I love taking you out to eat and watching you enjoying the food." In his parents' bedroom there was a portrait of his mother, which was so lifelike. He said, "That his father, who died a few months after his mother, said that he felt she was talking to him!" and I said, "Yes, I can understand that. I feel that she is talking to me too!" We did a lot of crying together, which was a great relief. On the final day he took me to a restaurant on the Champs Elysees, where we always used to go when we were younger and I would meet him after work at The Societe Generale. I would take the metro alone from Seine-et-Oise and wait outside the office for him to finish work, and we would go out, before returning home. All too soon it was time to go home and we went to the airport together. I got my plane to London and he carried on to Geneva. We were both crying. Would we ever see one another again? But that was a wonderful interlude and it boosted me up! Guy had been my penfriend and I had been writing to him since I was ten years old. We had first met when I went to visit him and his family, aged 14 and he was my first love, having a wonderful romantic time in Paris with just a few gentle kisses. We had kept in contact throughout the years and it was wonderful to be fully one's self with another person without any fear or anxiety.

September 1985

George Ofusu-Armaah, (my Ghanaian lawyer) rang to tell me that he had arrived from Germany, and we arranged to meet. I took him to Greenwich and we had lunch at the Trafalgar Inn, next to the Greenwich Naval College, and I showed him the Painted Hall and the beautiful chapel. He then met with my solicitor and tried to give any help that he could. It was nice to see him and he is such a cultured man and very well read, so you could have very interesting conversations with him, which was an absolute pleasure!

Whatever the outcome of the divorce settlement, this is the end of Part One of my life story. I hope to write Part Two after another forty years. Life begins at forty, so they say; so I am now walking at one year old.

What does the future hold? I put my hand in God's hand and trust that he will lead me on the right path to happiness in the future.

One night I had a dream and heard these words:
'Dream your dreams, may they come true!
May your future life bring happiness too!

Whether from a poem or something I have read, I don't remember, but it's a nice thought to end on, don't you think?

EPILOGUE

If I were to give any advice to a young, white, or black, British girl in love with a Ghanaian man today, in Britain. I would say that psychically there is no difference between black and white apart from the pigmentation. They feel, love, hate, suffer, are good, bad, wicked or evil – the same as any white. But there is a definite cultural difference! When they are studying in this country, most of them conform to British standards. As English is their official language (all their education in Ghana is done in English) some are great orators, able to converse easily on every subject. But once they return to Ghana; then begins the cultural problem. First of all his family: there is as much colour prejudice against mixed marriage (including black foreigners) as there is by whites in Britain, though things in Britain have improved, somewhat!

The Ghanaian man has been brought up in a society where polygamy (more than one wife) is still in existence in some parts of the country. I know that the attitude to sex and marriage in Britain is progressing, but in Ghana it is not. A man may have many girlfriends, especially if he is in a lucrative position, and especially, if he is married to a white or black foreigner; and their society encourages it. In 1964, when I first went to Ghana as a white married to an African, you were like the Royal Family here in Britain: you stood out in a crowd; people saw you, and knew you and whatever you were doing. At the time of writing this in 2004, however, there are many more mixed marriages, though not to the extent that you now see in Britain where people of all races and creeds are intermarrying. Whereas in Britain, where, when you get married your husband looks after you and the children, and that is his family; in Ghana the husband has an extended family, and his sisters, brothers and cousins will look to him for help, especially if he is the most educated one in the family with a good job and is successful in his particular field. Some tribes, are also inherited by their nephews, i.e. their sister's sons; so if your husband dies before you, you and your children would be turned out of your home. This happens to Ghanaian women all the time and they are left to fend for themselves and their children, whilst somebody else lives in their father's house. Nowadays there are a few exceptions where the man has made a will and a more enlightened family has honoured the will; but there are many more cases of them taking everything away.

In my time in Ghana I have seen many mixed marriages of whites (of all European races) and Afro-American or West Indians come and go. If you enjoy the luxuries of the modern world, I would advise you either to make sure that you buy a house in England, which you can rent to produce foreign exchange, or have some investment which brings in interest. In my day you couldn't get money out of Ghana but I believe that things have now improved. There are many personal things like cosmetics etc. that as a European you would need but which you cannot get a choice of in Ghana; so unless you have a source of income outside Ghana, you must do without. (I was lucky in that my mother used to send me all sorts of things.) The quality of life in Ghana is so much better than in Europe with the fresh air and the fresh food, fruit etc. which is outstanding.

When I first went to Ghana, we all had servants in the house, which was wonderful; but now with more and more people going to school it is more and more difficult to afford reliable help. Things like washing machines and Hoovers are hard to get and there are no credit systems to buy them. Also, things like fridges, freezers and air-conditioners (quite essential at times) are very expensive, so you should make every effort to take them with you. Even baby things like prams and cots and baby clothes are difficult to get at times, though I believe that things have improved considerably since my time, when even baby milk and medicines were sometimes difficult to obtain. Also the food is very different and some people cannot adapt, which can make life a misery. Personally I have always enjoyed trying new foods wherever I have been in the world and my diet is more African than European. I love my plantain, and fu-fu with palm soup or groundnut soup or light soup and yams and kelewele. (plantain chips fried with ginger and pepper and fried by the roadside) with fresh pineapples and mangoes (heavenly, to pluck ripe from the tree) and avocado and soursops and so many other lovely things. I have enjoyed sampling food wherever I have travelled, with ingera in Ethiopia and the wonderful dishes in India where we ate Indian food everyday. But there were times when I had to satisfy a craving for my favourite: plain old egg and chips with chip butties. When James used to travel I used to eat them everyday. There are many tinned and frozen food and other commonplace things, which you have to do without, and that can be hard for some people. One of my great cravings was for Black Magic chocolates or Cadbury's Fruit and Nut bars and if somebody brought me just one single bar, that was a great treat. (though, our chocolate doesn't travel well, in the heat, and melts, so has to be put in the fridge) as well as some lipsticks and make-up.

For one of my birthdays there was a shortage of bread. We didn't have bread for four months, as there was no control priced flour, so we could only make doughnuts from imported flour from Togo. I said, "What I really wanted for my birthday was bread with butter and marmalade!" I certainly learned the meaning of a few good phrases, such as 'half a loaf is better than none!' and 'you want jam on it, too!' In England you say them without any thought to the meaning, but when you have no bread or it costs over one pound a loaf you certainly appreciate their meaning! I eventually got my bread for my birthday when somebody went to London and brought a loaf of Mother's Pride back along with a pot of marmalade.

There are many Ghanaian customs, which the locals take very seriously, which Europeans cannot accept and it's hard to live amongst it. The African ju-ju is very much a part of life, though more sophisticated than before! People believe in it and even though many go to church, even the churchgoers visit the herbalist, as many are called now, when they feel the occasion demands! I do not want to put people off, but just to warn them to be prepared. The more prepared you are, the more chance of survival. The most important is to have a source of income here in Britain and if possible to always have an up-to-date return ticket; once you feel that you have a way of escape you don't need to! But if you feel trapped without any escape, that's when 'a molehill can become a mountain!' By 1985 the economic situation had gradually worsened over the years, and life was not as pleasant as it was in 1964 when I first arrived. But I must add that Ghanaians as a nation are a very pleasant nation and they give great hospitality to the guest. So you could be loved and revered by some, whilst, a few would hate and resent you, especially as there is a shortage of men in Ghana; so you lessen the chances for other women to get a husband, and maybe they would share yours! I myself regret nothing. I have had a wonderful adventure and made true and lasting black brothers and sisters. It has been a rich experience. I have even reached a point where I no longer see people's colour, only the good or bad in individuals, not the nation. I have not let the cultural differences affect me; embracing and enjoying fully, the rich vibrant colours, the sunshine and the flowers, smells and scents of Ghanaian, Africa, whilst enjoying the warmth of the people and climate, and the beautiful music of the drumming and highlife dancing steeped in history; not forgetting the beautiful colours and different patterns of the national Kente, hand woven for centuries with patterns, which, have individual meanings passed down from father to son. I have learned to love and understand them all, good or bad.

End of Part One ... to be continued!

AFTERTHOUGHT

This is a true account from memory of my personal experiencing of the phenomena of my personal everyday life experience. It is drawn from my long-term memory without conferring with or referring to any other soul. My aim is not to offend anyone, either by inclusion or exclusion. Memory can be most inaccurate – my memory and experiencing of it can be totally different from another's of the same event. It's like eyewitness accounts: as all are coming from different angles, they see and recall totally different things from the same event. Some names have been omitted to protect the innocent but I have not spared myself. This account was first written by hand in 1985 and not read again until 2002. I have found writing it very therapeutic, like psychoanalysing my life. I have decided to finish at the first forty years, as the life after is so totally different that I feel it needs another book to follow. If I do offend anyone I am really sorry and I say a big thank you to all my loyal friends who have supported me over the years. They all know who they are so there is no need for naming them. Thank you especially to my best friend in Scotland, and my two special friends in Burnt Oak, who have encouraged and supported me throughout my time of writing this account.

VALERIE JOY BROWN
WEST HAMPSTEAD, 2005